E-politics
Technology in American Government

Phillip B. Bridgmon
James Madison University

Mark C. Milewicz
Gordon College

KENDALL/HUNT PUBLISHING COMPANY
4050 Westmark Drive   Dubuque, Iowa 52002

Contents

Acknowledgment vii

Chapter 1 Introduction   1
    The Blessings and Curses of Technological
      Development   1
    Capturing and Assessing a Moving Target   4
    Justification and Theoretical Approaches   5
    The Plan of the Book and Summary
      of the Chapters   6

Chapter 2 E-government   11
    Electronic Government   12
    Government Structure   13
    The Federal Government   16
    Government and Business   37
    Government to Government   39
    History   40
    The Dream   40
    Digital Divide   41
    Evaluating E-government   42
    Government   43
    Politics   44
    Citizens' Use of the Internet   45
    The Pay Off   46
    Other Areas   47
    Summary   48

Chapter 3 Technology and Democracy   49
    Equality   52
    Freedom and Scenarios   55
    Digital Divide   56
    Direct Participation   59
    Voting   60
    Information   61
    Political News   62

	Influencing Government	63
	Summary	65

Chapter 4   **Electronic State and Local Government**   69
About the States   70
The Local Governments   70
The Digital Dominion   72
Leading the Way   87
Local Electronic Government   88
Summary   101

Chapter 5   **Congress and the Courts**   103
Congress   103
The Courts   111
Summary   121

Chapter 6   **Political Participation and Voting**   123
Democratic Political Participation in America   123
Democratic Political Participation in America
    and the Internet   129
Types of Participation   130
At Home vs. Home Voting: Another Perspective   133
Arguments for and against Internet Voting   135
The Internet and Information Gathering   136
Volume of Participation   140
Summary   147

Chapter 7   **Political Parties, Interest Groups,
and Social Movements**   151
Introduction   151
Political Parties   154
Interest Groups   161
Social Movements   172
Summary   176

Chapter 8   **Campaigns and Elections**   179
                 Introduction   179
                 Campaigns   181
                 Impact on Elections   195
                 General Conclusions about Internet
                     Use in Campaigns   201

Chapter 9   **The Media**   205
                 Introduction   205
                 Traditional Media   209
                 The Hypodermic Model   212
                 The Minimal Effects Model   212
                 The Theory of Agenda Setting   213
                 The Theories of Priming and Framing   214
                 New Media   217
                 The Negative Effect of Profit on News Delivery   221
                 Summary   231

Chapter 10   **Future Technology and Government**   233
                 Immediate Future   233
                 Efficiency   234
                 Effectiveness   235
                 Responsiveness   236
                 Where Do We Go from Here?   239
                 Summary   240

References   243

Acknowledgment

This project was inspired by the lifelong work of Daniel W. Pound. Dr. Pound served as our mentor, friend, and motivation as we progressed through the doctoral program at the University of Alabama. His untimely passing in May 2002 created a void in the lives of his family, friends, and former students. Without his influence, we would have taken on this project much later in our careers. We are sincere in our dedication of this work to his spirit.

This book is the result of many individuals who assiduously applied their skills toward its completion. Thanks to the staff at Kendall Hunt. We also owe a great deal of appreciation to Amanda Dainis, graduate assistant at James Madison University, who put much toil into this project. Additionally, we are both appreciative of the support we received from our colleagues and respective institutions. Truly, little to none is accomplished without help. Therefore, it is only fitting to thank our wives. Their talent and kindness are never lost on us. Our best to everyone.

Phil Bridgmon
James Madison University

Mark Milewicz
Gordon College

Introduction

The Blessings and Curses
of Technological Development

Over the past 100 years the rate of technological change in America has been profound. In a very short period of time Americans have experienced drastic changes to almost every facet of their lives. The developments in medicine, transportation, and communication alone are very impressive, and are often taken for granted.

For instance, in the field of medicine before 1900 there was no well-developed method for controlling pain. As 20th century medicine progressed, so did a doctor's ability to control discomfort through the use of anesthetics. The ability to control the level of consciousness and sensory perception of a patient has allowed doctors to perform types of procedures that were never possible in the past. A simple appendectomy or tooth extraction would be tremendously painful without the benefits of anesthesia.

Moreover, the aftermath of such medical procedures was risky due to the chance of infection. The development of antibiotics was revolutionary in that regard. In both instances, scientific advancements in pharmaceuticals have greatly improved the practice of medicine. When other drug discoveries are considered, along with modern developments in diagnostic tools such as x-rays, magnetic resonance imaging (MRIs), or endoscopies, what results is a revolution in health care that has profoundly increased life spans and the quality of life for human beings. During the American Civil War a damaged and infected foot was often amputated with the aid of a doctors' good saw and the patient's favorite bottle of whiskey. That same injury now involves the use of different tools and results

1

in a completely different outcome, not to mention a completely different experience for the patient.

Major technological developments have also changed the transportation of people and goods. Before 1900, transportation was slow, dangerous, and expensive. There were no automobiles, commercial flights, or interstates. As these things developed, people were able to take advantage of the added mobility to facilitate business and personal endeavors. In a very short period of time the average Americans' idea of speedy travel went from a horse, to a train, to a car, to a plane.[1] The rapid development of these things and the ease of movement that they provided also affected the American and global economies. Goods were more rapidly transported and more safely delivered. Perishable items could be shipped over long distances, particularly if the mode of delivery utilized refrigeration technology. This increased the variety and lowered the cost of goods available. Over time, moving people and goods has become much quicker, safer and economical. The economic and social benefits of these developments are significant.

Communication technology before 1900 allowed for only the slowest and most basic transmission of information. A handwritten letter or printed publications were personally carried by courier from sender to receiver. This process was slow and somewhat unreliable. For information to pass between individuals in different regions, it often took days, if not weeks. In the long period between the time of drafting and delivery, correspondence was easily dampened, mangled, lost or stolen. With the development of the telegraph, radio, television, fax machines, e-mail, cellular phones, and the Internet, information is now transmitted instantaneously and with a high confidence of reliable delivery. This has increased the volume of information available and facilitated an exchange of ideas and data at a rate that is unprecedented. This allows medical, political, or any type of time-sensitive or urgent information to be transferred almost immediately to almost any location around the world with tremendous accuracy.

In each of the examples above, technological developments have caused great improvements in the quality of life for human beings. We have become healthier, more mobile, and more communicative. However, this progress has also brought with it a number of problems. For instance, advancements in medical technology have

---

[1]Of course, the development of the space program in the 1950s is an obvious extension of these trends.

caused the costs of health care to increase. More and more Americans are unable to afford the services of the medical community. High quality health care has also increased the life expectancy of the average American. This has caused a strain on the social security system and on society in general by increasing the portion of the population that will be less likely to work and more likely to need support. Additionally, the use of antibiotics has resulted in the development of drug-resistant strains of bacteria that are now very difficult to treat. None of this was foreseen and is a direct result of certain technological developments.

Transportation advancements gave city workers the ability to leave the poor conditions of inner city life, resulting in suburbanization on a mass scale. This has resulted in economic segregation, and caused municipal and county governments to deal with new problems regarding revenue streams and the provision of city-services. Transportation advancements have also resulted in an increased pace of life which has been argued to negatively impact families. Transportation advancements have also affected the speed of industrial development and caused new challenges with global markets.

It has been argued that advancements in communication technology have also caused numerous problems. However, their effect is less well known. Do e-mail and the Internet cause families to relate less on a personal level? Has the profitability of the communication business caused a change in the news we receive or the programs to which we are exposed? If information is seen as a precious commodity, will developments in communication technology exacerbate the difference between the haves and have-nots in society? We already know the impact that the television has had on families and politics. What impact will new digital communications have?

The Internet alone poses a whole new set of advantages and problems for society and government:

- It makes information easier to obtain and knowledge more difficult.
- It facilitates both privacy and surveillance.
- It makes information more freely available, but it does not encourage public discussion of policy choices.
- It may encourage a sense of community or anomie (Noveck, 2000).

With every new technological development, there arrives a set of advantages and disadvantages that ultimately challenge the government.

However, the impact that communication technologies might have on American government is different. The medical and transportation examples show how these things have impacted what the government does, not how the government governs. They have impacted policy, but not altered the way the citizen and the government necessarily relate. Communication technology is different in that changes in this area directly impact the relationship between government and citizen. The exchange of information is at the heart of a democracy. Governments need to know what the people are thinking and the people need to know what the government is doing. The better this relationship, the stronger democracy will be. This area of study, therefore, deserves special attention.

Capturing and Assessing a Moving Target

The purpose of this book is to assess the impact of new communication technologies on American government. As has been previously discussed, each new technological development in society brings with it a new set of advantages and disadvantages. This work attempts to assess what advantages and disadvantages may exist for American democracy as result of advancements in communication technology.

Unlike the previous examples in medicine or transportation, we do not have the benefit of years of study on which to draw conclusions. We have some experience studying the impact of television, but the Internet is unlike any medium to come before. We are forced to reassess what we know. The rise of the Internet and other digital communication technologies are comparatively new developments. Therefore, the benefits and costs of these things as they relate to government and democracy are less well known.

By reviewing the literature that currently exists on this topic and by looking at the current political landscape, we will take what amounts to a snapshot of the communications environment in American government. We will then interpret what is occurring and suggest what implications may exist. This approach is beneficial in that it helps gather evidence in making an educated assessment of what impacts may be seen; however, it is far from definitive. Developments in this area of study are so rapid, predictions are somewhat risky, if not foolish. For that reason, we do not attempt to predict the future, but instead we pinpoint trends and paths for future research.

Justification and Theoretical Approaches

The topics of democracy and communication technologies are not as unrelated as they may seem. In fact, these ideas are closely related. The exchange of information is at the very heart of a vibrant democracy. The importance of this relationship is seen in the very definition of the term "democracy": government by the people. More specifically, in a representative democracy the people select individuals to represent their interests in government so that they may act on their behalf.

The key to this relationship is communication. If there is to be a government by the people, there must be effective ways for the government and the citizen to communicate. Moreover, a wealth of quality information should increase deliberation within the citizenry and improve the quality of discourse. It follows that the more effective the communication, the stronger the democracy may potentially be.

While most agree on the importance of information and communication in a democracy, there is no consensus on the impact that new communication technologies will have. Will the Internet, for instance, greatly improve the quality of democracy, diminish the quality, or have no effect at all? We tend to be in agreement that information is important to a democracy and that the Internet is a powerful new communication tool. There is no agreement, however, as to its impact. Opinions on the democratic potential of new communication technology are generally divided into one of three groups: Neofuturists, Dystopians, and Technorealists (Wilhelm, 2000).

Neofuturists believe that cyberspace will repair the weakened democracy. Democratic systems that suffer from low turnout and rising levels of mistrust and cynicism will be revitalized by new communication technology. Neofuturists maintain the notion that technological developments will strip the elite of their power and level the playing field in politics. In their opinion this process has already begun and will be unavoidable. Not unlike themes in Gene Rodenberry's *Star Trek,* the Neofuturist view presents new technology as a driving force in a society that is capable of solving stubborn socio-political problems.

More specifically, proponents of this view suggest that the Internet will empower citizens. The Internet will allow people to become much more politically informed and active in politics. It will provide for the creation of virtual town hall meetings where citizens nationwide can meet and discuss issues. Preferences on issues can be immediately registered on a national basis and reviewed by lawmakers. This utopian view holds that voting rates will likely increase as will the quality of government.

However, many feel as if this approach is misguided. Some argue that Neofuturists overestimate the ability of electronic gadgets to overcome human beings' shortcomings. It is possible that easy or convenient participation is not necessarily quality or thoughtful participation. Rather than improve our democracy, it is possible that digital communication will actually harm it.

Dystopians see new communication technology as being a harmful element to modern democracies. Rather than resurrect or restore political life, Dystopians see new communication developments disrupting the social and political fabric of the culture. Computer mediated communication, for instance, is seen as becoming a substitute for face-to-face communication. Moreover, the Internet facilitates passive participation and diminishes the likelihood of quality political deliberation. Dystopians feel that people lack the discipline to use technology effectively and will eventually suffer at its hands.

Technorealists occupy the center of these two positions. Taking a critical view of technology, they tend to see it as both a blessing and curse. They fail to think it will save us, but do not think it will destroy us either.

This book hopefully avoids falling into any of these categories. We do not proceed from any theoretical perspective and do not make any claim in predicting the future. What we do attempt is to take what we know about politics in America and see how those things might be changed by the introduction of computer mediated communication. The introduction of digital communications in society is still in its very early stages. We, therefore, only attempt to assemble a picture of how it is currently being used in politics, and how this is altering the way governments and citizens interact.

The Plan of the Book and Summary of the Chapters

This book is divided into two general parts. The first part assesses the impact new communication technologies are having on American governmental institutions such as the legislative and judicial branches. It also assesses this impact from the perspective of state and local governments. This first half provides a snapshot of how the government is using new technology in providing services and reaching out to citizens. The second half of the book assesses how citizens are using new technology to participate in American government. This half is an investigation into how the activity of individuals and groups are impacted by new technologies.

Chapter 2 contains a general discussion of technology and democracy. This chapter suggests that there are several scenarios one could entertain when examining technology and its ability to help or hinder citizen control of government. The most popular view is that there are obvious benefits to the use of technology in increasing the quality of our democracy. At the most basic level, technology allows us a greater capacity to communicate. If we choose to communicate about government, then technology will facilitate a greater exchange of ideas in the political realm. In that regard, it can facilitate quality political deliberation.

Chapter 3 addresses the currently fashionable idea of electronic government. This chapter spotlights how technology is transforming the way the government delivers services. Following a discussion of bureaucracies, we speculate how technology will alter the way government organizes its work. Moreover, we give several examples of how government services are being electronically delivered to citizens via the phone and Internet. We suggest that certain areas within the government will reflect more of technology's influence than others.

Chapter 4 discusses how Congress and the Courts are experiencing technological influences at varying levels. Members of Congress are seizing the tools of mass communication to help them carry out their duties and communicate their successes to their constituents. However, some members of Congress are using the Internet more cleverly than others. We take a moment in this chapter to mention these differences. Additionally, we suggest that our Court system is being influenced by technology at an administrative level. It is the access to court records and filing of cases where we see the most technological influence. Judicial decision-making, however, appears to be insulated from technology.

Chapter 5 is dedicated to how state and local governments are adapting to technology in fulfilling their functions. As we mention later on, all politics is fundamentally local. Our system of shared power necessitates coordination, explanation, and delivery of a complex set of policies. Technology can help us coordinate that activity. It can also help us avoid government service hassles such as lines at the Department of Motor Vehicles, problems requesting vital records, or the tedium of applying for social services. State and local governments are the true laboratories of democracy when it comes to using technology to deliver 'good' government. Technology has been very successful in improving the quality and delivery of services at this level.

Chapter 6 addresses the topic of participation and voting. In looking at how individuals use the Internet, we suggest that its political potential is not yet realized. This chapter looks at Internet usage and sees it as becoming more commonplace. However, it is not a purely political medium. People do not use the Internet in ways political scientists wish that they would. Additionally, the Internet seems a long way off from being used as a device through which we vote. We do see some benefits, however. The Internet does ease the burden of accessing governmental information and reduces certain impediments to political participation.

Chapter 7 investigates how parties, interest groups, and social movements are impacted. Much like the conclusions in the previous chapter, it appears that the internet and other forms of digital communications will not substantially change the political environment for these groups. However, the Internet will arguably impact the *way* business is conducted for these groups, particularly for social movements and protest groups. The Internet can accelerate group activity and allow for an ease of mobilization that is unprecedented. In fact, the groups that stand to benefit the most tend to be the ones that lack a well-established infrastructure. This makes social movements and protest groups a most interesting topic.

Chapter 8 discusses campaigns and elections. The obvious question here is whether or not the impact of this new medium on campaigns will mimic that of television's influence decades ago. With regard to that question, it is too early to tell. What we do know is that the Internet has not yet revolutionized campaigning. Internet campaigning appears to be developing into another weapon in the campaign arsenal, but we do not know at this point whether it will become a major or minor weapon. Currently, however, it does appear as if certain candidates have more to gain from the use of the Internet than others; the Internet may not help all candidates equally. One glaring problem appears to be that Internet use in campaigns currently runs the risk of failing in its most appealing potential. Rather than engaging and impacting non-voters and undecided voters, the Internet has shown the tendency to activate those who are in least need of activation—those who are already politically engaged.

Chapter 9 focuses on the media. This chapter recounts the development of the media and assesses what we know about its influence. We suggest that there are serious implications involving the new media in America. Its diversification and drive for profit are likely to be hurting democratic deliberation in this country. Unfortunately, the Internet does not appear to be helping. The traditional media players are extending their dominance to cyberspace and the salutary impact of information dissemination on the Internet appears to be marginalized.

Our final chapter offers a synthesis of these findings and suggests what direction and paths these topics may take in the future. It will revisit the general topic of communication technology in American democracy and offer some insight into the future development of this subject area.

E-government

The United States' government has ambled along from auspicious beginnings to one struggling to meet the demands of the Information Age. Indeed we have come from a distant place. Regardless of the transformation, modern day government has the same foundation as it did in 1789. The way it interacts with citizens, interest groups, the media, and with other governments has been altered by the Information Age. The underpinnings have remained constant, however. How could the framers have known of the lightening speed at which change would take place? Can we know how things will look in 200 years? This chapter examines electronic government: government on demand; instant access; and a world without borders. Electronic government holds many promises for accessing government and receiving government services. For some, though, the prospects for improved government through electronic means hold no promises.

Electronic government may be just another mechanism that changes very little of consequence. Diverging from these views are those who believe that the Information Age is dangerous and destructive. The fears of electronic government include elusive intrusions on civil liberties, disenfranchisement at the voting booth, and a deterioration of community. The actual affect of growing information technologies on government action does not rest in the extreme views. The true consequence is still forming, and has yet to be determined. Ultimately, we believe electronic government will settle somewhere in the middle of the many competing views. It will be a tool for effective and efficient government. No more, no less.

Electronic Government

At this point, defining electronic government will help start us down the right path of discussion. As we approach the subject, it will be helpful to maintain a common language and understanding. The term "electronic government" conjures up wireless government encapsulated in the Internet. Our ability to interact with government without actually walking the cold tiled hallways or hearing the echoes of clanking dress shoes pounding the floor of a government building is made possible by technology. For us, electronic government means getting government services anywhere and at anytime. We can extract these services in a number of ways: renewing library books over the Internet; filing tax returns over the phone; paying fines and fees using credit cards; and making direct deposits of government entitlements. These are just a few ways. Each day innovative ideas emerge that increase accessibility of government to citizens. Early efforts began slowly. Lately, however, the movement has been gaining speed.

Recently, a federal-level office devoted to electronic initiatives was created. We now have an e-government czar. Congress routinely entertains multi-billion dollar requests for various electronic initiatives. The United States government is the world's largest consumer of technology. The genesis of a commitment to making government more efficient and responsive by using technology began with the Clinton administration. The desire for the public's business to be transacted anywhere, and at any time, has only gained momentum. At the state level, we are seeing a similar commitment to electronic initiatives. Governments view technology as an agent of efficiency and accountability. These are some of the same virtues citizens claim they want from government. Electronic government may be the answer, but the changeover will be slow.

Despite the momentum favoring technology incorporation into the day-to-day operations of government, its full incorporation has been slow to develop. Government, the United States' in particular, is massive and broad in reach and scope. There are thousands of organizational interests. We might call them turf interests. Government offices are organized and arranged in a structure that is not easily changed. For these fundamental reasons, technology will not transform government. It is worth a brief look at the impediments to its full incorporation, and how those impediments, such as structure and culture, will be influenced by technology. Hence, rapid technological changes have the ability to transcend the age-old notions that government is incapable of change, doesn't have the necessary impetus for change, and will not change despite the benefits of efficiency.

Government Structure

German sociologist Max Weber explored the way organizations are construed for the purpose of delivering efficient and consistent services. His ideal type was that of a bureaucratic model. The term bureaucracy, when extracted from its heritage, simply means "rule of the desk." Bureaucracy is much more than a ruling desk or the person behind it. It is a blending together of power, rules, information, and regimented outputs. Bureaucratic organizations are designed as such due to their size, complexity, and place within a strict legal environment (constitutional government). The departments, bureaus, and offices of the federal government are based on this model. States and cities also employ this design.

It is worth reiterating that bureaucracies are ideal organizational types. Weber thought the top-down, hierarchical organization was best at handling the volume of work assigned to organizations such as governments. The characteristics of a bureaucracy also fit nicely within legal requirements that government treat everyone equally. These normative notions don't always manifest themselves empirically and require adaptation to political realities.

Bureaucracy

Government is an elusive concept for many citizens. The word "bureaucracy" conjures up deeply held resentment. Government is seen as being inefficient, daunting, and unresponsive. Rules and regulations cause frustration. Citizens call one office only to be transferred to another office. Calls are dropped while waiting for someone to answer. On occasion, no answer is forthcoming at all. The large buildings where government employees work aren't welcoming. They feel cold and are poorly lighted. Interacting with the government, for many, is a chore. For them, cutting through "red tape" is not an enjoyable task. Why may this be the case?

Citizens come in contact with government offices when something is needed or something is wrong. The potential problems range from a lost social security check to going to court and fighting for custody of a child. Governments establish rules and enforce them. When a citizen's behavior or desires warrant government attention the encounter can be unrewarding. In addition, government offices have specialized functions. Someone in agriculture may know very little about a lost social security check. The staff at the Department of Motor Vehicles can offer little help with a tuition reimbursement. Your local clerk of council cannot make adjustments to your cable bill. Each office of government handles the administration of a particular area, and their employees have specialized expertise and skills.

The institutions of government follow the bureaucratic model to varying degrees. Departments and agencies, or any organizations, can be adapted to their environment. Technology has an important role in shaping the organization's environment. Technology also shapes the essence of a bureaucracy, which has distinct characteristics: specialized labor functions, defined hierarchy, written rules, written procedures, equal impersonal relationships, and selection and promotion based on merit (Starling, 2002).

Specialized labor functions mean that a person has a particular duty within an organization. Decades ago typists typed. Teachers would go about the business of teaching students. Administrators removed the obstacles that hindered the day-to-day functions of labor. Over time, technological advancements have slowly stripped the need to specialize. To some degree, specialized labor functions have become less important in the Information Age (Fountain, 2002). Technology allows individuals to pursue broader occupational and professional interests. Within government, work roles have become less static. The onset of technology dependence has necessitated becoming more adaptable in the workplace. It is no longer wise for information technology expertise to be exercised by one person. The nature of contemporary public work demands the ability to use technology, assemble data, analyze information, and convey expertise to a wide array of audiences.

Hierarchy represents the lynchpin of bureaucratic theory. In most organizational systems there will be those in charge and those in charge of carrying out instructions. The hierarchy also allows for the work of the organization to be dispersed across levels of expertise and specialization. The ultimate success or failure of government institutions does not rest with one person or one level of the hierarchy (Simon, 1962). Technology expands the ability of government to solve and react to particular problems across the various levels. Through information systems and databases, street level bureaucrats have the ability to make decisions and deliver services without the normal wait associated with tapping the institutional memory before the advent of data systems and computers. Technology allows everyone in the workplace access to broader amounts of information. Information, we assume, is the most powerful commodity, next to power, in any workplace.

There have been several attempts to flatten government's structure from Weber's notion of a pyramid to one resembling a rectangle. The idea reflects the thought that empowered employees are productive (Maslow, 1943 and McGregor, 1961). Less hierarchical power would effectively create a stakeholder at the street bureaucratic level such as teacher, police office, librarian (Lipsky, 2003). In the bureaucratic model, power is concentrated in the upper levels, particularly in terms of decision making and planning. Others have a somewhat limited amount of power through discretion.

The desire to clearly articulate rules, responsibilities, and processes of an organization has several advantages. Efficiency and fairness being the most obvious. Work rules are clearly defined and easily available for government employees through the use of electronic government. Agency websites maintain virtually all rights, duties, and responsibilities. Workers do not have to guess about their role in the organization. Procedures are also similar to rules. Prescribed methods of dealing with particular situations are clearly stated and available.

Impersonal relationships are the easiest to recognize in an era of technology. In one vain, bureaucracies are not neutral or impartial in their interaction with citizens (Williamson, 1985). Everyone is not treated equally. In the other vain, however, if bureaucracies are to treat citizens impersonally, the technological era certainly facilitates impersonal interaction. We can interact with government, conduct business, and extract services without speaking to a bureaucrat. Technology serves as the conduit for creating impersonal relationships between government and its citizenry. This alienation is not desirable. Without citizen attachment to government, they may become less inclined to interact with it. Thus, technology may easily create the conditions that draw more citizens into government's machinations only to put them off with impersonal treatment.

The structure of government is not the only area that is fundamentally transformed by technology. It is worth understanding how government agencies are structured and how technology may alter government organization. Technology could easily create conditions where the word bureaucracy doesn't cause citizens to cringe. Until now, government has been seen as the problem not the solution (more about this follows later). Technology may undermine this negative view held by citizens. Many efforts are afoot at the federal and state level that move government fully into a transition toward electronic government.

The Federal Government

While government agencies have their foundation in a Weberian notion of bureaucracy, there are strong movements toward making government more accessible to the wired citizen. President Bush recently urged government agencies to work together by "working as a team across traditional boundaries to better serve the American people, focusing on citizens rather than individual agency needs" (e-gov, 2002). Again, we see the concern for boundaries and organizational self-interest as a foundation for government interaction. Government is a set of institutions that will struggle to shed this history of protecting itself. An additional aspect of the movement towards e-government is the idea of efficient government. In other remarks, President Bush indicated that e-governance "create(s) more cost-effective and efficient ways to serve citizens." (e-gov, 2002). Armed with these goals of better and efficient government, the federal government has a number of initiatives and goals related to e-government.

Initiatives

Several e-gov initiatives are outlined in Table 1. The areas of government interaction can be broken into three categories: government-citizen, government-business, intergovernmental. These interactions are important. Acceptance of government's legitimacy depends on their quality. Through technology, government seeks to improve the efficiency and responsiveness of operations. As such, numerous initiatives have begun to make government more efficient and user-friendly. Technology has the ability to help government slough off its bureaucratic image.

As members of Congress will testify, government-citizen interaction makes up a large part of their casework (Fenno 1978, Fiorina,1989). One such concern on the part of citizens is government benefits. Entitlement spending accounts for a majority of government spending (House Budget Committee, 2003). Entitlements are services provided by government to a person who meets certain

Text continues on p. 33.

Table 1

E-government Initiatives at a Glance

Project (Lead Agency)	Web Site	Description	Progress to Date	Next Steps
Government to Citizen				
GOVBENEFITS.GOV (DOL)	www.govbenefits.gov	Provides a single point of access for citizens to locate and determine potential eligibility for government benefits and services.	• Launched eligibility screening tool to identify social services citizens may qualify for • Re-launched site with additional functionality • Added all applicable federal benefit programs for citizens to the site • Established state level relationships and identified state benefit programs for inclusion on the site • Launched GovBenefits 3.0 featuring new state and federal benefit programs, a redesigned homepage, streamlined questionnaire, and a customer satisfaction survey	• Continue to work with all levels of government to develop a data standard that can be used to exchange benefit data • Release application to integrate USA Services into the citizen feedback process
Recreation One-Stop (DOI)	www.recreation.gov	Provides a single-point-of access, user-friendly, web-based resource to citizens, offering information and access to government recreational sites.	• First county/state data added to Recreation.gov as part of intergovernmental "Government Without Boundaries" initiative • Data provided for over 3,500 recreation sites managed by 10 Federal organizations and 4 states • Launched enhanced user interface and mapping capabilities • Established "RecML" data standard to improve data exchange among a wide range of partners (including non-government organizations)	• Pilot integrated recreation reservation system • Establish a consolidated government-wide recreation reservation system • Use of RecML as the vehicle to incorporate state and local data on the Recreation.gov web site

Continued

17

Table 1

E-government Initiatives at a Glance—cont'd

Government to Citizen—cont'd

Project (Lead Agency)	Web Site	Description	Progress to Date	Next Steps
IRS Free File (TREAS)	www.irs.gov	Creates a single-point of access to free on-line preparation and electronic tax filing services provided by Industry Partners to reduce burden and costs to taxpayers.	• Launched free e-filing web site with Industry Partners • As of September 2003, approximately 2.79 million taxpayers used Free File Alliance (FFA) services to file their taxes electronically during the 2003 tax filing season	• Complete FFA Operating Agreement • Receive and validate free offers proposals from prospective FFA members • Prepare Free File web pages on irs.gov • Conduct/complete usability testing on Free File pages • Conduct/complete FFA software evaluation process • Launch Free File to Public via media kickoff
E-Loans (ED)		Creates a single point of access for citizens to locate information on federal loan programs, and improves back-office loan functions.	• Established agreement between GovBenefits.gov and E-Loans to create the GovLoans Gateway as a part of the GovBenefits.gov site • Analyzed Pay.gov as a possible common solution for electronically collecting lender payments • Delivered a baseline report analyzing the technologies, systems, and processes lenders use to transmit data/reports to agencies during the loan lifecycle • Delivered design to provide non-HUD agencies/lenders with web access to default data on HUD's Credit Alert Interactive Voice Response System	• Create GovLoans Gateway—a web site to educate citizens on federal loan programs with links to federal agencies and private sector resources

Government to Business

Initiative (Agency)	URL	Description	Accomplishments	Future Plans
USA Services (GSA)	www.firstgov.gov	Develop and deploy government-wide citizen customer service using industry best practices that will provide citizens with timely, consistent responses about government information and services.	• Created an Office of Citizen Services at GSA to provide cross-agency customer service for citizens and integrated the Federal Citizen Information Center's (FCIC) call center with FirstGov.gov to provide citizens with the ability to contact the federal government via telephone, e-mail, letters, and fax • Added e-mail capability to FCIC's National Contact Center • Unveiled USA Services to the public	• Increase number of participating agency partners • Award new contact center contract thereby increasing capability to provide improved citizen response services • Assist agencies with system implementation for misdirected e-mail and telephone inquiries
E-Rule making (EPA)	www.regulations.gov	Allows citizens to easily access and participate in the rule making process. Improves the access to, and quality of, the rule making process for individuals, businesses, and other government entities while streamlining and increasing the efficiency of internal agency processes.	• FirstGov.gov links to all agency regulatory docket sites • Completed benchmarking study and evaluation of existing agency sites • Clinger-Cohen letter issued to consolidate redundant and siloed web sites • Public launch of cross agency front-end web application for receiving public comments on proposed agency rules	• Consolidate existing agency e-docket systems with EPA's system, including DOT, FDA, and DOL • Initiate business process reengineering of rulemaking process
Expanding Electronic Tax Products for Businesses (TREAS)		Reduces the number of tax-related forms that businesses must file, provides timely and accurate tax information to businesses, increases the availability of electronic tax filing, and models simplified federal and state tax employment laws.	• Nationwide deployment of the Form 94x/Employment Tax • Completed proof-of-concept for Pre-Screening Notice and Certification Request for the Work Opportunity and Welfare-to-Work Credits (Form 8850) • Nationwide deployment of Internet EIN	• Deploy Form 1120—Corporate Income Tax • Deploy Form 990—Return of Organization Exempt from Income Tax

Continued.

Table 1

E-government Initiatives at a Glance—cont'd

Project (Lead Agency)	Web Site	Description	Progress to Date	Next Steps
Government to Business—cont'd				
International Trade Process Streamlining (DOC)	www.export.gov	Makes it easy for Small and Medium Enterprises (SMEs) to obtain the information and documents needed to conduct business abroad.	• Defined solution architecture for simplifying export processes • Launched One Stop, One Form • Launched automated NAFTA certification of origin • Consolidated/merged content of USATrade.gov into the Export.gov portal	• Redesign Export.gov, integrating content from BuyUSA (Market Research and PTA) and enhancing functionality
Business Gateway (formerly Business Compliance One-Stop) (SBA)	www.business.gov	Reduces the burden on businesses by making it easy to find, understand, and comply (including submitting forms) with relevant laws and regulations at all levels of government.	• Launched BusinessLaw.gov • Integrated State and Federal EIN eApplication • Piloted Portal Maximizer for improved navigation • Created 4 projected digital compliance assistance tools: 1) INS' Alien Employee Visa Classification eTool, 2) OSHA Emergency Evacuation Procedures eTool, 3) EPA's Auto Dismantler & Recycler Environmental Audit Advisor, 4) Motor Vehicle Waste Disposal Wells Advisor • Harmonized Electronic Miner Reporting proof of concept (saving 25,000 hours in reporting time for mining firms) • Completed the Small Business Paperwork Relief Task Force Report to Congress	• Complete additional compliance assistance guides designed to help businesses comply with relevant regulations in the environment, health and safety, employment, and taxes • Develop a "forms gateway" for federal forms systems • Expand harmonized minor reporting (Mine.gov) to include additional federal agencies and additional states • Use XML-schemas to streamline, harmonize, and automate information collection requirements that affect three other industry specific "verticals"—food, chemicals, and health care

Consolidated Health
Informatics
(HHS)

Adopts a portfolio of existing
health information interoperability standards (health
vocabulary and messaging)
enabling all agencies in the
federal health enterprise to
"speak the same language"
based on common enter-
prise-wide business and information technology
architectures.

- Government-wide health IT governance council established
- Portfolio of 24 target domains for
  data and messaging standards
  identified
- Four messaging and one health
  vocabulary standards adopted
  government-wide; additional vocabulary standards being reviewed
- Partnered with 23 federal agen-
  cies/departments who use health
  data for agreements to build
  adopted standards into their
  health IT architecture
- Regular meetings with industry to
  prevent major incompatibilities in
  partnership with the National
  Committee on Vital and Health
  Statistics

- Develop the Business
  Gateway portal into the
  Federal cross-agency portal
  for businesses, integrating the
  content and functionality of
  SBA.gov and
  BusinessLaw.gov into one
  comprehensive site:
  Business.gov
- Deploy subject matter
  experts and report recom-
  mendations
- Assess government-wide investments in standards' licenses and support
- Define change management
  role for the initiative
- Provide requirements government-wide for health IT architecture standards
- Identify appropriate pilots,
  demonstrations and deploy-
  ments

Continued

21

Table 1

E-government Initiatives at a Glance—cont'd

Project (Lead Agency)	Web Site	Description	Progress to Date	Next Steps
Government to Business—cont'd				
Federal Asset Sales (GSA)	http://www.firstgov. gov/shopping/ shopping.shtml	Identify, recommend, and implement improvements for asset recovery and disposition, making it easier for agencies, businesses, and citizens to find and acquire/buy federal assets.	• Developed a draft Governance Model • Launched study of government Utilization and Donation practices • Final Request for Proposal (RFP) posted for Personal Property Asset Class vendor solicitation • Formed and hosted the Source Selection Evaluation Board and Source Section Advisory Council for the Personal Property Asset Class vendor selection	• Continue agency MOU partnership development • Finalize Source Selection for the Personal Property Asset Class by selecting a vendor • Launch Personal Property Asset Class Sales Solution • Utilize agency partnerships to develop a final Utilization and Donation Program Recommendations Report • Post Final RFP for Real Property Asset Class • Launch e-marketplace sales solution for Real Property Asset Class • Complete report on the viability of the Financial Instruments Asset Class • Further define transition plans for migration of FAS e-marketplace solutions to managing agencies

Government to Government

Geospatial One-Stop (DOI)	www.geodata.gov	Provides federal and state agencies with single-point of access to map-related data enabling consolidation of redundant data.	• Created draft standard to ensure consistency among data sets that describe transportation routes and allow governments to share data about transportation related issues. Pilot project demonstrating the utility of the standard completed. • All draft standards available for review on www.geo-one-stop.gov • Inventory of existing Federal data holdings complete • Launched GeoData.gov • Harmonized Draft Framework Data Standards submitted to ANSI for review and approval process	• Establish unified grants program for awarding of grants/cooperative agreements to state and local governments for geospatial acquisitions • Establish active Data Channel content stewards for all channels and processes for maintaining the currency and quality of content in the Portal • Manage Phase 1 of the GeoData.gov portal as an operational tool to develop best practices strategy • Establish a GSA Multiple Award Schedule contract for interoperable geospatial portal components that will be used to acquire a Version 2 production portal • Complete ANSI public review, comment and adjudication of Framework standards

Continued.

Table 1

E-government Initiatives at a Glance—cont'd

Project (Lead Agency)	Web Site	Description	Progress to Date	Next Steps
Government to Government—cont'd				
Disaster Management (FEMA)	www.disasterhelp.gov	Provides federal, state, and local emergency managers on-line access to disaster management related information, planning and response tools.	• Released upgraded DM Interoperability Services (DMIS) to include new tools such as alerts, web-services map capability, open source intelligence, specific needs request, and regional weather • DMIS used in 34 actual emergencies and 61 disaster preparedness exercises with over 291 DMIS operating groups (with 201 waiting for access) in 46 states • DisasterHelp.gov has over 10,600 registered users in 8 months	• Release on-line templates for storing event and site information centrally • Release Playbook module that provides templates and best practices for creating response plans • Continue Agency MOU partnership development • Continue to support and participate in industry EM-XML consortium to help develop interoperability standards for disaster information • Continue developing and receiving input from partner agencies for providing better information sharing on DisasterHelp.gov

SAFECOM
(DHS)

Serves as the umbrella
program within the Federal
government to help local,
tribal, State and Federal
public safety agencies
improve public safety re-
sponse through more effective and efficient
interoperable wireless communications. As a public
safety practitioner driven
program, SAFECOM is
working with existing
Federal communications initiatives and key public
safety stakeholders to
address the need to
develop better technologies
and processes for the cross-
jurisdictional and cross-
disciplinary coordination of
existing systems and future
networks.

• Developed grant guidance for
  public safety interoperability
  equipment grants to local, tribal,
  and State organizations adopted
  by FEMA and COPS
• Chartered and held the first
  meeting of the Federal
  Coordination Council—an
  Interagency working group for
  public safety communications
• Integrated the Public Safety
  Wireless Network Program
• Released the beta version of the
  Interoperable Communications
  Grant Clearinghouse database
• Released a Request for
  Information for technology concepts and existing or under-
  development products or services
  to provide for the interoperability
  of public safety communications
• AGILE and SAFECOM released
  the first draft of the Statement of
  Requirements for public safety in-
  teroperability

• Fully integrate grant guidance
  across federal grant programs
  with interoperable commun -
  cations funding
• Develop and operate an interoperable communications
  center and grants clearinghouse on the web that will
  allow public safety users to
  identify the best solutions for
  their jurisdiction
• Develop and promote technical assistance publications
  that include common interoperability terminology for
  public safety and further addresses communications-
  related issues to improve the
  use of Incident Command
  Systems
• Develop fully interoperable
  demonstrations across the
  country and create interoperability models out of the successful demonstrations
• Continue to support the
  development of standards
  that will enable multi-
  jurisdictional and multi-
  disciplinary interoperability
• SAFECOM will release a
  Broad Agency
  Announcement to identify innovative technologies to fund
  through demonstration
  projects

Continued.

Table 1

E-government Initiatives at a Glance—cont'd

Government to Government—cont'd

Project (Lead Agency)	Web Site	Description	Progress to Date	Next Steps
SAFECOM (DHS)—cont'd				• SAFECOM is working with the joint DOJ/DHS 25 Cities Project, which will help make the top 25 high threat metropolitan areas interoperable • SAFECOM is participating on the White House Spectrum Policy Initiative Taskforce which will make recommendations to the President
E-Vital (SSA)		Establishes common electronic processes for federal & state agencies to collect, process, analyze, verify and share birth and death record information. Also promotes automating how deaths are registered with the states.	• Eight states (CO, HI, MO, MS, MN, IA, CA, OK) can electronically collect, process, analyze, and disseminate electronic birth records • Three states (MN, MT, SD) and New York City have signed contracts to implement an improved death registration process	• Develop pricing models for on-line access to birth and death information • Roll out infrastructure for on-line access to birth and death information • Implement death registration software in New Jersey and New Hampshire • Implement death registration software in New York City, Minnesota, Montana and South Dakota

GRANTS.GOV (formerly E-Grants) (HHS) www.grants.gov	Creates a single portal for all federal grant customers to find, apply and ultimately manage grants online	• Conducted Find system pilot • Completed unified grant application core data standards • Launched Grants.gov web site • Launched Find system • Phased 100% of agencies' competitive announcements into Find system • Completed Apply pilot • Deployed Apply system initial release • Conducted Apply system training	• Phase agencies' programs into the Apply system • Begin Phase II for managing grants on-line • Integrate Find and Apply systems • Enhance Find and Apply system functionality • Define Reporting data standards • Deploy Reporting functionality • Define Mandatory Grants Application data standards • Deploy Mandatory Grants Application functionality

Internal Efficiency and Effectiveness

E-Training (OPM) www.golearn.gov	Create a premier e-training environment that supports development of the Federal workforce through simplified and one-stop access to high quality e-training products and services, and, thus, advances the accomplishment of agency missions.	• Launched GoLearn.gov • 176,000 registered users and 134,000 course completions to date • Variable training costs have been reduced to less than a penny per student • Launched IT security courses mapped to GISRA and NIST requirements • Launched Module 3 which includes initial establishment of IT COP/Knowledge Domain through the IT Workforce Development Roadmap; e-mentoring; upgraded performance support tools; and initial standardized reports	• Migrating existing Transportation Virtual University customers (approx. 40 agencies and/or agency components) to GoLearn.gov to provide single point of entry and fee-for-service capability • Shut down/migrate any additional on-line training systems across government to GoLearn.gov • Establish "communities of practice" working with stakeholder groups and customize the roadmap for the Acquisition, HR, and Financial Management occupations. Anticipate a Module 4 release in September 2004 • Migrate approximately 27 agencies to the GoLearn platform in FY04 (total 58)

Continued.

Table 1

E-government Initiatives at a Glance—cont'd

Internal Efficiency and Effectiveness—cont'd

Project (Lead Agency)	Web Site	Description	Progress to Date	Next Steps
Recruitment One-Stop (OPM)	www.usajobs.opm.gov	Outsources delivery of USAJOBS Federal Employment Information System to deliver state-of-the-art on-line recruitment services to job seekers including intuitive job searching, on-line resume submission, applicant data mining, and on-line feedback on status and eligibility.	• Re-launched upgraded USAJOBS web site • Job-seeker requested enhancement package implemented • Averaging almost 200,000 visits per day since launch on new platform • Over 185,000 new resumes created in first three months of operation	• Continue to enhance site features • Implement integration with Federal agency hiring systems to streamline the job application process and reduce redundancies • Migrate agency job search engines and resume builders
Enterprise HR Integration (OPM)		Streamlines and automates the electronic exchange of standardized HR data needed for creation of an official employee record across the Executive Branch. Provides comprehensive knowledge management workforce analysis, forecasting, and reporting across the Executive Branch for the strategic management of human capital.	• Deployed Release 1 • Loaded Release 1 Repository with eight years of CPDF data • Defined Release 2 Logical Data Model and Data Elements • Defined Portal User Roles for Release 2 and beyond • Analyzed database security design and Implementation approach for Release 2	• Implement Release 2 Physical Data Models • Begin Release 2 Business Intelligence design • Complete Release 2 requirements for eOER • Design Role-based mock-ups of Release 2 Portal

| E-Clearance (OPM) | Streamlines and improves the quality of the current security clearance process. | • Loaded clearances into OPM SII system
• Deployed single point of access to clearances that links the OPM SII system with the DOD JPAS system
• Deployed SF 86C (Certification) form
• Opened E-Clearance learning lab
• Began imaging investigative records
• U.S. State Department has deployed the eQIP System | • Finalize testing of Federal security questionnaire (SF86)
• Continue implementing imaging government-wide
• Continue to train and prepare agencies for eQIP deployment
• Deploy e-QIP |
| E-Payroll (OPM) | Consolidates 22 federal payroll systems to simplify and standardize federal human resources/ payroll policies and procedures to better integrate payroll, human resources, and finance functions. | • Non-continuing agencies aligned with E-Payroll Providers
• Provider entrance sessions completed, customers and migration dates on target
• Payroll Advisory Council formed and monthly sessions conducted
• Standardization focus group formed to develop policy and procedures for payroll delivery standardization opportunities
• Completed migration of DoE
• Received draft partnership merger proposal | • Complete first quarter migrations (ABMC, NRC, STB, non-DOT components of DHS)
• Publish policy and procedures for standardized payroll processes
• Manage remaining Executive agency migrations
• Finalize merger recommendations |

Continued.

Table 1

E-government Initiatives at a Glance—cont'd

Internal Efficiency and Effectiveness—cont'd

Project (Lead Agency)	Web Site	Description	Progress to Date	Next Steps
E-Travel (GSA)		Provides a government-wide web-based service that applies world-class travel management practices to consolidate federal travel, minimize cost and produce superior customer satisfaction. From travel planning and authorization to reimbursement, the E-Travel Service (ETS) will leverage administrative, financial and information technology best practices to realize significant cost savings and improved employee productivity.	• Developed government-wide inventory and business case defining cost/benefits and high-level agency migration requirements • In final stages of completing MOUs with 24 BRM agencies • 18 BRM agencies have begun migration plans with 12 agencies targeting 2004 to begin migration • ETS contract award has been awarded • Finalized exception language and incorporated agency comments for the final Federal Travel Regulation amendment requiring the use of ETS by Dec 2006	• Continue customer service support from the ETS PMO to insure agencies experience a successful migration to ETS • Finalize agency MOUs and migration plans • Full implementation of world-class E-Travel Service • Publish final amendment to Federal Travel Regulation requiring the use of ETS
Integrated Acquisition Environment (GSA)	www.fedteds.gov www.bpn.gov www.ppirs.gov www.fedbizopps.gov	Creates a secure business environment that will facilitate and support cost-effective acquisition of goods and services by agencies, while eliminating inefficiencies in the current acquisition environment.	• Launched Past Performance Information Retrieval System • Issued Business Rules for Intragovernmental Transactions • Merged SBA Pro-NET registration with CCR registration • Registered all agencies for intragovernmental transactions • Launched Federal Technical Data System (FedTeDs.gov) • Proposed Central Contractor Registration rule published in Federal Register for public comment	• Pilot a central place for contractors to post their certifications and representations as required by the Federal Acquisition Regulations (FAR) • Populate a central directory of all multiple agency contracts • Launch updated management information system initial operating capabilities (FPDS-NG) • Prototype of intra-governmental orders and payment transaction exchanges

| E-Records Management (NARA) | www.archives.gov/ records_management/ initiatives/erm_ overview.html | Provides policy guidance to help agencies to better manage their electronic records, so that records information can be effectively used to support timely and effective decision making, enhance service delivery, and ensure accountability. Four major issue areas: Correspondence management, Enterprise-wide electronic records management, Electronic Information Management Standards, Transferring permanent records to NARA. | • Issued guidance for transferring permanent e-mail records and attachments to the National Archives
• Issued transfer guidance for permanent scanned images of textual records
• Expanded methods of transferring electronic records to the National Archives
• Endorsed revised DoD standard for common set of requirements for records management applications government-wide
• Issued guidance for transferring permanent PDF records to the National Archives
• Released Guidance for Coordinating the Evaluation of Capital Planning and Investment Control Proposals for Electronic Records Management Applications
• Registered, into a NIST repository, XML schemata capable of supporting automated transfer and accessioning of e-records | • Release methodology for determining agency-unique requirements not contained in DoD 5014.2-STD
• Issue guidance for transferring permanent digital photography records to the National Archives
• Issue guidance for transferring permanent GIS records to the National Archives
• Issue guidance for transferring permanent web records to the National Archives
• Methodology for developing and implementing an ERM proof of concept pilot
• Analysis of lessons learned with applicability to electronic records management government-wide automated transfer and accessioning of electronic records |

Continued.

Table 1

E-government Initiatives at a Glance—cont'd

Project (Lead Agency)	Web Site	Description	Progress to Date	Next Steps
Cross-Cutting E-Authentication (GSA)		Minimizes the burden on businesses, public and government when obtaining services on-line by providing a secure infrastructure for on-line transactions, eliminating the need for separate processes for the verification of identity and electronic signatures.	• Gateway prototype deployed • Drafted Guidance released creating authentication assurance levels • Four agencies (DOD, TREAS, USDA, NASA) cross-certified with Federal PKI Bridge • Draft Credential Assessment Framework completed • Credential Assessment conducted on one Credential Service Provider	• Add additional applications for the Centralized Validation Service for PKI • Issue final guidance creating authentication assurance levels • Draft Authentication and Identity Policy Framework for Federal Agencies • Establish list of trusted credential providers • Define authentication architecture based on standards for interoperability • Complete Strategic Business Plan • Demonstrate architecture in Pilot • Establish interoperability laboratory

Figure 1

requirements. Once the criteria are met, the citizen is eligible for the benefit. To help administer these programs, government has created an online access point for the various entitlements. The "govbenefits.com" website provides a point of entry for individuals seeking government assistance. Through the site, anyone can determine his or her eligibility for almost all entitlement programs. Future goals for the 'govbenefits' portal include allowing application for the respective benefits to be conducted on-line.

The creation of an entry point for government benefits is possibly the most important electronic advancement made by government. If current trends hold, entitlement benefits will continue to gobble up government's resources. Part of the offset to this demand includes administering the various programs more efficiently. Electronic government has this potential. Its success depends on integrating all benefit programs and linking them to state resources, which are the future steps.

Social security is a type of entitlement program moving ahead with online efforts. Figure 1 is the site page for social security.

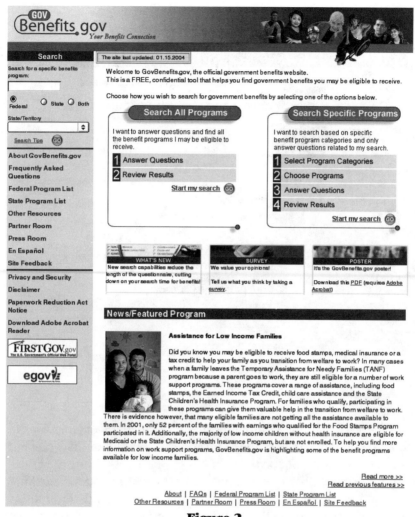

Figure 2

At their site, those who qualify for Social Security and Supplemental Security Income can be determined, and benefits can be secured online. The site easily links users to eNews, other online services, and job opportunities. Contacting the Social Security Administration can be completed online or over the phone. Numbers are available online. The site is also available in Spanish, as well as other languages.

Users of the social security site or govbeneifts.gov site find user-friendly sites that lessen the need to know which agency handles the services specifically needed by the potential recipient. Figure 2 is the site page for govbenefits.gov. Users only need to know which category they fall into in order to be linked with the office that handles their issue. At the sites, users can learn about the program and thus educate others about the services that government provides. These sites ultimately provide access to those that need the services the most. Thus government is made more responsive and efficient (the overarching goals if you remember).

Taxes

Taxes are legally required payments. Complying with the tax code is burdensome for most citizens. Many choose to let someone else handle the unseemly duty of filing federal, state, and local tax forms. For those folks, the forms are mind numbing and arcane. Their reluctance to wade into tax forms, special deductions, and the maze of rules creates a dislike of government and paying taxes. Presently, tax preparation software lessens the need to know all the tax laws or possess forms needed for filing. The federal government and several states are beginning to ease utilization of this software and the Internet. Citizens can now e-file their tax returns.

Filing income tax returns will someday be a paperless endeavor. In 2003, tens of millions of returns were filed using the Internal Revenue Service's (IRS) enhanced e-file system. Through a partnership with software providers, the IRS was provided free preparation and filing on-line. This not only reduces the burden of complying with tax liability, but also reduces costs to both citizens and government. Most states have similar systems. Before e-file, the federal government successfully used tele-file or telephone aided filing. For those using the easiest (EZ) tax form, the process was as simple as punching in numbers when prompted by an automated system. Returns under both systems are processed and completed within a couple of weeks (assuming no errors).

Through these electronic initiatives, it is possible the IRS can overcome many of the stigmas attached to its existence. Not only can citizens file free returns, they can also check on the status of their returns. Refunds and payments can be made electronically through direct debiting and crediting. The angst taxpayers feel will never be totally relieved. Certified Public Accountants and other such consultants need to be concerned about an impending reduction in the use of their services to prepare and submit tax forms for citizens. It is worth noting that professional tax services have availed themselves of such technology long before it became possible for mass participation in e-filing.

Employment
The federal government employs millions of citizens (Light, 2003). Recruiting, training, and retaining such a massive labor force consumes significant resources. Through usajobs.opm.gov, the federal government can advertise and recruit potential employees with greater efficiency. Applicants can search for jobs and even submit applications and resumes online. By creating a single portal for all agency job openings, the federal government can streamline recruiting by diminishing agency needs to create and maintain uniformity in the search process. Job seekers enjoy the ease of searching all agencies according to their knowledge, skills, and abilities (KSA). This is important as KSA statements are required for public work.

Like most groups, the federal labor force is undergoing change. Pressures to eliminate certain jobs because they can be performed by the private sector threaten accountability of public employment and its security. Despite this real concern, an aging workforce is the primary issue that top government officials will address in the near future. Retiring public employees will need replacing within the next decade. Hiring officials are turning to the Internet for help. Potential applicants can now search and review job postings. Applying for many positions is also permitted over the Internet through templates and file uploading capabilities. In addition to the Internet, job hotlines are utilized for those who don't have ready access to computers. Potential applicants can then use traditional mail service regardless of how they discover the availability of a particular position.

Once selected, employees must be trained. Technology makes training easier. Computer simulations can create scenarios that mirror those encountered on the job. The Department of Defense and NASA have used such technology to train pilots and astronauts. Similar programs are used to train workers on rules, regulations, and procedures. At a basic level, technology is used to present training materials to employees. Technology and training can be passive or active. The applications range widely.

We predict that technology will continue to transform the nature of recruiting employees. After the terrorist attacks of September 11, 2001, the safety of mail service came under scrutiny after a series of anthrax discoveries. Applicants using the United States Postal Service were required to reapply. Those using electronic means to apply did not experience delays in their applications. The ease and safety of using the Internet to seek public employment is quickly becoming the norm. It is not an unsafe stretch to believe that someday all initial applications for government work will be processed through electronic media.

Loans
The United States government makes loans of all types. Student loans provide money for college expenses. Small business loans help fledgling enterprises lift off the ground. Other types of loans— like mortgages—involve both direct lending and insuring risk, as well as help individuals and families secure homeownership. While an e-loan gateway is being planned, it has yet to be implemented. There are agency-specific loan sites. One of the most well-developed is the Department of Education's tools for processing and repaying student loans. The Federal Application for Student Aid can be completed online. Once part of the system, students are assigned a personal identification number (PIN), which allows access to their account. Management of the account is then as easy as logging on.

Recreation
Governments at all levels provide valuable recreation opportunities. National, state, and local parks include an abundance of activities, from canoeing to camping, golf to ping-pong. Recreation.gov seeks to offer an easy way for citizens to discover information regarding these places. In May 2002, county and state data were added. Future goals include creating a reservation system and improving mapping abilities. States also provide similar services that have not yet been incorporated into the federal site.

Government and Business

The role of government in making and enforcing rules is fundamental. However, laws and rules are developed within an environment of politics. It was Woodrow Wilson who envisioned government functions, including rule making, that were less influenced by politics. The development of good administration was required for the advancement of the human condition. It is customary for Congress to leave many of the technical applications of a program up to the agencies administering them. The process for developing these guiding principles is known as rule making.

Rule making involves creating regulations which individuals and businesses will follow. Rule making is characterized by a process. This essential administrative function is a subject of controversy. Politics is attached to all aspects of the process. For this reason, Congress formally asserted the boundaries of the bureaucracy with the Administrative Procedures Act of 1949 (Thomas.gov). Rule making is governed by the protections of public notice and due process. Moreover, past executive orders issued during the Reagan administration required impact statements, cost-benefit analysis, and justification for the new rule or change to an existing rule. Thus, rule changes don't just happen. Those who will be affected by the proposed rule are allowed an opportunity (procedurally) to comment before rules are formally adopted. Those found in violation of a federal rule have the legal guarantee of due process.

In order for the rule-making process to be successful there has to be informed participants. Rules that make it through the process can only be followed if they are known. Technology has the ability to serve both actors in the process and those who must adhere to agency rules. Even if it did not, those affected would discover the agenda through traditional means—legislative staff, watchdogs, and other interest groups who monitor the federal government's rule-making efforts.

Proposed rules and rule changes, as well as executive orders, can be found in the Federal Register. The Register is published weekdays. The sum of all adopted rules can be found in the Code of Federal regulations at regulations.com. At this site, the Federal Register is also accessible. As required by the Administrative Act of 1949, whoever wishes to participate in the rule-making process can do so. The website makes this participation easier. At the regulations.com website, you can also visit firstgov.com which links to agency docket sites and in turn, list rules that will be considered during upcoming meetings. Future plans for the regulations.com site call for improvements such as streamlining all rule-making functions into the single portal.

Another example of e-governments influence has been upon businesses complying with the myriad of federal statutes and codes. At businesslaw.gov, government has made accessing and understanding business law easier. The site was launched in December, 2002. Businesses can now register online, as well as petition for a state identification (ID) number. They can also obtain an IRS Employer Identification number (ID). This number is important for paying business activity taxes, and remitting payroll charges for employees. It also allows for some regulatory reporting. For example, the site saves 25,000 hours annually in reporting for coal miners alone (e-gov.com, 2003). Current plans for upgrading the site include better search capacities and industry-specific ports.

Government to Government

The relationships fostered and developed between governments are extremely important. Federalism is the philosophy of shared power among the various levels of government in the United States. History is filled with examples of states in conflict with one another over trash-dumping, water resources, and taxes. States have taken issue with the power and coercion exercised by the central government. Around the 1930's, the states began looking to the central government for help in addressing pressing policy concerns caused by the Great Depression. After adopting the income tax early in the 1900's, government quickly began developing the capacity to handle wars, depressions, and civil rights. The Great Depression dislodged any reluctance the states held in regards to limiting the central government's scope. Seizing on a dire situation, President Franklin D. Roosevelt expanded government programs and thus the federal government's role of shaping the macro economy and coordinating massive social programs was initiated.

Many of the issues that occur in a federal system deal with money and resources. The United States is not different in this regard. The U.S. federal government is generally looked to for help in ameliorating the effects of natural disasters, drought, terrorism, and creating the proper climate for economic growth. Several electronic initiatives improve services in these areas; others are still waiting to be developed. One such area receiving attention is disaster management. At the site disasterhelp.gov, emergency planners have access to information and resources used to address natural disaster situations.

The area of most importance is how the federal government shares its resources through grants.gov. The federal government transfers hundreds of millions of dollars each year to individuals and states. Much of the transfers occur through entitlements. Significant resources reach the recipient through an application process. The website grants.gov is an entry point for all federal grant recipients. At the site you can search for and complete applications. When researching grants, the site provides useful information. Plans to enhance the site include creating a unified application to decrease costs and full search capabilities.

History

Electronic government started when Al Gore created the Internet. We, of course, are joking on this point. While the former Vice-President may not have created the actual Internet, he did spearhead the latest effort at making government more efficient through information technology. Most likely, the reliance on technology to streamline government operations stems from his preference for technology. This is not surprising given his substantial role in developing the systems that make modern technologies work. Al Gore's work through the National Performance Review (NPR) was not the first effort to create more efficiency within government. It has been, by most accounts, another effort at reforming government that produced minimal success. The importance of the NPR is that it seeks to make government more efficient and productive through the use of information technology.

At the beginning of the NPR's work, the need to cast off government's old way of doing business became apparent. There was very little need to proceed with efficiencies and technologies if they were simply going to be rife with the negative connotations associated with a bureaucratic organizational structure. With a team of street level bureaucrats, as well as experts in reinventing organizations, a set of proposals was developed. The results of their efforts were 1,200 suggestions for making government work better and more efficiently (Access American, 2003). Thus, the e-government movement at the federal level had its impetus from a reform effort. President Clinton vowed to adopt the suggestions of Al Gore's committee. To celebrate, a big party was held on the White House lawn to unveil the new initiative. Most all electronic initiatives can give thanks to this event as their birth.

The Dream

The primary goal of reinventing government with the help of information technology is centered on improving access and creating more efficient government operations. Taking advantage of government services can be a daunting task. Many citizens simply do not know where to start when negotiating the bureaucratic maze that can easily overwhelm even the most knowledgeable citizen. With greater technologies becoming available and implemented, governments can deliver services with much more ease, efficiency, and service. To solve the problem of knowing where to go for a particular problem or service, governments are creating one-click pages whereby any government service is no more than one click of the computer mouse from the correct website. From there, visa applications can be filled out and printed, tax forms can be submitted, and information concerning government benefits can be viewed. Most common transactions can be handled online from home or library, or anyplace that will allow private business to be conducted on the computer. These information technology (IT) applications potentially provide greater access.

Digital Divide

In order to take advantage of government's use of technology to deliver services, citizens must have access to the Internet. The use of computers in the United States continues to grow. The U.S. Census estimates that a majority of households have a personal computer (PC) (Census, 2000). This bodes well for those hoping that information technology will increase the access of government services to citizens. For those who have trouble locating access, or for those who do not know the basics of computer usage, access to government is an empty goal.

The Digital Divide consists of folks without computer access or computer knowledge. It is the space that separates folks with the ability to take advantage of all the promises that technology has to offer (Reich, 1991).

Despite the barriers to accessing government through the computer or telephone, survey evidence reveals that citizens are embracing the idea of e-government (Washington Post, 2003). The Council for Excellence in Government reports that 70% of those surveyed had Internet access. This estimate seems a bit inflated and could include access at home, work, school, or other place. Most importantly, people are using this access to become electronic citizens and take advantage of government services via the Internet. Fully three-fourths of Internet users have used a government site to get information or carry out a transaction (Council, 2003).

Not only are citizens using the Internet to access government services, but they are also reporting high levels of satisfaction with their experiences. Of those using e-government access, three-fourths (Washington Post, 2003) believe technology is making it easier to interact with government, particularly in getting information about government programs and services. Two-thirds (Washington Post, 2003) believe that transactions have become more efficient and less cumbersome. It is not difficult to believe these perspectives. Throughout this discussion, we have maintained that technology holds promises. Allowing citizens to access information and complete the most basic transaction appears to be a promise being delivered.

Evaluating E-government

It appears that those using the Internet to access government services have some positive notions of electronic government. Users of electronic government sources are happy. Electronic government is in its infancy, however. As with most major advancements and changes, the proper direction and foundations take time to develop. Electronic government seems to be subject to similar forces. West (2000) concluded that the practices of state and federal agencies to be varied, and generally lacking in their overall development.

West's evaluation project mailed surveys to the chief information officers in all 50 states and those from 38 federal agencies. The examination also conducted content analysis of approximately 1,800 websites. Table 2 lists information that is commonly sought out by citizens, and at the very least, information that proves useful for obtaining additional information. Some important findings from the survey are: those with disabilities would have trouble using most government websites; roughly a fourth of these sites have services available online; some sites had commercial advertisements; and federal sites were better overall than state sites.

These findings are consistent with other surveys, and are not totally surprising. In order to improve the delivery of electronic services, the government will have to invest the capital resources to upgrade the quality of electronic government websites, expand the range of uses and accessibility, and commit to making electronic government more than a place to get a form or discover office hours. Many Information Technology (IT) directors see that the best time to expand electronic initiatives is now.

The final components to making e-government successful are education and access. Citizens need to be comfortable conducting transactions online. They need to be computer literate. While the number of savvy users increases, there are those who still do not have access. Also, some are simply unwilling to use technology to interact with each other, or to carry out day-to-day activities.

Government

Government is a set of institutions that carries out public functions. These institutions are guided by constraints, primarily legal and political ones. In the United States, the Constitution provides the framework for government action. Politically, Congress is thought to be most pressured by political constraints. It, too, is constrained by the Constitution. The executive branch houses the bureaucracy, and is headed by the President.

It is somewhat surprising to citizens when they realize that government touches virtually every aspect of their lives. Government regulates things from the official time of day to protecting consumers, and oversees, enforces, and takes an interest in almost every activity. As citizens in the United States, we don't recognize the pervasive reach of government. Ideological conservatives rail against bloated government waste and inefficiency. Even within these sensitive groups, there is rare understanding or appreciation for the vastness of government.

At the federal level, government agencies and bureaucrats insert themselves into the lives of citizens more so than a member of Congress or a Supreme Court justice. Members of Congress and the Supreme Court can make policies, interpret laws, and suggest remedies to social ills, but they don't carry out their policy prescriptions or rulings. It is up to the bureaucracy to interpret, implement, and access government's activities. More will be written later about how technology is changing the way the legislative and judicial branches operate, but for now, their importance is minimal to the overall notion of electronic government. It is the agencies and departments that actually deliver government services that are most affected by the e-government revolution.

Given the massive size of the government bureaucracy, it is understandable that changes will be slow. Organizations such as government departments have unique organizational cultures that affect their acceptance and adaptation to new ways of carrying out their functions. The insistence that e-government become more than a disseminating function of government places pressure on the bureaucracy to change and adapt. We believe this pressure is the key to a successful transformation toward e-government.

Organizational culture works to ensure that work gets done (Gulick, 1937). Boundaries and obstacles, such as job descriptions and pay level, provide cues to job prestige and importance, but the work of the government requires success. Part of organizational culture is relationships, which is code for organizational communication patterns. Technology has the ability to increase communication. We can do this anytime over any distance. Technology also exposes the workings of an organization's culture or ways of interacting to achieve a desired objective. Predicting how technology will change culture is not our work, but speculating about the relationship of how culture shapes the use of technology does fall within our interests. We believe that despite the movement toward e-government, the core of organizational culture is still the same.

Organizational culture is an extension of how the organization is structured. Government structure, how workers are arranged to carry out tasks, has implications for the types of outputs it will produce. These implications include how quickly government can respond to an inquiry, process an application, prosecute a criminal, or give aid to the needy. When most citizens hear the word "bureaucracy" it conjures up negative feelings. With expanding technologies there exists a diminished basis to maintain these feelings.

Politics

The movement to enhance electronic government services derives from political and ideological pressure. Conservatives believe that business practices should apply to government. This usually manifests itself in such phrases as "run government like a business." Others see the benefits businesses have reaped through adopting information systems that reduce their costs and make them more competitive. Ideologically, if information technology can reduce the size of bureaucracy then the result is smaller government; this view is compatible with those who believe that less government (regulation) equals greater freedoms (Friedman, 1962).

The collision of the various political and ideological pressures with the rapid rate of technological advancement leaves electronic government at a crossroads. The federal government is the largest consumer of information technology (Washington Post, 2003). New legislation such as the Electronic Government Act (2002) provides the framework for advancing new initiatives, sharing the savings associated with the new technologies, and ensuring the security of the new changes (White House, 2002).

There is very little argument that President Bush's administration is squarely behind the idea that information technology and e-government should advance. Comments by the administration's e-gov czar indicate that we are in the beginning stages of moving government services online and toward a market-based, goals-oriented model (Office of Management and Budget, 2003). Opposition from those not of the President's party also seems to behold the promises information technology holds for government.

Joe Lieberman has hailed e-government as the "Next Generation Government" (Senate, 2001). As part of the Congressional Internet Caucus, technology in future government services is considered the best way to achieving a citizen friendly, responsive government. Government will either harness the new technologies or will lose its place as a positive presence in society (Senate, 2001). He, along with others, has championed the cause of e-government.

Senator Lieberman's concerns hark back to the discussion earlier in this chapter about organizational structure and management models. If government chooses to apply technology to the old bureaucratic structure, the delivery of government services will be the same, just delivered through a different medium. According to the authorizing legislation such as the E-government Act (2001, 2002), this fear is easily addressable even though e-government is, as Senator Lieberman characterizes, "a loose-knit mix of ideas, projects and affiliations, often uncoordinated, sometimes overlapping (Senate, 2001)."

As we stated earlier, E-government is in its infancy. Support for using technology to improve services is the next logical step. The promise of more efficient and responsive government may become tangled in old bureaucratic alliances. Authorizing legislation is the first step in a two-step process. The second step is Congress' willingness to fully fund many of the initiatives that spring forth under the E-government Act. The Act creates a permanent department with budget authority within the Office of Management and Budget (OMB). Given the OMB's strategic location, e-government programs may very well see the resources needed to develop their potential and deliver on their promises.

Citizens' Use of the Internet

In order for government to become more than just an information source, the types of services citizens seek need to move beyond discovering information, which is the most common activity. Most users of the Internet surf the web for facts, agency descriptions, documents, and opportunities (Larsen, 2002). The most common type of information sought by consumers is that related to tourism or recreation (Pew, 2001). Many sites allow users to make reservations, which probably accounts for their popularity.

Students, and parents, find government websites useful for doing work related to school or jobs. Over two-thirds of respondents to a Pew survey indicated they had surfed the net for similar information. Almost two-thirds sought out information about what an agency actually does. This is not surprising given the vast nature of government services. These types of queries are what are expected of users. Electronic government requires users to move beyond the standard log-on-and-find expectations of government.

Transactions such as filing taxes, renewing licenses, and applying for jobs are the types of services e-government should deliver. These transactions are sought out by few citizens (Pew, 2001). In order to realize the efficiencies technology offers, more citizens will need to log on and be comfortable making business transactions. Their reasons for not doing so are already numerous. Security and privacy issues pose the gravest concern. Entering in social security numbers and credit card numbers is still risky to many. This is an impediment.

The Pay Off

Technology has the potential to be cost-effective. It is believed that technology can reduce the costs of government services therefore saving taxpayer money. These savings are part of the impetus for the dedicated efforts of incorporating technology into government practices. Precisely gauging the savings associated with new technologies is difficult due to the intertwined nature of technology and government structure (Fountain and Urzua, 2001). Rough, conservative estimates place the savings around 12 billion dollars in 2001. (Fountain and Urzua, 2001)

The use of technology in daily operations illustrates the immediate potential savings. Using e-mail instead of placing a long distance call or mailing numerous documents have the potential to save thousands of dollars per employee. E-mail limits costs associated with purchasing and handling paper. Technology also reduces the costs of transactions. The costs of processing payments, billing, and completing related transactions are estimated to be cut in half. In our social security discussion, assume that benefits were applied for and received electronically through direct deposit. The government would save on a phone call (toll-free) asking for information. The citizen saves herself the time of driving to the nearest federal building. Once there, it is not uncommon to lack documents required to complete an application. Thus, another trip is required later. This example could be traced out to the end, but we think you get the picture.

Technology creates efficiencies and opportunities. With these opportunities, opportunity costs arise. Opportunity costs reduce resources and limit the ability to take advantage of alternatives. As a student, if you are deeply engaged in reading for class, you are unable to drive to the music store. The inability to go to the music store is your opportunity cost. As technologies make government leaner and more efficient, the counterbalancing demand to extend government services to those on the other side of the divide may become a normative argument. Additionally, investing in technology requires more investments. The money invested in technology cannot be used in other places. As with education spending, there are those with great and loud voices that view technology investments as luxuries. Others would disagree. The federal government's position on technology investment tends to view the investments as positive. While it is intuitive that technology pays off (like a college education), our understanding of the rewards is evolving. It will take some time before we can firmly calculate all the possible costs and benefits. Future experience will help us with that task.

Other Areas

Technology may someday allow for a full range of political participation, including voting. Citizens can now e-mail or fax their elected representatives. At the local level, cities and towns can place a meeting agenda on the web rather than printing and publishing it each week. The cost savings easily climb into the thousands of dollars. States allow for the renewal of auto registrations. Like a wobbly new spring calf, we too are getting our legs. Future possibilities are endless.

Voting via some medium other than punch cards and bubble sheets is not too distant. Online voting could be conducted from any computer. Voice recognition software could allow voting to expand to phone users. Technology potentially could allow anyone eligible to vote to do so more easily. Not only can technology enhance participation, but it also may strengthen democracy. The flipside, of course, is that technology could further divide and alienate people, leaving participation in the pathetic state it currently enjoys.

As strange as it may seem, jury duty is being transformed by technology. What is being touted as "cyber justice," "cyber juries," and "cyber courts," are ideas that would allow justice to be dispensed via electronic means. Through streaming media online, video conferencing, and telecommunications (wireless and otherwise), we can see and interact with one another from a great distance. Even across the street is not an insurmountable distance. Current technology allows a group of people the luxury of interacting with one another while maintaining different locations. This capability is only going to improve.

Summary

Government structure and operations are at a crossroads. Technology is readily available and has the ability to transform how government interacts with all of its constituents. There seems to be political support for providing the resources needed to make sure e-government is reality, not rhetoric. Old bureaucratic machinations are still in place, however. Citizens are not fully availing themselves of current services, or simply do not have the desire to interact with government electronically.

Although e-government has been around several years, it is still in the beginning stages of development. Initial research points toward a trend of greater reliance on electronic government. This alone may be enough to rapidly cause the electronic capacities of government to increase. We hope this prediction is accurate.

We see only great things for government operation and technology. Time and space can no longer discriminate or discourage someone from seeking out government services. Information is no longer a commodity that can be hoarded and hidden from others. Technology has the ability to make access to government more equal. The truest equality will come when everyone has the understanding of government's structure, special functions, and the processes it uses to solve problems. Hopefully this chapter has shed some light on all these requisites.

Technology and Democracy

3

Emerging technologies hold promise in promoting the quality of democracy. Technology allows citizens to interact and influence government through unconventional media with minimal effort or expertise. As technologies grow and become more commonplace, their usage in keeping up with and making claims on government will also grow. During this maturation process it will be possible for the quality of our democracy to expand and fulfill the promise of full incorporation. Democracy is not like electricity, which flows through electric wires with its potential only released through the flip of a switch. Its nature is more fluid, like shades of gray.

The United States was founded on the promise of self-determination. Our belief in democracy rests on the citizenry being able to influence government, compete over scarce public goods, and exchange ideas on matters politic. For all this to happen, the citizenry must be engaged and engaged on civic matters. Voting, phoning elected representatives, attending local meetings, and working in campaigns are examples of being connected to the process.

Democracy is not an all or nothing proposition. It exists in varying degrees, and depends on the practices of government and citizens. Theorists have attempted to place a finer point on understanding the notion of people controlling their destiny through making collective decisions. Their fruits produce a collection of similar concepts that allow us to judge our democracy. Several important concepts related to democracy form the basis for visualizing how technology may someday allow all citizens more access and influence on the functions of government.

At the heart of democratic theory is the idea of citizen participation and input. Government policies should reflect the sentiments of the majority while protecting those in the minority. Madison helped allay the fears of those weary of the passions of the masses (Federalist No. 10). It was Thomas Jefferson's view that the answer to responsible government was not to eliminate the ability of citizen's to participate, but to educate them so that they may become viable actors in democratic government. These views of democracy separate the theory into two distinct varieties: direct and indirect.

What is the best mechanism for allowing citizens to express their views on public matters? Actually there are several methods for resolving conflict and making decisions concerning public matters. One only needs to survey the social choice literature to discover that voting is not always the best method for choosing among alternatives. At this point, though, we are ahead of ourselves. Our question is how the public's interest gets translated into policies and other government outputs. The two methods we will discuss are direct democracy and our representative system.

Direct democracy means that all eligible citizens can participate in decisions of government. For all questions and issues, everyone has equal voice and opportunity to influence what government chooses to do. While it would be nice if everyone could participate by voting on policies, the mechanics of direct democracy are workable in more intimate settings. With the United States population reaching a few hundred million, the prospects for direct democracy have dwindled. Thus, the Founding Fathers correctly adapted our version of democracy to a representative form. Our democracy is not direct, but indirect.

Direct democracy empowers citizens. In some states, citizens have legal tools available that allow them to control the policy process. Initiative, referendum, and recall are the most common avenues for citizens' control over government policies, and in the case of recall, their representation. Initiatives and referendums are essentially similar policy tools the masses may use to enact policy. Both require votes by the electorate. Initiatives are policy questions placed on the ballot as a result of a citizen-led process. Referendum questions are put to voters by a legislative body. Recall allows citizens to end the term of an elected representative at any time through a process culminating in a recall vote. If a recall vote is successful, the representative subjected to the vote seeks other work.

The tools of direct democracy work best in small districts. They are used regularly in those states that permit them. It is fashionable to question the ability of citizens to control their own fate by deciding policy questions for themselves. We believe, like V.O. Key, that voters are not fools. That citizens are not interested in most public matters may be a result of feeling powerless to shape government. We doubt those claims that the great masses are ill equipped to understand and render decisions on complex or even simple policy questions. If they are ill equipped, it is because they don't have much practice in these areas.

Understanding impediments to direct citizen rule, such as time, distance, education, and intense passions of organized interests, the Founding Fathers designed a republican form of government whereby an elected agent—President, Senator, and House Representative—represents citizens. Thus, an indirect form of democracy has proven palatable. Most citizens like their elected functionaries, even though they may disdain government. These affections for their delegates contribute to the legitimacy of and the authority for government to enact policies on behalf of the governed. Through their participation and acceptance of what their elected representatives produce, consent is conferred, even if only tacitly.

The persistent question that accompanies a representative form of government addresses the quality of its representation. It is an obvious question and commonsensical, yet it is not asked often enough. If a representative keeps a hand on the pulse of her constituents and diligently serves them, is this enough to qualify as good representation? The short answer: it depends. It depends on how accurately public opinion is gauged. It depends on the power and influence the representative has to address the constituent's needs.

Generally, a representative has three roles he or she can fulfill when representing their constituents: delegate, trustee, and politico. Delegates strictly adhere to the attitudes and opinions of those they represent. On any particular issue he will take steps to discern the position of his constituents. In contrast, the trustee serves under the assumption that her constituents trust whatever stance she may develop on a policy question. The politico vacillates among the trustee and delegate role. He takes on the most appropriate role depending on the issue and how in touch the constituents are to the process.

These roles have consequences for the quality of representation citizens may receive. The trustee and politico roles pose the most recurrent dilemmas. Politicos are good at the craft of politics, but may be perceived by the electorate as whimsical and weak leaders. Trustees who are out of touch with the constituents govern without regard for the true public interest. They develop a hubris that is nourished by what they perceive as unbridled power gained from their position as an elected functionary. Under these scenarios it is easy to see that a republican form of government is not without concerns. Some of these concerns will be explored later in the chapter concerning parties and interest groups.

Beyond our general discussion of representation, democracies flourish when an educated citizenry has the ability to exchange ideas and debate issues freely. When free expression is stifled, the marketplace of ideas no longer works efficiently in the public interest. The inability to question government priorities and actions of elected functionaries, or to openly criticize injustice leads to citizen oppression. Good democracies are those that can be characterized as free and open.

Open democracies conduct business where citizens may observe deliberations, debates, and position taking. Government documents are available for review by citizens and the media. Opportunities exist for input in public meetings. Agendas are released in advanced. Meeting times are posted, and regular schedules established. In honest governments, decisions are made that everyone sees and ultimately everyone knows. Open government means open secrets (www.opensecrets.com).

Free expression is the ability to state opinion without fear of reprisal for taking the position. If public expression on political matters resulted in economic, physical, or emotional harm to one's self or family, psychologists tell us that this will normally lead to fewer public statements and positions on public matters. Humans naturally want to protect their families and their well-being. External events— usually politics—that don't immediately impact this desire to protect and prosper won't be a priority. As students of politics and government, you know that politics directly impact individual well-being, health, job availability, and the ability to provide things such as food for the family. Political activity and livelihood shouldn't be linked. Yet, they were hand-in-hand at the founding of the United States, and they are now as well.

Equality

Of the primary features of democracy, it can be argued that in the United States we have varying degrees of each. Certainly in the 2000 presidential election it can be argued that the majority did not rule

(Al Gore won the popular vote but lost in the electoral college). The two features that are most affected by technology are equality and liberty. It is worth exploring these separately before returning to traditional forms of participation.

Equality means different things to different people. When discussing democracy, equality refers to social, legal, and political equality. Very few would argue that we have pure equality in the United States. Women and minorities still struggle for equality in pay and employment. Indigent citizens will tell you that the legal system is not built for those without financial resources. Many disenchanted voters claim they don't vote because they don't feel that they matter. Thus, establishing that our democratic practice produces and maintains inequalities is not a difficult argument to make. The question most appropriate here is whether or not technology can ease some of the fundamental inequalities.

Before turning our attention to whether or not technology can ease the inequalities that impede democracy, agreement on the cause of the inequalities has to be reached. This question yields lively debate both on the causes and consequences of maintained inequality. Inequality is caused by a faulty government structure and failed policies according to the socialist democratic paradigm. The resulting concentration of wealth also concentrates political power. They would suggest dispersing economic wealth in order to equalize political power. Thus, better government policies toward wealth redistribution are required.

Others contend that a lack of faith in the invisible hand of the free market and poorly conceived policies in the areas of wealth redistribution both suppress freedoms and exacerbate disjointed priorities and poor decision making (Friedman, 1960). Thus, less government is needed in order to produce a balanced playing field where citizens are free to engage in alliances that create freedom and are beneficial. This strain of libertarians claim that democracy and freedom would be enhanced if less government regulation was the norm.

Despite these causes of political inequality and their respective remedies, both have resources and wealth as a common base. Both acknowledge that concentrated wealth is to be blamed on failed government policies. The democratic socialist would argue that better policies are needed to rectify the imbalance, while the libertarians would argue that government has had its opportunities and should end all failed programs. Since it is unlikely that either of these extremes will take place, inequalities have to be overcome by individuals and their own devices. This is where technology brings considerable influence.

As Reich (1991) describes in his lucid argument concerning the future of individual economic success, technology can be the great liberator. Computers and the Internet allow individuals to transcend traditional limits of time and distance. With the click of a mouse, messages can be sent to someone on the other side of the world. Surf a few web pages and you can obtain an item needed to decorate a home. More importantly, you can compare prices, quality, and terms of sale on just about any good or service provided.

Technology not only allows us to communicate and find the best deal on goods and services, its most important contribution is its ability to make transactions more efficient. As we become more efficient and productive, our quality of life is raised. While it is true that everyone who has access to technology and uses its power will see an increase in living standards, the time saved by using technology can be put to civic use, continuing education, or some other contribution to community. Thus, technology has the potential to create the conditions whereby everyone has equal access to the tools of productivity, efficiency, and mutually-beneficial transactions.

Other Equalities

In so far as technology could ease some economic inequalities, the argument that other forms of inequality will fall like dominoes once the first one tumbles is difficult to make. Political and legal equality are the easiest to envision disappearing. As attorney Johnny Cochran has observed, the color of justice is not black or white, but rather, it is green. He contends that in the U.S. legal system, defendants are presumed innocent until proven broke. Cochran is alluding to legal inequality. Politically, Dye (2001) would argue that with enhanced economic standing comes greater political influence. His theory of elite policymaking is predicated on concentrated monetary wealth. If technology can somehow serve to broaden wealth, it is possible that political inequality would lessen if Dye's theory is correct.

Social inequality is also a great threat to the quality of democracy. Since it is not caused by government structure, but rather human proclivities, technology has less potential to undermine its support system. Social inequality is symbolized by the unequal access to education, power, and wealth based on social characteristics such as gender, race, or religion. As mentioned earlier, women still struggle for equal pay. Legal challenges are common on issues of affirmative action and equal access to education and jobs. Religious intolerance has been prevalent since the United States' founding. Remember the Salem Witch Trials?

Part of the cause of social inequalities is surmountable through education and access to information. Technology has a role in both of these areas. Education levels traditionally translate into better paying jobs and advancement potential. Education, particularly higher education, is becoming a more realistic option for many historically disadvantaged groups. Technology will not only allow these groups to discover beneficial opportunities, but will also aid in taking advantage of those opportunities.

Equality may not be needed to maintain a strong democracy. Dye (2001) contends that his theory of top-down policymaking in fact does not threaten our democratic notions at all. It may be that the other threats to a quality democracy are not consequential either. The inequalities are important if citizens are not politically equal or powerful. If inequalities serve to disadvantage or punish unfairly, then our system of governance is not just or democratic. These aforementioned fundamentals of democracy serve as a basis for theorizing about the potential influences technology may have on democratic constructs. It is worthwhile to examine some scenarios in order to protect an additional fundamental tenet of democracy, and that is liberty.

Freedom and Scenarios

Benjamin Barber (1998) outlines three scenarios for the future of technology and the fate of our democracy. While they don't treat the issue of equality directly, the scenarios get at the heart of our overarching practice of democracy. First, at one end of the spectrum, we should expect technology to lift the quality of democracy. Those holding this position see technology as a panacea. If we only had more technology with more children and adults trained to use it, the conditions of workers and society would improve. Technology then has very little detractors at this end of the spectrum. Barber contends that even though market forces demand and produce improvements in business and industry, it is not certain these forces will produce efficiencies in our civic life.

Secondly, Barber contends that in order for U.S. democracy to be improved by technology, more of its power must be harnessed for the public interest. Similarly to public radio and public television, the public needs cheaper access to digital technologies that have multiple applications. Computer and Internet availability in libraries is the beginning. Voter kiosks at supermarkets and other interactive technologies are the next step. Importantly, technology must be dispersed among all citizens. Otherwise, it will continue to be a currency used exclusively by those with power and influence.

Last, and at the other end of the spectrum, technology has the potential to weaken the quality of democracy. If used for ill purposes, governments could use power to violate certain Constitutional protections such as privacy. The popular 1980's movie "Terminator" deals with several subjects that pertain to our discussion. An issue in the movie addresses the way in which computers ravaged the world and throw it into a submissive role to the cyborgs. Could computers take over the world? Back in present day Earth, contemporary concerns fret over trampled civil liberties, identity theft, and loss of freedom. Also tied in part to the other end of the spectrum is the concentration of technology as manifested in the digital divide. There is always a fine line when dealing with the extremes.

There is a moderate position with regards to technology and democracy. We hinted at it earlier in our discussion. Technologies have the potential to provide information and allow citizens to exchange ideas concerning government. It will allow workers to become more productive (Reich, 1990). Thus, technology enables citizens to tend to public matters without losing economic power. Technology also provides the basis for a new community that replaces our well-worn social institutions (see Fountain, 2001 and Putnam, 1998).

Of these three scenarios, only one is ideal. Much will have to happen for the acceptable scenario to deliver on its promise. We have already mentioned dispersing the power of technologies to everyone. When and if everyone realizes the power, they must be willing to use it in the public interest. We agree with others: we are at a fork in the road. Will we do what is necessary to make sure technology is a public good? The impediments to successful incorporation are embodied in the digital divide.

Digital Divide

Technology can do three things to civic engagement and the quality of participation: it can help it, hurt it, or change it very little. The belief that the information revolution will have very little to do with how well citizens are connected to government are weak. Most observers point to the potential of growing information technologies to yield better relationship between citizens and government (pick any politician and ask him or her about the prospects for improved government through the use of technology). At the same time, there is a bit of a hedge against the possibility that the fundamentals around the world may exacerbate existing inequalities (Norris, 2001).

The promise of the information revolution is deliverable if most individuals have access to information technologies. Similar to wealth, information technologies are currently concentrated in countries that can afford them. The United States leads the way in consuming technology (Norris, 2001). Within the United States, the concentration again remains in the hands of those with the wealth and education to buy and use computers and other digital devices that make information cheap and disseminating information easier.

Given the varying rates of usage of the Internet for different purposes, it is worth exploring the various scenarios technology can have on civic life. Can technology widen the gulf between those with power and those without? What roles will traditional groups, such as political parties and interest groups, fill in the future? Is the digital divide something to worry about?

The digital divide is a space. Between those who have the ability to use information technologies to improve the human condition and those without the ability is ground that must be closed in order for technology to ameliorate the inequalities our current democratic practice produces. For the sake of argument we will assume this divide exists.

Our first question regarding the digital divide: can technology widen existing inequalities? The answer is "yes:" technology can worsen existing inequalities. This can happen very simply. If technology becomes concentrated in the hands of traditional institutions and political actors—government, parties, and interest groups—then it will not benefit those who need its power the most: disengaged, economically disadvantaged, the non-participant.

Since technology and its interaction with government are in its infancy, the concentration scenario just outlined is a viable possibility. Indeed, when it comes to technology and politics, some authors have concluded that technology will yield nothing more than politics as usual (Margolis and Resnick, 2000). They claim that the traditional political participants will adapt new technologies to their existing political activities, and that it will do very little to alter the nature of politics.

If the established groups adapt technologies to their existing behavior, the digital divide won't grow. It won't go away either. This can be both good and bad. Fundamentally, the divide matters if one believes our current system of governance meets the requisites for a quality democracy. If it doesn't meet them, the current actors may use new techniques to enhance their strength. More will be said about this in the chapter pertaining to parties and interest groups. It is becoming more apparent that the divide will not be widened as a result of their usage of technology, but because the power of technology is concentrated within the hands of those who already have power.

It is becoming more common for various media to be owned by a few large companies. Since these conglomerates hold the reins of technological dispersion, their benevolence will dictate the size of the digital divide. If what is past is prologue, this is doubtful. Recently, members of Congress have questioned the skyrocketing costs of cable and Internet services. They have outpaced inflation, and done so in the face of a deregulated communications industry. This wasn't supposed to happen. The result is that more and more citizens are being excluded from the advantages of multiple news sources and broadband Internet access.

The threat to the divide thus comes from unequal access to the development and distribution of multimedia. In addition to the lack of access, this concentration of access limits the number of messages citizens will receive concerning government. As students of the media and public opinion will attest, the media may not tell citizens how to think, but it certainly tells them what to think about. Concentrated access limits debate, suppresses ideas, and mutes legitimate public concerns.

It is not certain that the current divide will take on new forms. We shall see. What is certain is that unequal access currently exists. It is also apparent that this will go unabated. Closing the gap may not be possible due to the power of special interests that will work to protect the current scheme. If the trend toward concentration continues, we will have a bonafide digital divide. As outlined here the problems this poses hinders the advancement of democratic quality.

Despite the divide, technology serves those who use it. Our attention now turns to the possibilities technology has for democracy. The discussion is part normative and part speculative. We do maintain that the speculation is well within the bounds of history and future possibilities. Thus, we discuss the ways and potential ways technology can be used to enhance democracy and citizen attachments (efficacy and participation) to government.

Direct Participation

Direct democracy allows all stakeholders a voice in the deliberation process. In all policy decisions, everyone that is so inclined can influence the process. In a polis that is small, this is workable. We simply have too much history to overcome for direct democracy to become the norm in the United States. Under wild conditions we could make the transitions, but power has become concentrated, roles established, and order achieved with our current representative system. Technology, however, helps governance transcend traditional boundaries that impeded direct participation systems.

Time and distance were once the greatest barriers to direct democracy. Technology eliminates the barriers of space and time. The next barriers to direct participation are traditional questions related to freedom, power, and methods of social choice. How can we translate emerging technologies into tools for direct participation in deciding policy outcomes? We believe the answer is not found in allowing citizens direct control over the policy process, thus supplanting their elected representatives. Yet, it can be found in technologies that allow citizens to learn about and contribute to public discussions.

In the spirit of Thomas Jefferson, technologies aid citizens in their ability to follow, keep up to date, and communicate with government and officials. Governments at all levels maintain a web presence that provides information concerning meeting times, decisions by boards, statutes and codes, and even the ability to make inputs on public matters. Therefore, we envision technology following a path that buttresses current government practices and traditional forms of citizen participation rather than uprooting a system of governance.

We also reject the notion that the effects of technology on government will be neutral. Technology will influence the ways we have become accustomed to: running for office, making decisions, and interacting with one another in the polis. These subtle changes will be important even though they will not fundamentally alter the current system. What then will be the effects on participation? At this point it is pure speculation. Examining a few mechanisms may shed some light on the prospects.

Voting

Traditional voting in elections requires you to trudge down to the local voting precinct and bubble in a form, pull a lever, or punch a card. The good citizens of Florida had a bit of trouble with the latter form in the 2000 presidential election. Current methods of voting for candidates have changed very little over the course of our brief history. The way we count ballots has changed a bit, but the methods are still fundamental. Whenever we have had some changes in voting method or counting, technology has been the catalyst. We are again at the point where technology will influence and alter the voting process.

Most jurisdictions have some variation on automatically counting votes as they are made. Optical scanners are the form of technology most precincts are comfortable with. In this system marked ballots are fed into a machine that records the vote. Others still use the lever style found in the traditional voting "booth". Those who cannot afford advanced technologies such as these may have a centralized counting station where all precincts converge to have their ballots counted. Cutting edge technology transcends these traditional methods. Through touch screen technology, the task of voting no longer requires paper or pencils or clunky voting booths that fold into a suitcase. But these methods are variations on a theme. All of them require the voter to venture to a central location to fulfill their duties as a citizen. Technology may be harnessed to go beyond simplifying the voting system to also making it easier for the individual.

Voting could take place over the Internet or telephone. This is controversial and very unlikely to develop. Detractors point to fraud, security, and privacy concerns. The actual process of voting over the Internet or phone is simple. Over the telephone, an interface could be developed that mirrors phone registration systems on college campuses. Even better, the websites that allow secure transactions for credit card payments, airline reservations, and doctor visits can be adapted to allow citizens to vote.

Cash-strapped governments are unlikely to expend the resources needed to adapt to web-based or telephonic voting. We feel comfortable with this position because lesser technologies compatible with traditional methods of voting haven't been readily adopted either. Thus, a paradox exists concerning voting. How can a country as devoted to voting and citizen participation as the United States devote very little toward the mechanisms of those processes? We are unsure at this point. However, we are certain that our democracy suffers because of the paradox.

When citizens are deprived of their only opportunity to influence government, they are robbed of their natural right to direct their destiny. Countless contemporary examples of voter fraud, disenfranchisement, and confusion at the polls beg for a better system of casting ballots and electing representatives. Political scientists bemoan low voter turnout as a weakness of our democratic practice. The most prevalent factor contributing to depressed turnout and participation is the structure of our elections system (ranging from registration requirements to the ability to vote when absent). Technology holds the promise of ameliorating these conditions.

Registering to vote and being allowed to vote over the phone or Internet strips away the barriers to participating in politics. Turnout in presidential elections would increase several percentage points by removing these obstacles alone. Technology in this case makes it easier to vote. When a potential voter calculates lower costs to time and energy, they are likely to vote even if registering or absenteeism is an issue. Thus, turnout could be increased by expanding voting opportunities.

Information

Voting is the most basic act of participating in politics, and should not be taken as the end of the matter in terms of enhancing democracy. More voters showing up at the polls is great if they arrive with knowledge. Technology lends itself to voters having the information they need to actively participate in politics from voting to contacting their elected official after the election has passed. There are many forms of participation in between these two that technology can also help.

Sources of information for those interested in politics are abundant and increasing. The sources of information are diverse, catering to every conceivable ideology or partisan edge. With this in mind, consumers of political information on the Internet—the most diverse holder of political information—have to cautiously pursue credible information. Several trusted sources are readily available.

Major news networks maintain companion websites. Cable news programs usually have extensive websites devoted solely to politics. Interest groups (public) solicit donations, and spread developments electronically via e-mail and other traditional forms of communication. Government agencies, bureaus, and offices readily post guides and information concerning government activities. On just about any government site, interpretation of the information found there is scarce. If you are seeking perspective, a specialized venue is more appropriate.

Political News

Most citizens get their news from television. Before the advent of cable news channels, this posed more serious concerns for information holding by the public. As with voter turnout, political scientists question the depth and quality of civic information held by the masses. For too many citizens, identifying their elected representative is a difficult chore. Imagine how much more burdened they would be if asked how their elected representative voted on a particular policy question, how much money from interest groups the representative accepts, who their biggest donors are, or what issues they currently are working to resolve.

The answers to these basic queries are not readily held by the masses. Some may argue that they are unimportant. Citizens only need to know if they are working in a secure job, that their children attend safe and adequate schools, and that they have family and friends. Elected officials take care of public matters. Not the average citizen. But does our democracy, or any quality democracy, demand more from its citizens? Are voters not fools only when they can determine if government and officials are creating the conditions for prosperity and managing externalities in a proper manner? We contend that in order for democratic government to flourish, citizens must elevate their concern, interest, and level of information they possess regarding the activities of government.

If citizens possessed more information, their representatives would take them more seriously. At some level, elected officials continuously keep in mind how things they say, write, or do will be portrayed by voters. Comments by elected officials allude to their awareness. What is their fear? They fear the loss of their elected office by making a misstep with the public. They know that somewhere someone is paying attention to their actions. If elected officials knew that more than just elite media or salivating politicians waiting to take their place were watching them, they may be more responsive to a wider audience and therefore enhance democratic representation.

Influencing Government

Our federal system doesn't allow citizens a direct vote on national policy matters. Despite this limitation, citizens can make waves by holding better information or having developed policy positions. To fully take advantage of their knowledge they must convey it to their elected representatives. Through contacting elected representatives, citizens can influence how their elected officials vote on an issue. Through new technologies, communicating with elected officials is easier.

Before telephones, citizens conveyed their interests through campaign contact, long trips to Washington, or in chance meetings with their elected officials. The mail system also provided an option. Each of these avenues is not without problems. Campaigns did not occur often (at least not daily). Train or carriage trips were time consuming. Letters got lost or ignored. These methods simply do not occur frequently enough or allow all voices to be heard in the policy process.

Telephones and cars helped some with communication, but these tools were also concentrated in the hands of the wealthy. Not everyone could afford cars and phones even though Henry Ford had the idea that everyone should be able to own a car. Neither of these technological advances expanded the inclusion of all voices in the governing process. If history is a judge, neither had tremendous impact on governance at all.

The two most politically transforming devices in the last century are the radio and the television. Students of politics know well the powerful draw of Franklin Roosevelt's fireside chat. It is the forerunner of the modern weekly radio address. In these chats, Roosevelt could talk to citizens on fully developed topics, not in sound bites. He could offer comfort, encouragement, and allay fears. The fireside chat could draw in regular citizens into a process previously reserved only for the elite.

Around the time of the fireside chat, new groups were being incorporated in the political process, namely women and immigrants. Thus, representation was being expanded. The electoral strength of Franklin Roosevelt can be attributed to the attachments these new voting blocks had for his policies and charisma. Roosevelt took advantage of the greatest technological tool he had—the radio—in order to forge his political strength. It didn't hurt that he was passing out a New Deal and jobs either. The point here is that Roosevelt is probably the first politician to use technology for help in the governing process.

The television era of politics was ushered in during the Kennedy/Nixon debates of 1960. In those series of debates, the major networks combined forces to air all the debates on all three networks. Some comedians who grew up in this era have made a small living by joking that if the President was on television, their whole night of entertainment was compromised. In the first of those famous debates, television viewers gave the edge to Kennedy while radio listeners believed Nixon had the stronger performance. Since then, mastering the television age of politics has influenced all politicians. It has also held consequences for governing and the quality of democracy (Bennett, 1996).

Bennett (1996) makes a strong argument for what he calls a "governing crisis." Part of this crisis is the emptiness of campaigns and political discourse. Technology has been a catalyst for the draining of public ideas and leadership. Modern campaigns must master the sound bite, and the imagery and craft of weaving meaningless messages. Voters are not informed by modern campaigns. Even the format in the Kennedy/Nixon debates is not used in modern debates. Politicians refuse to divulge policy positions in great detail. The public rarely asks for more than superficial treatment of the issues. The result is a non-responsive government that lacks capacity and vision to address public problems.

There is very little doubt that television affected governance more than any other technological development in the past century. Perhaps new technologies will never influence the ways politicians speak to the polis. It is hard to imagine that their effects will be neutral. For the wired citizen, the Internet may supplant television as their source of political news. It may also be the medium they choose to use to influence government. In fact, under some conditions it is essential.

During the anthrax scare after the terror attacks of September 11, 2001, communication with members of Congress was limited to phone, fax, e-mail, and that which took place in person. Staffers seeking Hill appointments were encouraged to apply via e-mail. Those who applied while the anthrax scare gummed up the mail works were asked to reapply using an electronic method. This example demonstrates that communicating with elected officials can be helped by technology. Democracies require the ability to communicate ideas and positions to others. Technology certainly helps in this area.

Summary

This chapter hopefully conveys the importance of technology in promoting democracy. The unique nature of democracy allows it to be molded and shaped according to the desires of the majority. Early in this discussion, several scenarios were presented that predict where our democracy may be headed. Two of the three possibilities discussed here are not positive.

That technology can hurt the quality of a citizen-controlled government is an a priori assumption. We simply have very little evidence at this point to say with confidence that technology has indeed harmed our notions of citizen input and their control over government. The possibility of harm is not far fetched. If our discussion of the digital divide is correct, and technology becomes more concentrated, the gulf between those with power and those without will widen. This in effect will serve to marginalize and cut off masses of citizens. Ultimately, they will be left with little influence.

It may also be possible for technology to have no net effect upon democracy. We don't maintain that technology will have zero effects. Rather it is our position that the fundamentals of democracy that are enhanced will be negated by those where technology has little ability to improve. For examples, technology eliminates time and distance as obstacles to communication. Rapid development of broadband technologies allow faster and varied communication. News sources are readily accessible from almost anywhere. These are being improved to help strengthen democratic quality. These advances will be negated if technological advances are not widely available for whatever reason. They can easily become tools of existing, and unequally influential, political actors. After costs and benefits are calculated, the axis of democratic quality may not be tilted in either direction.

While the last scenario we addressed dealt with an all-positive view of technology, it is also possible for technology to have unqualified success in promoting the ability of citizens to influence and get things from government. Our treatment of electronic government will be treated in more detail in the next chapter. Here, though, we can discuss success. What would a healthy democracy look like in a rapidly developing technological environment? The answer to this question is found in how we define success.

It can be argued that our current system of democratic government is fine. If existing actors hoard new technologies, nothing negative will happen. Politics will carry on as usual. Therefore, we don't need to worry about technology not being widely available (so they would say). Success can then be defined in terms of access, responsiveness, and efficiencies.

Electronic government (e-government) gives citizens more access. Access to government goes beyond documents and rules, but includes the ability to interact with government (pay taxes, apply for entitlements, jobs). Citizens can engage government without being intimated or inconvenienced. This positively promotes the legitimacy of government and democracy by extension.

Responsiveness can be defined as how quickly government addresses demands and issues. Technology helps government process requests quicker and with greater efficiency. This quicker turnaround time allows citizens to maintain their current standard of living, and perhaps make some improvements in overall quality of life. Governments that quickly address citizen needs are more democratic as they are being responsive to citizen demands. Efficient governments far exceed private enterprise in delivering services with very little lost to overhead. Technologies will make a lean public sector even leaner. Efficient governments have the ability to address a wider range of public issues with fewer resources. Depending on the intensity in which groups compete, it is possible that a group's pressure would ease and more inclusion could occur. Moreover, arguments by the Libertarians would not be on solid footings. They contend that government exacerbates inequalities through unfairly regulating the market. Their arguments are essentially over the issue of efficiency. If government can provide services as efficiently as the free market, their arguments become meaningless arm waving.

We envision a democratic government in the digital age as one that is accessible, responsive, and efficient. Under our earlier scheme whereby everyone is politically, socially, and legally equal, we would still have a distance to traverse. But, we also qualified our view of democracy in that we likened it to a spectrum of black, white, and gray when we held that democracy is not an all or nothing proposition. The quality of democratic governance is shaded with each new policy, program, and law. Technology also does its part to fill in the overall way we go about debating public questions, controlling externalities, and distributing public goods.

As we mentioned earlier, the effects of technology on government and citizens are not fully recognizable. Along with others, we have speculated based on what we know about our current democracy. Ultimately, we think technology is a multiple-use tool that is being adapted to all sorts of concepts in determining its usefulness. From electronic commerce to electronic government and in between, rapid technological growth is just beginning. The first few steps down the path may be rocky or contain a pothole or two. We don't foresee a turbulent path in perpetuity, however. Like the radio and television before it, the Internet will find its niche. We look forward to its positive contribution toward democratic governance.

Electronic State and Local Government

State and local governments have long been considered laboratories of democracy. At the state and local level, thousands of government entities offer a vast array of social, legal, and political arrangements. Within each town, city or state, there are opportunities to try out different methods of governing and policies. When a method works, we try to replicate the success in other places. In this sense, policies can be viewed as bubbling up rather than filtering top down (see Dye, 2001 for a complete discussion of top down policy making). It is at the state and local level where innovation can take place and policies are implemented. As Tip O'Neil believed politics is mostly recognized local. Some of this is true for electronic government.

All states and many local governments have a virtual presence on the Internet. Some websites and services are better than others. In this chapter, we attempt to examine some state and local governments that are committed to the idea of electronic government, and have been rated highly by organizations that focus on government delivery of services via the Internet. Our focus shines a spotlight on the states of Michigan and Virginia, as well as local governments.

Within our discussion concerning the governments of these states and several cities, we will attempt to weave together a framework for understanding why governments at all levels are choosing digital technologies to help them with governing. Do elected officials believe these new technologies will save money? It could possibly be that they conclude that the Internet will make government more responsive. It could also boil down to a fundamental acknowledgment that technology is the newest way to deliver government services. We firmly believe the movement toward technology is the creation of efficiencies and a desire of public officials to improve "customer service" for their citizens. We shall see.

About the States

Virginia is a southern state located in the Mid-Atlantic region. Wedged between North Carolina and Maryland, it is typical of most southern states in terms of geography. Mountains in the western part of the state give way to a piedmont that rolls up an extensive coastal region. Several parts of Virginia are wealthy (northern Virginia, parts of Richmond, Charlottesville, and pockets in the Shenandoah Valley), while others are more susceptible to economic ebbs and flows (Southside Richmond, and southwest Virginia). Even with diverse geography, people, and economic proclivities, the state is committed to the notion of electronic government. Virginia prides itself in being the digital dominion, as well as the Internet capital of the world (Warner, 2003).

Michigan is a wealthy, industrial, upper Midwestern state as diverse in geography and economics as Virginia. The industrial anchors of Detroit and Grand Rapids sandwich a fertile farming region in the central part of the state. Upper Michigan is a virtual wonderland of natural beauty and recreation. Bordered by Great Lakes on three sides, Michigan has an extensive maritime history to go along with its distinction as the automobile capital of the world. Michigan is a recognized leader in the development of technology applications and the life sciences.

Both states have solid reputations as leaders in electronic government. Both rank highly in their use of and commitment to digital government. Each year, both states spend billions on computers, hardware, software, and network maintenance (Governing, 2003). These efforts have paid off with recognition and adulation. For these reasons it is worth taking a look at what these states are attempting and achieving in regards to electronic government.

The Local Governments

Several cities and counties in the United States have been recognized for their usage of technology. In their respective classifications, Roanoke, Virginia, Richmond, Virginia, and Tampa, Florida are leaders in the electronic government movement. These local governments represent models to be replicated by others of similar size and demographics. Other localities can also examine their practices in hopes of exposing the better aspects of electronic government. Before we dive into the mechanics of e-government at the local level, it is worth getting a sense of governance at this level. It is indeed different than national government. The distinction between federal and state/local government does bring along differences. Governing at each level of government is not the same.

Local Governance

Local government is the level of government most recognizable to citizens. They interact with teachers, and see patrol cars around their neighborhoods, utility workers preparing infrastructure, and garbage trucks once or twice weekly. For a good many citizens, all government and politics is local, as we mentioned earlier. This fact is not meant to disparage citizen knowledge of how government works beyond the local level. Our intent is quite the contrary. We contend that local government is important to citizens. If local leaders neglect technological advances that improve the quality of government, the citizens are the ones who ultimately suffer.

Boundaries within the public sector are easily blurred. Understanding the level of government that services a particular problem is compromised due to the interwoven nature of public administration. That is, almost all policy problems are addressed by each level of government simultaneously. It may be possible for more than one level of government to have jurisdiction over a particular problem. In addition to government, the non-profit, also known as the third sector (public and private being the others), is involved in the delivery of public services. Some examples serve to illustrate these points.

In the case of an elderly person who is poor and in need of health care, whom should they seek for help? Private-sector physicians can help with health issues. But we said our focus is on a *poor* elderly person. This individual is covered under the Medicare system (federal insurance program for senior citizens). Some private doctors accept Medicare patients, some do not. Looking beyond the health issues, our senior in this example has no nearby family. She obviously needs an outlet for socialization in addition to help with nutrition, spiritual matters, personal finances; and legal matters and future health issues. Non-profits exist to serve this wide array of needs to some degree. Local governments provide facilities and transportation, as well as subsidize the efforts of senior non-profit agencies. State governments provide grants to local government and non-profits that helps address some of these issues. They also maintain Medicaid, in addition to the federal Medicare programs (combined state and federal insurance program for indigent citizens). Indeed knowing what level of government provides each service is complicated. It is easier to identify local government as the provider of all services.

Due to the confusing nature of federalism and a growing reliance on non-profits and the private sector to deliver services to citizens, it is incumbent upon governments at all levels to coordinate. Simply passing a citizen's call to someone else that may pass it further is unacceptable. Technology helps coordinate the massive third sector and the interrelated nature of government service delivery. Communication is easier among governments (there are over 80,000 of them by the way), and citizens can use technology to determine what services are offered by the different levels of government. Our focus here is the state and local levels, and it is at the local level where much innovation is taking place.

The Digital Dominion

Virginia

Virginia became the first state with a cabinet-level Secretary of Technology (Strategic Plan, 2003). Harnessing technology to improve government services, generate economic development, and maintain a competitive edge are a few of the stated reasons for focusing heavily on developing technology. Technology is inescapable and pervasive, and applicable to almost any government function. Overall, Virginia does well in the area of economic development and the delivery of social services. The Center for Digital Government rates these areas highly in their most recent survey of the states (Digital State, 2002).

The Commonwealth of Virginia's strategic plan for technology reveals a host of accomplishments and indicates it does not intend to resting on its laurels. Among its fellow state governments,

Virginia was the first to implement many technological enhancements: a web portal, a best motor vehicles services site, real time election results, mobile wireless services, and live online help (Warner, 2003). These initiatives represent the promise of electronic government.

Virginia's strategic plan was crafted during troublesome economic times for most states. The influences of dwindling resources in crafting a future plan for technology innovation and implementation cannot be discounted. A quick review of the plan yields several goals: save the taxpayers money, and make government more efficient, effective, and convenient. In essence, the political leadership in Virginia believes technology will help them pursue economic development, streamline government operations, and make government more accessible. We will take a look at each of these in turn.

Economic Development
Virginia's political leadership recognizes that the nature of economic success is changing. Technology innovations beg for new organizational structures in order to completely take advantage of its promise. If states choose not to approach technology as a future mechanism for economic development then they are likely holding their citizenry back by several decades. Virginia's situation, while a bit unique, is not insuperable by other states.

Thanks to its proximity to the nation's capitol and unique group of corporations, northern Virginia has seen an extraordinary increase in economic development. Extending to the south from Washington D.C., northern Virginia consists of a swath of technology-related business. These enterprises—AOL Time Warner, Xerox—represent the symbols of salvation from the industry's downturn toward the end of the 1990's. The northern Virginia region provides a solid base of wealth that is transferable to other parts of the state. Political leaders hope that technology will help to spread this wealth to other Virginia regions.

Other parts of the state have not fared as well. Localities face high unemployment rates when a plant or manufacturing business shuts down unexpectedly. Like many workers, they have to retrain and gain the skills necessary to compete in a high-tech service-based economy. Most of the replacement jobs will be grounded in technology. The reality of future economic success in all parts of Virginia will depend on an educated workforce that his highly adaptable to a technologically advanced economy. These higher technology jobs will increase the productivity of workers. This will give them greater job security while enhancing quality of life. This can only happen if there is a focus by elected officials on technology coupled with a willingness to make the necessary investments. Virginia makes this effort, and appears to have long-range dedication to using technology to improve the lives of its citizens.

Service Delivery

In addition to economic development, Virginia is committed to using technology to deliver services to its citizens. Virginia claims to be in the midst of building a digital government. From this perspective, digital government moves beyond electronic government. It takes on several features: 1) citizen-facing, 2) transformational, 3) accountable, 4) efficient, and 5) fundamental.

The initial step taken by Virginia is to create some uniformity within the state's web portal. Surveys of state agencies revealed that very little cohesion existed in terms of the look, feel, and usability of state agency websites. The result of this finding is the desire to make all state websites customer-facing and uniform. This will give users a common format to refer to when utilizing sites from different state agencies.

As another result of these surveys, the Commonwealth of Virginia will also implement an increase in the number of services that can easily be conducted online. Professional licensing is a prime example. Currently, fewer than five percent of professionals can renew their licenses online. None can file an application for a new license. Another area of concern is paying the state what it is owed through an electronic payments portal. Despite these areas in need of improvement, Virginia excels in several others.

Social Services

The Center for Digital Government gives Virginia a top ranking in its most recent survey of social service delivery (Digital Government, 2003). Figure 1 provides a brief list of services available online by entering the states web portal at www.myvirginia.org. The services available after clicking "online services" range from using an eligibility screener to determine eligibility for public assistance to planning your vacation through the Virginia Tourism site. Let us take a closer look at a few selected sites to see how Virginia provides online services to its citizens.

Commonwealth of Virginia

Wireless Site | Text Only Site | Web Policy | Contact the Governor of Virginia
Contact Us | State Web Site List

 virginia.gov

Enter search keyword   [Search]

Home > Online Services > Citizen Services

> **Virginia Communities**
> **Family & Education**
> **Business and Employment**
> **Online Services**
  > Business Services
  > Citizen Services
  > Voter and Election Services
  > Commonwealth Calendar
  > Emergency Notifications
  > Information about RSS Feeds
  > Premium Services
  > Translations
  > Wireless and PDA Services
> **Government**
> **Visiting Virginia**
> **Featured Sites**
> **About VIPNet**

Community Services| Driver and Vehicle Services| Education Services| Election and Voter Services| Employment Services| Health Professions| Legal Information for Public Use| Legislative Information| Shopping with the State| State Employee Services| Taxes| Travel and Tourism

Community Services

Assistance Eligibility Screener
This service can help you find out if you are eligible to receive temporary cash or food stamps.

Birth Certificates
Have your birth certificate mailed to you.

Child Care Database
Search for licensed child day care in your area.

Child Support Services
Individuals who have a child support case may access data related to their child support payments, balances due, and case status.

Commonwealth Calendar
Virginia government meetings open to the public.

Consumer Assistance Portal
The Office of Consumer Affairs at the Virginia Department of Agriculture and Consumer Services serves as the central clearinghouse for the collection, evaluation, investigation or referral of consumer complaints.

Hunting and Fishing Licenses Online
Buy your hunting and fishing licenses online.

Restaurant Inspection Reports
Health inspection reports online.

Virginia Communities
A database of local resources, including communities and government sites.

Virginia Information and Referral System
Database of service providers.

Driver and Vehicle Services

Address Change
Use this feature to update your address with DMV.

Administrative Hearing Request
You can request an administrative hearing if you have been issued an order of suspension due to an insurance verification request

Compliance Summary Request
You can use this feature to find out how to reinstate your Virginia driving and/or vehicle registration privileges.

Create a Plate
Say it on your plate! Virginia offers more than 180 special license plates. Plus, you can personalize your plate with your unique message.

DMV Online Transactions
Complete list of services available online from the Department of Motor Vehicles (DMV).

Driver's License Renewal
Save yourself a trip to DMV. Click here to renew your driver's license

Driver's License Replacement
Have you lost or damaged your driver's license? You can purchase a replacement online.

Insurance Verification
If you have received a letter from DMV requesting information about your vehicle liability insurance policy, you can furnish that information using this feature.

Online Payment of Moving Violations and Pre-payable Offenses
Pay for speeding tickets, moving violations and other pre-payable offenses issued from 67 participating localities.

Organ Donor Status Change
Use this feature to change your organ donor status

PIN Administration
A Personal Identification Number (PIN) is required to access certain transactions on our website

Plate Purchase
Want a new look for your vehicle? Purchase a new license plate today

What's Hot

Contact Virginia Government
Contact resources for Virginia government.

Plan your Virginia vacation
The Virginia.org trip planner is a special feature that lets you create your own travel brochure, with just the information about Virginia that interests you the most.

Watercraft Registration Renewal
Once you have received your renewal notice with your assigned PIN code, you may renew your watercraft registration online.

Purchase Hunting and Fishing licenses online
Purchase Hunting and Fishing licenses online from the Department of Game and Inland Fisheries.

Online Payment of Moving Violations and Pre-payable Offenses
Pay for speeding tickets, moving violations and other pre-payable offenses issued from 67 participating localities.

Figure 1

Prospective Purchaser Inquiry
Purchasing a vehicle? Check DMV's records first. Get a vehicle history today!

Record Request
Want to know what's on your DMV record? View your driver or vehicle record online or have it mailed to you today.

Registration Card Replacement
Has your registration card been lost or stolen? Use this feature to purchase a replacement

Report a Vehicle Sold or Traded
If you have sold or traded a vehicle, update your DMV record.

Sample Knowledge Exam
Can you pass the test? Try our sample knowledge exam and see how well you know Virginia's motoring laws and safe driving techniques.

Souvenir Plate Orders
Want a souvenir plate for your office? Order a souvenir plate today.

Trip Permit Purchase
If you are a Virginia resident, you may purchase a 3-day permit to operate an unregistered vehicle from a point of origin to a point of destination.

Vehicle Registration Renewal
Renew your vehicle registration online, any time of day.

Watercraft Registration Renewal
Once you have received your renewal notice with your assigned PIN code, you may renew your watercraft registration online.

What Have I Done Online?
View details about your past online transactions.

Education Services

Find It Virginia
With your Virginia Public Library Card, you can research any topic.

Lesson Plans
Post and search lesson plans through the Commonwealth of Knowledge site.

Library of Virginia Foundation Online Donation
Individuals may contribute through the Library of Virginia Foundation.

Library of Virginia Online Research Requests
Provides public access to the library and archival resources.

Longwood University Application Payment
Pay for your Longwood University application online.

Submit a Tip
Submit anonymous school safety tips or concerns via the '4SAFEVA' site.

Election and Voter Services

Absentee Ballot Status Lookup
Determine the status of your absentee ballot.

Campaign Expenditure Search
Campaign Expenditure Search online.

Election Results
Election results online.

Help America Vote Act of 2002
In order to receive the maximum in federal funding, Virginia must produce a State Plan. The HAVA Advisory Committee (with representatives of various constituency groups, private citizens and election professionals) and the SBE staff produced the Draft Plan now available for public comment.

Polling Place Lookup
Find local polling place and state and federal elected officials by entering home address.

Voter and Election Services
Voter and Election Services available online.

Voter Registration Verification
Voter Registration Verification.

Employment Services

CareerConnect
CareerConnect is a customer service network designed to assist workers, students, individuals seeking employment, and employers with an abundance of educational, employment, and career-related information.

Employment Application
State employment application.

Find Unemployment Services
Unemployment services through the Virginia Employment Commission.

Recruit Job Posting Notification
E-Mail job posting notification system at VirginiaJobs.

Figure 1—cont'd

Search for State Job Openings
Recruit job listings with the
Commonwealth of Virginia.

Unemployment Claim
Claim for unemployment benefits
through the Virginia Employment
Commission (VEC).

**Virginia Employment
Commission Continued Claim
for Benefits**
You can now file your weekly
continued claim for benefits over the
Internet. Do not file for the previous
week until Sunday or thereafter. You
must have your SS# and Pin # to file.

Health Professions

Licensee Search
Department of Health Professions
(DHP) Licensee Search.

Practitioner Information Search
Virginia Board of Medicine
Practitioners Information Search.

Legal Information for Public Use

Attorney Records Search
This search will provide information
about attorneys practicing law in the
Commonwealth of Virginia.

Case Management System
The Supreme Court of Virginia
offers circuit court searches and
district court searches.

Identity Theft
Information on how to protect
yourself from Identity Theft.

**Search for Attorney General
Opinions**
Search for Attorney General opinions.

**Sex Offender and Crimes
Against Minors Registry**
Search the violent sex offenders
database through the Virginia State
Police.

Supreme Court Decisions
Find Virginia Supreme Court
decisions.

Unclaimed Property Search
Unclaimed property search from the
Department of the Treasury.

**Virginia Worker's
Compensation Commission
Opinions**
Search the Virginia Worker's
Compensation Commission Opinions
database.

Legislative Information

Citizen bill tracking
In partnership with the General
Assembly's Division of Legislative
Automated Systems, DLAS, the
Virginia Information Providers
Network, VIPNet, is offering a free
legislative tracking service.

Code of Virginia Search
Search for Virginia Laws.

Find your legislator
Find your Legislator through the
General Assembly site.

Legislation Information System
Search for bills and legislation.

State Song Contest
Submit comments about the State
Song Contest.

Shopping with the State

Blue Book Purchase
Purchase the Secretary of the
Commonwealth's Blue Book Online.

Forestry General Store
Department of Forestry (DOF)
General Store.

Library of Virginia
Library of Virginia store.

Marine Products
Virginia Marine Products Board
shopping cart.

Figure 1—cont'd

Seedling Store
Department of Forestry (DOF) seedling store.

Shop eVirginia
Shop for products and specialties offered by Virginia government entities. Shop eVirginia includes a variety of items from across the Commonwealth.

Virginia is for Lovers
The Official Virginia is For Lovers Online Shop featuring Virginia is For Lovers merchandise.

State Employee Services

Payline
Your source for personal earnings, benefits and leave information.

Taxes

iFile for Individuals
iFile for individuals allows individuals to file their Virginia taxes online.

Travel and Tourism

HOV Calculator
Determine how much time you could save by commuting with the Virginia Department of Transportation's (VDOT) HOV Calculator.

Park Reservations
Make reservations online for camping facilities at Virginia State Parks.

Smart Travel
Make highway travel plans with the Department of Transportation's 'Smart Travel' service

Travel Plans from Virginia Tourism
Plan your Virginia vacation and travel excursions through the Virginia Tourism site.

Figure 1—cont'd

Using the link for determining eligibility assistance takes us to a welcome page. Figure 2 shows the various online services that citizens seeking assistance may use. By clicking the all categories link, the online screener provides information on all types of assistance. The next page of the online tool asks a series of questions related to family size, expectant mothers, bill payments, and number of disabled family members (see Figure 3). Once finished with the online survey, Internet users may submit their responses to the screening tool.

Figure 4 is the page that will appear once the online eligibility survey is completed. This page explains the various social service programs in terms of program names and descriptions. The center category indicates preliminary eligibility. Of particular importance on this site is the information provided for further assistance. Those wishing to fill out an application for benefits will find directions to the nearest benefits office, as well as a toll-free number. The benefits of such a system are numerous. Knowing which program is suitable for your particular needs saves you time and helps avoid embarrass-

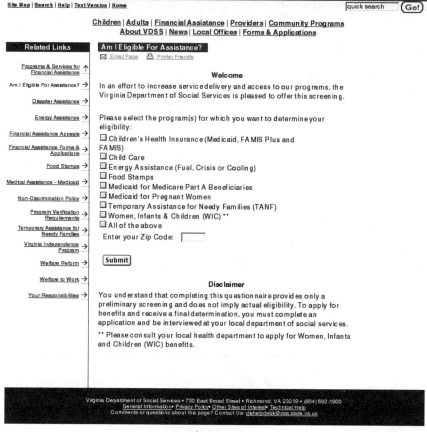

Figure 2

ment. Benefits offices can spend time managing applications and determining benefits rather than extensive investigations into eligibility.

Motor Vehicles

Registering cars and issuing licenses are the basic tasks of the Department of Motor Vehicles. Once a citizen has registered a vehicle or obtained a license, the basic task becomes renewal and information updates. Through Virginia's "vehicle services" link, citizens can manage their vehicle information online. Whether the task is changing an address or reporting a vehicle sold or transferred, the services provided by the Department of Motor Vehicles is saving the most important thing most citizens have: time.

Site Map | Search | Help | Text Version | Home   quick search [Go!]

Children | Adults | Financial Assistance | Providers | Community Programs
About VDSS | News | Local Offices | Forms & Applications

Related Links
Programs & Services for ↑
Financial Assistance
Am I Eligible For Assistance? →
Disaster Assistance →
Energy Assistance →
Financial Assistance Appeals →
Financial Assistance Forms & →
Applications
Food Stamps →
Medical Assistance - Medicaid →
Non-Discrimination Policy →
Program Verification →
Requirements
Temporary Assistance for →
Needy Families
Virginia Independence →
Program
Welfare Reform →
Welfare to Work →
Your Responsibilities →

Am I Eligible For Assistance?

✉ Email Page   🖶 Printer Friendly

Please review your answers below, if you need to change an answer please click the "Change Answer" button.
If answers below are correct click on the "Submit" button to continue.

Question	Answers Displayed
Where do you live?	Augusta
Does anyone in your house pay to cool or heat the house? If so, how many people live with you in your house? (including yourself)	No - 0
How many people live with you in your household unit? (including yourself)	2
Is there a child under 5 in your home?	No
Is there a child in the age 5-12 in your home?	No
Is there a child in the age 13-17 in your home?	No
Is there a child age 18 in your home?	No
Is anyone pregnant in your home? If so, enter the number of child(ren) she is expecting.	0
Do you have a child in your household, 13-17 years of age who is physically or mentally incapable of caring for himself or is subject to court supervision?	No
How many people are 60 years of age or older or permanently disabled in your household?	0
How much money do you have?	$0.00
If you own any motor vehicle(s), what are the amounts of the two most valuable vehicles?	Vehicle 1: $0.00 Vehicle 2: $0.00
How much unearned income does your household receive each month?	$0.00
How much money does your household earn each month? (Enter the amount before taxes)	$0.00
How many SSI recipients live in your household?	0
How much SSI does your household receive each month?	$0.00
Do you have Medicare Part-A?	No

[Submit] [Change Answer]

Virginia Department of Social Services • 730 East Broad Street • Richmond, VA 23219 • (804) 692-1900
General Information• Privacy Policy• Other Sites of Interest• Technical Help
Comments or questions about this page? Contact Us: dishelpdesk@dss.state.va.us

Figure 3

Site Map | Search | Help | Text Version | Home

quick search **Go!**

Children | **Adults** | **Financial Assistance** | **Providers** | **Community Programs**
About VDSS | **News** | **Local Offices** | **Forms & Applications**

Related Links

Programs & Services for
Financial Assistance ↑

Am I Eligible For Assistance? →

Disaster Assistance →

Energy Assistance →

Financial Assistance Appeals →

Financial Assistance Forms &
Applications →

Food Stamps →

Medical Assistance - Medicaid →

Non-Discrimination Policy →

Program Verification
Requirements →

Temporary Assistance for
Needy Families →

Virginia Independence
Program →

Welfare Reform →

Welfare to Work →

Your Responsibilities →

Am I Eligible For Assistance?

✉ Email Page   🖨 Printer Friendly

Thank you for completing our questionnaire. Below are the results based on the answers that you gave.

Finishing this questionnaire was just the first step to give you an idea whether you might be eligible. It does not mean that you are or are not eligible. To get benefits you must complete an application at your local department of social services. You also must give any information and proof needed to determine if you are eligible. Click on the program link to find more information for a specific program.

A "MAY NOT" result does not mean we cannot help you. These results were based on your answers to the questionnaire. If you need help, please contact your local DSS office.

Programs Eligibility Screening Results

Program Name	Results	Program Description
Child Care	May not be eligible. The reason for disqualification may be: • You may be disqualified because you do not have a child under the age of 13 living with you. • You may be disqualified because you do not have a special needs child living with you.	The Child Care program assists low-income families by providing financial assistance with the cost of child care services. The program also offers information on the selection and monitoring of quality child care. There must be at least one child and one adult in your household to be eligible. Income of adults who do not have a legal responsibility to support the children for whom assistance is requested and their siblings is not counted in the eligibility determination. Child support paid to another household is deducted from the income counted in the eligibility determination.
Children's Health Insurance (Medicaid, FAMIS Plus and FAMIS)	May not be eligible. The reason for disqualification may be: • You may be disqualified because you do not have a child under the age of 19 living with you.	Children's Health Insurance in Virginia provides comprehensive medical services to children under age 19 with countable income within 200% of the federal poverty level. Children who receive a "may not be eligible" because their family income is higher than the income limits may be eligible because of deductions that are allowed for work and child care or because the income of a stepparent or brother or sister is not counted in determining a child's qualification for the program.
Energy Assistance (Fuel, Crisis or Cooling)	May not be eligible. The reason for disqualification may be: • You may be disqualified because you do not currently pay to heat or cool your house.	The Energy Program has three seasonal components. Applications are accepted for Fuel Assistance from the second Tuesday in October to the second Friday in November, for Crisis Assistance from November 1 to March 15 and for Cooling Assistance from June 15 to August 15. Help is available with fuel or utility bills for heat, purchase, maintenance or repair of heating or cooling equipment, security deposits, or electricity for operation of cooling equipment. Assistance is not available year round and is not intended to cover the total cost of heating or cooling a home.

Figure 4

Food Stamps	May be eligible.	Food Stamps are benefits that can be used like cash to buy food for a more nutritious diet. Each eligible household receives a card that can be used like a debit card at any store that has a sign displaying the Cardinal Card or the Quest sign.
Medicaid for Medicare Part A Beneficiaries	May not be eligible. The reason for disqualification may be: • You may be disqualified because you do not have Medicare Part A (Hospital Insurance). • You may be disqualified because of the number of eligible people.	Medicaid provides limited coverage for Medicare beneficiaries with countable income within 135% of the federal poverty level and countable resources of no greater than $4,000 for an individual or $6,000 for a couple. Medicaid pays for Medicare premiums and may pay for Medicare deductibles and copayments. Prescriptions are not covered.
Medicaid for Pregnant Women	May not be eligible. The reason for disqualification may be: • You may be disqualified because you did not report an unborn child.	Medicaid for Pregnant Women provides comprehensive medical services for pregnant women who have countable income within 133% of the federal poverty level. Pregnant women who receive a "may not be eligible" result may be eligible when Medicaid income disregards and budget unit policy are used or when there are high medical bills.
Temporary Assistance for Needy Families (TANF)	May not be eligible. The reason for disqualification may be: • You may be disqualified because there is no child under age 18 living with you.	TANF (Temporary Assistance for Needy Families) provides cash and employment assistance to help families become independent.
Women, Infants & Children (WIC)	May not be eligible. The reason for disqualification may be: • You may be disqualified because you do not have a child under the age of 5 living with you. • You may be disqualified because you did not report an unborn child.	WIC is a special, supplemental nutrition program for Women, Infants and Children sponsored by the United States Department of Agriculture. WIC helps women and children get the nutrition services and foods that they need to stay healthy. WIC has also been show to help a baby develop better mentally.

Required Documents

Different programs have different verification requirements. The programs and the **minimum** verifications for the programs are listed below. Sending in the verifications with your application may reduce the time needed to determine your eligibility.

Child Care: Income verification is required.

Children's Health Insurance: Income verification is required. It is not necessary to be interviewed at the local Department of Social Services and mail-in applications are accepted.

Energy Assistance: Income and heating and/or cooling expense verification are required.

Food Stamps: Identity (driver's license or picture I.D.), residence, income, resource and shelter expense verifications are required. An interview is also required.

Figure 4—cont'd

Medicaid for Medicare Part A Beneficiaries: Income and resource verification are required. It is not necessary to be interviewed at the local Department of Social Services and mail-in applications are accepted.

Medicaid for Pregnant Women: Income and verification of pregnancy are required. It is not necessary to be interviewed at the local Department of Social Services and mail-in applications are accepted.

Temporary Assistance for Needy Families: Income, resources, social security numbers and children's birth verifications are required. A face-to-face interview is also required.

Women, Infants & Children (WIC): Income (Medicaid card, pay stubs, TANF printout with case number, Food Stamp Notice of Eligibility, this year's W-2 form, and/or income tax returns) and residency (utility bills, rent/mortgage receipts, Medicaid card, VA driver's license, or TANF/Welfare photo ID).

The worker who reviews your application will tell you if any other verifications are needed. It is not necessary to be interviewed at the local Department of Social Services and mail-in applications are accepted.

Where to Visit:
You may visit any of the local agencies listed below to apply for benefits for Food Stamps, Temporary Cash Assistance, Children's Health Insurance, Medicaid for Pregnant Women, Energy Assistance, Child Care, and Medicaid for Medicare Part A Beneficiaries.

Staunton/Augusta
68 Dick Huff Lane
Verona, VA 24482
540-245-5800

You may call **1-888-942-3663** to find out the nearest local health district office to apply for Women, Infants & Children (WIC) benefits.

Begin a new Eligibility Screening

Virginia Department of Social Services • 730 East Broad Street • Richmond, VA 23219 • (804) 692-1900
General Information• Privacy Policy• Other Sites of Interest• Technical Help
Comments or questions about this page? Contact Us: dshelpdesk@dss.state.va.us

Figure 4—cont'd

In addition to the online services, Virginia DMV offices have implemented new kiosks that allow the completion of certain services via automatic systems, similar to an automated teller machine (ATM). These kiosks, combined with the Internet and telephone services, have provided significant savings to both the agency and its customers. For example the testing system, Knowledge Automated Testing System (KATS), saves customers over 1300 hours per day (Strategic Plan, 2003, 9). Cost savings for state government are estimated to be roughly eight million dollars per year. All of these have been achieved in the face of higher demand and stagnant staff levels.

Virginia is committed to electronic government, and they are not alone in their endeavor. Michigan also realizes the benefits of electronic government and administration, and is another leader in adapting technologies for public use. We now turn our attention to Michigan's electronic government practices. Comparing a Southern state with an upper-Midwest state heavily dependent on industry as a source of economic growth, reveals the similar practices, and common problems faced by state governments hoping to adopt electronic government initiatives. The differences between Virginia and Michigan allows us to compare electronic government practices that are working across state governments despite regional differences.

Michigan (Go Blue!)

Michigan is in the upper quartile of state spending on technology (Governing, 2003). The Center for Digital Government ranks Michigan number one along with Arizona, Kansas, Virginia, and Washington in the delivery of online social services (Digital Government, 2003). Along with nine other states, Michigan is tied for second in the law enforcement and courts category for online government. More importantly, Michigan is tied for second in the promotion of digital democracy, management, and administration. Michigan is doing several things in the electronic government realm very well. Each of these areas will now be taken in turn.

Social Services
"Michigan.gov" is the gateway to all electronic government services provided by the state of Michigan. Conveniently located on the main page is a directory of online government services. By accessing the complete list of electronic services, users are routed to a comprehensive list (see Figure 5). These services range from the usual suspects such as electronic filing of taxes to participating in online government surplus auctions.

Delivering social services is an area where Michigan has excelled. It is also the area that is the most demanded by citizens. Those seeking social services—energy assistance, food stamps, rental assistance, etc.—are the most vulnerable within society. By making it easier for eligible beneficiaries to obtain benefits, the state fulfills its ultimate responsibility to protect its citizens. In the area of social services, several states are tied at the top. Cathilea Robinett, executive director of the Center for Digital Government, attributes the intense competition to political leadership, and a commitment to automate social services delivery (Digital Government, 2003). Michigan actually climbed from eighth in 2001 to first in 2002. Our other state under review, Virginia, vaulted to number 1 from 21 in 2001.

Figure 5

Michigan is lauded for its use of a screening tool that asks a series of questions to determine the need for assistance by persons with ailing family members. Jim Hogan, senior project manager for Michigan Human Services Development, points out that most citizens are unaware of the public help available to them. In his words, "people don't know what they don't know." This lack of knowledge buttresses the need for expanded electronic government. The more important point is that government, at any level, has yet to completely provide adequate online services for all eligible citizens. The move to automate some of these basic social services is a step in the right direction. Not only does it allow the states to get benefits to those who need them, but it also saves money. This essentially permits more resources to be put into the service rather than maintaining an antiquated bureaucratic structure.

Due to welfare reform rules in the mid 1990s, the states have been required to improve the delivery of social services. Since many of the most basic benefit programs have time limitations, states have seen the need to improve the ways their citizens seek out and obtain employment. Most states have some form of online job bank. Michigan's employment system utilizes Michigan Talent Bank. Virginia also utilizes an Internet job bank. These systems allow the states to move citizens from unemployment to work, thus lessening the burden on the social services system.

Criminal Justice
Michigan has long been recognized for its commitment to law enforcement, training of personnel, and the justice process. While the state has yet to obtain a lofty ranking in the overall management and administration of its criminal justice system, it does provide some useful online tools in this area. Moreover, new governor Jennifer Granholm has hinted at the expanded use of cyber courts in moving cases through the justice system.

Michigan allows Internet users to search the criminal history of past offenders using the Criminal History Record Search through the Criminal Justice Information Center (CJIC). The center is the state's repository for information on all offenders. All law enforcement agencies, prosecutors, and courts send information to the center. All offenses punishable by more than 90 days in jail or carrying jail time and fine totaling $100 or more are included in the system (Michigan.gov, 2003).

The Michigan Department of Corrections also maintains an Offender Tracking Information System (OTIS) that provides users with the status (location, release date, parole eligibility) of offenders under the care of the department. According to the OTIS site, the database contains information on more than 300,000 prisoners, parolees, and probationers. These simple tools, CJIC and OTIS databases, provide citizens with the necessary information to participate in the justice process and secure their homes and property, particularly in the case of past victims. Past victims are usually vigilant in the monitoring of their offender's progress through the justice system. As the victim's rights movement gains more political momentum, we expect to see more electronic tracking systems. At the state level, politicians have sought to respond to protecting victims' rights. Past victims have demanded louder voices in sentencing, probation, and parole hearings. These electronic tools provide the means to, at the very least, participate in the process.

Courts
In January 2001, Michigan's Governor, John Engler, signed legislation creating the first cyber court in the United States. The court simply works like others, save close human interaction. In business and commercial civil matters exceeding $25,000, participants can file their case in virtual or cyber courts. Either party can petition to have the case heard in a traditional manner. In the cyber court, motions, briefs, and arguments take place over the Internet and videoconferencing. Justice in the court is rendered by a judge, not a jury, and can be appealed. The usage of the cyber court positions Michigan, like Virginia, as a force in the future development of technology use. The cyber court is part of a larger technology influence on the courts, which will be discussed in the next chapter. From digitizing the courtroom to holding proceedings with participants in different locations, technology is transforming jurisprudence. Michigan is leading the way.

Leading the Way

While many states are pushing ahead with technological innovations in state governance, a select few are leading the way. We have examined Michigan and Virginia. If asked, the Chief Information Officers (CIO) in these states would agree that they have accomplished much in regards to electronic government. They would also probably agree that much is left unfinished. Electronic government within their states, as well as all states, is in its infancy. Nevertheless, a recent report on the overall theme of the 2003 Managing Technology conference sheds light on where states may be headed in and in what manner they intend to arrive.

The need to do more is the primary theme emerging from the 2003 Managing Technology Conference. Virginia Governor Mark Warner delivered the keynote address in which he high-lighted Virginia's efforts to better manage information technology (IT). Both Governor Warner and the other participants alluded to the fact that technology can save money if managed correctly. Moreover, all attendees at the conference agreed that technology is important in the running of government. CIO Aldona Valicenti of Kentucky claimed that technology is a "thread in the fabric of government" (Governing.com, 2003). Since we are weaving together this treatise on electronic government, we readily agree with officer Valcenti.

We have examined two states, which by all means is not an exhaustive look at what the states are attempting in the area of electronic government. Other examples are compelling, and we encourage you to survey what your state offers in the realm of digital governance. If you are fortunate, you may live in a state with a commitment to technology. If not, you can become an advocate for its incorporation. There is another half of the state and local equation, though, and that is the local efforts at electronic government. We have now arrived where, according to Tip O'Neil, all politics lives.

Local Electronic Government

Before turning our attention to the technology programs of some selected local governments, it is important to clarify some concepts related to the ability to deliver electronic government. Political will drives the adoption of technological innovation at the local level. Capacity impinges upon political will and usually hinders adoption of electronic governance tools. What we mean by both of these will be clarified as our discussion continues. In the short term, political will means a desire to use technology, and capacity involves monetary resources.

We have chosen to examine three local governments. Using the Center for Digital Government's ranking system according to population, we are using those cities ranked at the top of their respective classification. Tampa, Florida is tied for first in the "population over 250,000" category. Richmond, Virginia is tied for second in the "125,000 to 250,000" category. Roanoke, Virginia tops those in the "75,000-125,000" class.

Tampa

Tampa, Florida is a coastal city on the Gulf of Mexico. Like most cities in Florida, Tampa has experienced rapid growth and the consequences that come along with it. City government has also experienced rapid advancement in their adoption of digital technologies at city hall. In late 2002, the Center for Digital Government and Government Technology Magazine recognized Tampa's electronic government efforts by naming its official website, TampaGov.net, as the "best municipal website in the United States" (TampaGov, 2003).

Tampa's reasons for adopting electronic government services are rooted in improving service, creating efficiency, and enhancing access. Through a common portal, users of Tampa's website search the myriad of services easily, by using links that cut through the maze of potential pitfalls. The portal for TampaGov.net is pictured in Figure 6. With very little effort, users can select from the list of online services clearly displayed, or use the "Find It Fast" function. "Find It Fast" also includes a drop box of government functions, frequently asked questions, as well as the site's top ten requests. Users of the site find it easy to navigate, conduct transactions, and find information.

The city's online services do not cater to only residents. Visitors may access maps and local attractions. As many local governments turn to tourism to bolster economic development, we will see more of these types of services. Business is also a prominent target of Tampa officials. The other side of economic development is the job market. Businesses can pay taxes online, as well as access departments that handle zoning and permit requests.

As would be expected from an award-winning city, Tampa charts how it became the best website for local government in the United States. Table 1 contains the chronology of events pertaining to Tampa's electronic government project. As noted by Table 1, the project was initiated and finalized in 2000. Like most other governments, Tampa's electronic government plan initially began as an effort to engage in electronic commerce. In Tampa's case, the Mayor wanted the city to be able to transact business between citizens and government over the Internet.

Tampa's electronic government events culminated in November of 2000 when the city council approved the vendor contract

Figure 6

with National Information Consortium (NIC). Since then, Tampa has reached several milestones on its path toward electronic government fame. Table 2 lists the City of Tampa's achievements. As the list reveals, the first accomplishment was placing the Museum of Art store online, marking its first electronic commerce venture. Next, Tampa set out to make information available concerning locations with high rates of traffic accidents. In spring of 2001, the ability to make payments to the city via credit card was established. In a little over a year following this move, the city took in $1,000,000 in electronic

▓ Table 1

2000 E-government Initiative Events

The following is a chronology of events pertaining to the City of Tampa's E-government project.

January 10

Luncheon meeting with Mayor Greco, Rick Smith, Henry Ennis, and John McGrath—Mayor directs Rick & John to come up with a strategy/plan to allow the City to transact business over the Internet; to report back in 90 days; to utilize staff from appropriate departments to assist in this undertaking.

March 23

Meeting with Mayor Greco, Rick Smith, Henry Ennis, and John McGrath—Present the strategy of advertising an RFP to seek a private sector venture partner to assess, design, build, operate and manage the City's Internet Portals. The Mayor directs Rick & John to finalize the RFP.

April 13

Rick Smith and Dave Kennedy present a briefing to the City Council on the City's Internet Strategy in response to City Council motions on March 9, 2000: (Buckhorn-Alvarez) That Rick Smith, Director of the Planning and Management Department, be requested to appear before Council on APril 13, 2000 to discuss E-Commerce and to also discuss how the City can take advantage of the technology available in order to bring the government to the public via the net or the web. Motion carried. Motion: (Saul-Sena-Ferlita) That Rick Smith, Director of the Planning and Management Department be requested to appear before Council n April 13, 2000 to discuss opportunities for the public to provide input regarding Councils decision making process. Motion carried.

April 14

Rick Smith presents overview of the City Internet Strategy at the Mayor's Meeting with City Department Heads.

April 18

Rick Smith and John McGrath present a briefing on the City Internet Strategy at Sam Halter's staff meeting includes Deputy CAO, Water, Sewer, Solid Waste, DPW, Parks, Recreation, and Intergovernmental relations (includes—Mike Salmon, Dave Tippin, Braid Baird, Wayne Brookins, Jack Morriss, Joe Abrahams, Ross Ferlita, and Debbie Stevenson).

Rick Smith and John McGrath present a briefing on the City Internet Strategy BCS Managers (includes—Steve LaBrake, Sandi Cedola, Nick D'Andrea, Teresa Meyer, John Barrios, and Bill Doherty).

Rick Smith and John McGrath present a briefing on the City Internet Strategy to Admin Sarah Lang.

April 24

Rick Smith, John McGrath, and Steve Cantler present a briefing on the City's Internet Strategy to Julie Harris and Annette Spina (Curtis Lane unable to attend—Annette to brief him).

Continued.

▓ Table 1

2000 E-government Initiative Events—cont'd

April 25
Rick Smith and Steve Cantler present a briefing on the City's Internet Strategy to City Clerk (Janette Martin).
Rick Smith and Steve Cantler present a briefing on the City's Internet Strategy to TCC (includes John Moors and his staff).

April 26
Rick Smith and Steve Cantler present a briefing on the City's Internet Strategy to the TPD Command Staff.
Rick Smith and Steve Cantler present a briefing on the City's Internet Strategy to the TFR Command Staff.
Rick Smith and Steve Cantler present a briefing on the City's Internet Strategy to the Tampa Museum (includes Emily Kass and her staff).

May 1
Rick Smith and Steve Cantler present a briefing on the City's Internet Strategy to Accounting and Business License Divisions (includes Ron Ibarra and Butch Hill).

May 2
Rick Smith, Steve Cantler, and John McGrath present a briefing on the City's Internet Strategy to Purchasing (includes Joan McConnell).

May 8
Rick Smith and John McGrath present a briefing on the City's Internet Strategy to Revenue & Finance/Budget (inclues Henry Ennis, Jim Stefan and Martha McCurdy).

May 10
Rick Smith, John McGrath, and Steve Cantler present a briefing on the City's Internet Strategy to City Attorney (includes Jim Palermo, Gina Grimes, and Sam Hamilton).

May 18
Issued E-government Request For Proposals (RFP)

June 1
Published E-government RFP Addendum 1—Pre-Proposal Vendor Meeting Attendance Record

June 6
Published E-government RFP Addendum 2—Overview of Major Application Systems

June 14
Published E-government RFP Addendum 3—Clarification & Responses to Proposers Questions

June 23
City receives proposal from Gartner Group to aid in assessing Egovernment RFP proposals.

July 6
E-government RFP closed—8 proposals received.

July 25
RFP evaluation team completes initial assessment of proposals and narrows
selection process to two submissions—American Management Systems
(AMS) & National Information Consortium (NIC).

August 21
Gartner Group presents research on AMS & NIC proposals.

August 23
NIC onsite presentation of proposed services.

August 28
AMS onsite presentation of proposed services.

August 31
Evaluation Committee selects NIC proposal as first choice and to begin contract negotiations.

September 13
Initial draft of NIC contract received.

October 31
Completed contract negotiations with NIC.

November 16
City Council approved e-government contract.

---

payments. These milestones helped Tampa achieve its recognition as
the "best city website". In early 2003, one million web page requests
were processed. The latest capability includes corresponding with
city offices for various services. Tampa does not appear to be losing
its momentum. The recent recognition seems to have only ignited
the city's officials to maintain their path of leadership in electronic
government.

Richmond

The City of Richmond, like Tampa, places a strong emphasis on using technology to deliver government to its citizens. Its website is
easy to navigate, and yields useful information to users. At the official website of Richmond, the most prominent feature that symbol-
izes the essence of our treatise is the "eCitizen" link (See Figure 7).
The "eCitizen" link takes you to the Richmond Electronic Services
Gateway. At the site, users can access the most frequently requested
services, make online payments, and get most forms and documents.
Electronic government is best captured on the site's introduction: "In

▓ Table 2

TampaGov Milestones

2003
01/31/2003 1st month of activity exceeding 1,000,000 pages requested
02/19/2003 Message Center service requests & action inquiries and general correspondence

2002
02/21/2002 Cemetery records
04/08/2002 Find it Fast! site search capabilities
04/08/2002 Off-duty police services
05/07/2002 Dynamic custom maps
06/13/2002 5th generation home page implemented (archived image)
06/28/2002 Crime activity maps
06/28/2002 Employment application submission
08/04/2002 1st Place in 2002 Best of the Web
08/16/2002 Museum membership applications & renewals
08/18/2002 $1,000,000 reached in total City revenue collected via the web site
08/16/2002 Neighborhood indicators and profiles facility
10/29/2002 MyTampaGov transaction tracking of web payments incorporated
11/21/2002 1st Place in 2002 Digital Cities Survey
12/31/2002 ~10 million web pages requested during 2002

2001
01/15/2001 Museum of Art online store (1st eCommerce service)
01/16/2001 High traffic accident locations
01/31/2001 Boards & Commissions membership info
03/15/2001 City of Tampa Television Channel 15 live webcast
03/30/2001 TampaGov branding and comprehensive site redesign— www.tampagov.net (archived image)
04/05/2001 Police incident and traffic accident reports
04/05/2001 Secured web payment processing using credit cards established
06/01/2001 Consolidated news & public announcements
06/13/2001 Parking citation inquiries/payments
06/22/2001 Parking lot/garage monthly permit applications/payments
07/26/2001 Business tax renewal payments
08/30/2001 Egovernment saving calculator
10/15/2001 Permit applications/payments & inspection requests
10/22/2001 Personnel managed job postings
11/01/2001 Utility bill inquiries/payments
11/01/2001 MyTampaGov established
11/07/2001 Fire calls for service
12/31/2001 ~6 million web pages requested during 2001

2000

01/10/2000 Mayor directs staff to create a strategy to allow the City to transact business over the Internet

05/10/2000 Purchasing bid package info

05/18/2000 E-government Request For Proposals released

06/01/2000 E-government RFP Addendum 1 - Pre-Proposal Vendor Meeting Attendance Record

06/06/2000 E-government RFP Addendum 2 - Overview of Major Application Systems

06/14/2000 E-government RFP Addendum 3 - Clarification & Responses to Proposers Questions

07/06/2000 E-government RFP closed - 8 proposals received

07/17/2000 Traffic related advisories

07/17/2000 Police calls for service

11/16/2000 E-government contract established with Florida Local Interactive (FLI)

12/08/2000 Business tax receipt inquiry

12/14/2000 Consolidated calendars

12/31/2000 >3 million web pages requested during 2000

1996 to 1999

09/18/1996 City of Tampa web site introduced - www.ci.tampa.fl.us (archived image)

05/14/1998 City Council draft agendas

06/04/1998 City Council action agendas

06/11/1998 Community Redevelopment Agency agendas

02/07/1999 2nd generation home page implemented (archived image)

03/09/1999 Employment application forms

04/01/1999 City Council meeting transcriptions

09/18/1999 3rd generation home page implemented (archived image)

12/31/1999 >1 million web pages requested during 1999

---

the future, you will have the ability to access many of the services here that currently require a trip to city hall" (City of Richmond, 2003). Let us take a look at how Richmond approaches electronic government.

Most of Richmond's online services are information and document-based. Figure 7 indexes the most requested types of information. Requested services range from adoption inquiries to complaining about tall weeds. Yes, local government is a bit different than state and federal government. Richmond's list of frequent requests represents the mundane and the interesting. It also illustrates the difficulties local governments face in delivering services via various technologies. Some services, weed removal for example, may not be deliverable through the Internet. At least one can complain

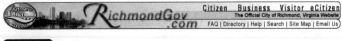

FAQ
Forms and Documents
Frequently Requested Services
Request City Services Online
Sign-Up For My Richmond Gov
Edit Your Richmond Gov Account
Information Technology
Online Payments
Publicly Accessible Computers
Send a Richmond City Postcard!

Providing services to citizens on the Web is a major undertaking supported by City Council and the City Manager. Currently, we are providing many of the forms and documents that citizens request most frequently in a read-only PDF format. In the future, you will have the ability to access many of the services here that currently require a trip to City Hall.

If you have suggestions for items that should be on our E-Citizen "to-do list", please Email the E-Citizen Team.

Home | Citizen | Business | Visitor | eCitizen | Help | Directory | FAQ | Search | Site Map | Contact Us
© 2000-04 City of Richmond, Virginia. All Rights Reserved. Disclaimer & Terms of Use

Figure 7

about tall grass using their computer, therefore beginning the process that will eventually fix the problem.

Richmond's eCitizen portal lists various online services by category type (Figure 8). The first feature listed prominently is Jobs With The City of Richmond. Unfortunately, the only service available to users is a downloadable application form. The rest of the application process takes place traditionally by sending the completed form in the mail. Ironically, a complete list of job openings is not easily available on the eCitizen page. It is customary to discuss only strengths of an award winning city's web practices, but we feel compelled to shed light on the fact that finding an open job with the city of Richmond is not easy. On the city's homepage, under "hot links", current job openings are posted by category. You still won't be able to apply for them online though.

Businesses in Richmond can avail themselves of several on-line services: business licenses can be obtained online, and, once up and running, businesses can apply to have their property assessments reviewed if they believe they are paying too much in taxes. For individuals, personal property tax returns can also be completed online. These timesaving measures for businesses make the businesses themselves more efficient. These management efficiencies

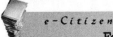

Forms And Documents

business | citizen | city sells | community development | finance | human resources | human services | jobs | minority business enterprise | online documents | parks, recreation, & community facilities | procurement services | public safety

Business

- Admissions, Lodging, Meals Tax Coupon (ALM)
- Application for Review of Assessment of a Commercial and Multiple Dwelling Property
- Application for Review of Assessment of an Industrial Property
- Business License Application

- Business Personal Property Tax Return
- Business Tangible Personal Property Tax Return
- Contractor's Certification of Worker's Compensation
- Encroachment Application
- Hauling or Moving Permit Application

Citizen

- Adopt-a-Spot/Street Activity Form
- Adopt-a-Spot/Street Agreement
- Application for Certification of a Vital Record (birth and death records)
- Application for Review of Assessment of a Single Family Property
- Families and Children Medicaid Application
- Dog/Cat License Application

- Graffiti Removal Release of Liability
- Pet Lost and Found Form
- Request for Motor Vehicle Reassessment
- Social Services Benefits Application
- Supercan Request
- Volunteer Cleanup Application
- Tax Relief for the Elderly & Disabled

City Sells

- Private Bid Form

- Public Bid Form

Community Development

- Application for Certificate of Appropriateness
- Application for Community Unit Plan
- Application for Land Disturbing Permit
- **Application for Tax Exemption for Rehabilitated Structures**
- Building Permit Certificate Application
- Certificate of Zoning Compliance Application
- Certificate of Occupancy Application
- Credit Card Payment Form
- Demolition Permit Application
- Designation of "Responsible Land Disturber"
- Electrical Permit Application

- Elevator Permit Application
- Fee Schedule
- Freedom of Information Request Form
- Gas Piping Permit Application
- **Inspection Request Codes**
- Mechanical Permit Application
- Plan of Development Application
- Plumbing Permit Application
- Rezoning Application
- Sign Permit Application
- Special Use Permit Application
- Subdivision Application
- **Tank Permit Application**
- Urban Design Committee Application
- Wireless Communication Facilities

Finance

- Admissions, Lodging & Meals Tax Coupon
- Business License Application
- Contractor's Certification of Worker's Compensation
- Dog/Cat License Application
- Replacement of City Decal Request Form

- Request for Motor Vehicle Reassessment
- Tax Relief for the Elderly & Disabled
- Tax Escrow Payment Program Application
- Tax Escrow Payment Plan Coupon
- Business Personal Property Tax Forms

Figure 8

Human Resources

- Application for Leave
- Certification List
- Certification of Health Care Provider
- Disciplinary Review Checklist
- DPU Interview Utilization
- Education Level
- Emergency Contact
- Employee Separation Checklist
- Employee Exit Form
- Employer's Accident Report
- Employment Application
- Essential Job Functions
- Exemplary Service Award Nomination
- Family and Medical Leave Act(FMLA) Fact Sheet
- Grievance
- Grievance Instructions
- Grievance Reply

- Grievance Non-Compliance
- Grievance Notification
- New Appointment Checklist
- Notice of Employee Separation
- Performance Evaluation Plan
- Personnel Requisition
- REAP Referral Form
- Request for Personnel Action
- Secondary Employment Request
- Shared Application
- Shared Donation
- Substance Abuse Policy
- Supervisor's Form Guide
- Supervisor's Guide to Performance Evaluation
- Supplemental Recruitment
- Tuition Assistance Application

Human Services

- Record of Complaint & Results of Investigation
- Application for a Department of Health Permit
- Application for a Death Certificate

- Coordinator's Check List For A Temporary Food Event
- Application For Temporary Restaurant Permit

Jobs

- Employment Application

Minority Business Enterprise

- Employment Profile/Certification Report
- Past-Good-Faith-Efforts Form for MBE
- Minority Business Participation Commitment Form for Pre-qualification (MBE-1)

- Sub-Contractors List & Participation Verification Form (MBE-2)
- Monthly Compliance Monitoring Report – (MBE-3)
- Minority Business Participation Form

Online Documents

- Adopted Biennal Fiscal Plan Year 2003-2004 & Year 2004-2005
- 2000 Census Report
- City of Richmond's Downtown Plan
- Downtown Plan Update
- City of Richmond's Annual Financial Report
- City Council-Appointed Authorities, Boards, Commissions - Vacancy Report

- City of Richmond's Master Plan
- Old Manchester Neighborhood Plan
- Shockoe Bottom Land Use and Development Strategy
- City of Richmond's Adopted Capital Improvement Plan 2004-2008
- City of Richmond's Adopted Biennial Fiscal Plan 2001-2003
- West Main Street Corridor Plan
- City Organization Chart

Parks, Recreation & Community Facilities

- Adopt-a-Tree Program Request for Site Evaluation
- Camp Registration Form
- Pine Camp Application

- Registration for Programs or Classes
- Richmond Racers Swim Team Application
- Senior Program Application

Procurement Services

- MBE/ESB Participation Commitment
- Vendor Bidder Application
- Professional/Non-Professional Commodity List

- Commodity Sub Class Listing
- Commodity Sub Class Listing 2

Public Safety

- Citizen Police Academy Application

- Criminal History Record Request
- Record Request

 *Note: In order to view and print these documents, your computer must have the Adobe Acrobat Reader utility installed. If this software is not installed on your system, you can download it for free from Adobe

Figure 8—cont'd

result in higher profits, possible expansion, and increased hiring. As economic development becomes a central tenet of local government, we anticipate more government-to-business services applications for the Internet to develop in order to lessen costs associated with complying with government regulations.

Virginia receives high marks for promoting democracy through online initiatives. As the capital city, Richmond follows this lead by making several documents available online that enhances citizen participation in local government. While participation may not be enhanced, the level of information certainly has the potential to be bolstered. Richmond officials post their budget and proposed spending items for future years online. Citizens can readily get access to see where their money is going. The downtown development plan is also available online. Citizens can now plan along with city planners for the upgrades, changes, and events taking place within their communities. Closely mirroring the downtown plan is a list of capital improvement projects for a four-year period. These documents sustain the core of government operations as they provide a list of what capital projects will be conducted. Using the city's organization chart and a list of boards, commissions, agencies, and missions, navigating the Richmond city electronic government is not difficult once you have learned which office has domain over a particular issue.

Richmond is also a leader in minority business recruitment. Through online initiatives, Richmond has sought to increase the number and strength of minority-owned business ventures. Avenues exist for minority businesses to receive notification of public business, and compete for public business through a bidding process. In addition to attracting this minority-owned businesses, Richmond allows for certification and participation through several online programs such as the Employment Profiles-Certification report and Compliant Monitoring report. All of these are accessible through the city's website.

Finally, Richmond is working on improving efficiency through various management initiatives. In the realm of public finance administration, Richmond has several features that ease the pain of separating taxpayers from their hard earned money. In addition to the ability of businesses to pay taxes to the city online, the elderly and disabled can apply for tax relief. Personal property tax compliance can be accomplished through requests for motor vehicle reassessments and decal replacement requests. Various lodging and escrow applications are also available online. Each of these makes it easier to comply with tax laws. This ease of administration is a major factor in the adoption, design, and collection of various charges. Electronic initiatives, beyond the software used to track revenue collections, are increasing the effectiveness of governments' collection of owed monies.

Roanoke

Just across the state from Richmond sits the city of Roanoke, which is located in the western part of Virginia in the Roanoke Valley. One visit to the city's website, roanokegov.com, demonstrates that Roanoke is in a class by itself when it comes to technology and government. The political leadership is visibly proud of its number-one ranking in the small city class by the Center for Digital Government in 2002 (Digital Government, 2003). We will now examine a few things Roanoke is doing well in regards to electronic governance.

Unlike Richmond, the city of Roanoke allows job seekers access to a comprehensive list of available jobs and the ability to apply for them online. Special features allow users to also update and check the status of their application. As local governments like Roanoke continue to compete for job candidates from a wide range of experiences, education, and diverse backgrounds, tools such as online personnel systems save time, financial resources, and promote a more qualified pool of applicants.

Beyond an online personnel system, Roanoke has created a special feature that allows citizens and businesses to easily send money to the city coffers. From the homepage, users only need to click once to select the type of payment they wish to make. Sending payments then requires selection of where the money will be debited, and a click to send. Each transaction completed online saves the sender time, postage, and hassle. No longer can checks get lost in the mail. We suppose at some point the cyberdog could eat some payments, but as these online systems develop, more attention is being paid to security, accessibility, and privacy. They will continue to get better in these areas. Roanoke will benefit through managing less cash, checks, and currency. Financial data can be easily assembled through various software programs. Thus, fiscal administration is improved through the online payment system.

Roanoke is not different from other cities in their desire to be responsive to the needs of their citizens. Through an easy-to-use online form, citizens can request city services and register problems. The online form asks for standard information such as name, address, and phone number. It also provides space for a general description of the reason you are requesting help (Roanokegov.com, 2003). By using the online forms, citizens can make complaints without the anxiety of interacting with another human being. Citizens also do not need to know which office or department handles their particular issue. After the user inputs the nature of the problem, the receiver of the message is able to route it to the appropriate office for service. Since local governments are structured similarly, the potential responsiveness is increased, while citizen dissatisfaction is decreased. Simply put, technology lessens the communication barriers inherent in a bureaucracy. No longer will citizens have to make several calls and face numerous dead ends before finding someone who can address their problem.

Roanoke does several other things well also. Their comprehensive plan details where Roanoke would like to be several years in the future, and is available online, as well as a calendar of community events. The city's website contains significant information to make all constituents—private citizens, businesses, and non-profits—better informed. When each of these groups has more information concerning the public business of their city, they can become better participants in community decisions. They also have more means of communicating their preferences and perspectives. Some are hesitant to embrace the rapid rate of technological change due to the fraying of social bonds, but their fears may be unfounded at this point. We envision the other side of the coin with regards to technology. It can create and enhance a sense of community. This community may be virtual, but it has all the earmarks of a community nonetheless.

Summary

We see state and local governments using technology to efficiently manage and carry out the public's business, and offer citizens easier ways to interact with government. As noted earlier in this chapter, the most contact that citizens have with government takes place at the local and state level. It is therefore important for state and local governments to begin improving existing technologies, and adapting new ones as they develop. The benefits of adapting technologies to state and local government include improved management efficiencies, better responsiveness, and enhanced participation in the governing process.

It is our assumption that state and local governments desire the benefits that technologies offer. If they don't, it will be somewhat perilous if you agree that the future economic, social, and democratic success of society depends on adapting technology to the pillars of an open, free, and accessible government. Michigan and Virginia both envision technology as the future economic energy of their states. Both states have science and technology corridors bridged by the ingenuity of their significant urban areas and the quality of their university systems. Tampa, Richmond, and Roanoke each approach technology usage slightly differently, but with resounding success. That they vary in size with each having its own set of policy problems only further enhances the case that technology can be used for good purposes with recognizable results. These results achieved by these governments will become the benchmarks by which other state and local governments will be judged.

We hope this brief review of what a few state and local governments are doing with technology gives some insight into future possibilities. It should also serve to compare other localities' usage of technology. States are laboratories of democracy. Each is unique. Technology appears to be able to span these differences, and render itself useful in a variety of settings. It appears the accolades heaped on Michigan, Virginia, Richmond, Roanoke, and Tampa are well-founded. Their usage of technology should be modeled elsewhere according to local conditions.

Congress and the Courts

Congress and the Courts are not immune from the influences of technology. We have discussed how bureaucracy, placed organizationally within the Executive branch of government, is using technology for practicing better management methods and delivering more efficient services. For Congress and the Courts, technology is slowly being adapted to their methods, affecting several areas of business: overseeing the bureaucracy, providing resources to agencies, passing laws, and judging disputes. The process of adapting technological advances to Congress and the Courts is ongoing, and the current state of legislative and judicial operations at both the state and federal level are best summarized as being in a state of transition. To address this transition, our discussion summarizes the primary role of Congress and the Courts within a system of shared power, and how their roles are being influenced by technology. Our plan is to discuss Congress, then move to a general discussion of the Courts later in this chapter.

Congress

Congress has its legal foundation in Article I of the Constitution of the United States. Its powers are enumerated and detailed in Section 8. Of the three branches of government, Congress was expected to be the key governing institution. After all, Congress is the branch of government directly elected by the people. It was the Framers' intent that our federal government would work to serve them. Congress was to fulfill this role of service to its people.

Congress has important duties given to it by the Constitution. Its members have the ability to make laws, regulate interstate commerce, appropriate funds, and raise money. These are a few of the enumerated powers granted, but they represent the primary role Congress plays in American politics. There is little reason to think Congress, as an institution, was accidentally created as the first branch of government. Therefore, we can think of Congress as the keystone establishment in Washington, D.C. (Fiorina, 1989).

Membership

The House of Representatives is comprised of 435 voting members. Non-voting delegates from U.S. territories and the District of Columbia are also included. House members serve two-year terms, which makes them perpetual candidates. The Senate includes two senators from each of the 50 states. Senators serve six-year terms with roughly a third standing for reelection every two years. Unlike the House, the Senate is not subjected to complete turnover every election cycle. Members of each chamber are drawn from upper strata of the socio-economic spectrum. Their primary vocational interests center around the law.

Congressional Structure

The majority party provides the leadership for each chamber of Congress, respectively. Congress still relies on senior members for leadership. The elite few in the congressional leadership control committees, staff, and the agenda for Congress. Its overarching structure permits members to develop expertise on various policy questions and focus attention on the specialized needs of an institution that encompasses 435 distinct interests. Committees divide up the work presented to Congress, and insure that a wide range of policy questions will be discussed, investigated, and hopefully addressed through some legislation or appropriation.

The Congress Connection

The importance and structure of Congress would be of little interest to students of American government and politics if they alone were the extent of any discussion. However, these concepts lend serious weight to the discussion of the work that Congress accomplishes.

Several years ago, political scientist David Mayhew (1974) detailed how Congress and its work provide a visible electoral connection.

It is assumed that all members of Congress (MOC) seek to hold their seats as long as they can attract half the votes plus one more (Bevill, 1993). Therefore, MOC must attend to casework, take policy positions, and explain their work to the voters who elect them to office. The structure of Congress helps the members with these endeavors. Each MOC has an office, staff, and a small budget they can use to run an office that serves their constituents. Committee memberships permit MOC to work in policy areas that are important to their districts. Some committee assignments are more powerful than others, and are frequently used as rewards for some members.

Technology has the most realistic chance of influence on the duties of the MOC. Some of the most obvious changes involve how members of Congress relate to their constituents. We can see these changes in the methods of communicating to constituents, and of addressing the problems they may have with government casework. How members of Congress go about campaigning for office is also influenced by technology. Additionally, Congress' role within a system of shared power has utilized technology to lobby regulatory commissions such as the Environmental Protection Agency.

Congressional Elections
Congressional elections are easily characterized as being largely uncompetitive. For example, House incumbents have recently enjoyed reelection rates over 90%. In any given year, only a handful (30-40) of seats will be truly competitive. Part of the lack of competition in House elections is caused by the structure of congressional elections. Finance laws hinder would-be opponents from raising the money needed to beat an incumbent. District factors, such as partisanship of the district, almost always ensure that the incumbent will not face major party opposition. In fact, for most incumbents, the biggest threat to being reelected is surviving an intra-party challenge in the primary. Technology has very little effect on the structure of elections. Technology shapes elections during the campaigns of the candidates. These campaigns have influence on the way any MOC will ultimately govern. Our attention turns to a brief discussion of how technology is used in the campaign process.

A sampling of Senate and House races in 1998 showed that by October of that year, more than two-thirds of candidates for open seats in the U.S. Congress had a website (Dulio, Goff, & Thurber,

🇺🇸 Table 1

**Candidates with Campaign Sites on the Internet
(Major Party Candidates Only)**

	Percentage of Candidates with Sites in 1998	Percentage of Candidates with Sites in 2000
Candidates for U.S. Senate	72%	91%
Candidates for U.S. House	35%	66%
Candidates for Governor	95%	83%

Table adapted from: "Political Campaigning on the Internet: Business as Usual?" Elaine Ciulla Kamarck, p. 88. *In Governance.com: Democracy in the Information Age.* Elaine Ciulla Kamarck and Joseph S. Nye, Jr., Eds. Brookings Institution Press: Washington, D.C., 2002.

1999). Table 1 shows the '98 data in more detail. Here, widespread use of the Internet is seen except for the House elections in '98 (this is partly explained by the approximate 100 seats that were uncontested, which led to minimal campaigning).

Additionally, both parties' candidates appeared to use the web equally. In the 1998 races, just over 71% of Democratic candidates used the web in their campaigns, while a little over 68% of Republicans did the same. Clearly, as a novelty or not, the Internet had, by 1998, become a more widely used campaign resource.

By the election of '98, nearly 73% of candidate websites were being used to solicit campaign contributions, with both parties exhibiting approximately equal rates of activity in this regard (Dulio, et al., 1999). This did not, however, mean that all of these websites were soliciting secure "online" donations. As shown in Table 2, the majority of websites soliciting contributions were doing so in a fairly traditional manner.

The '98 election cycle definitely shows an increase in use of the Internet, but this technological advance appears to be measured in inches, not yards. While more candidates were using the Web, few of them were using it as a direct interface for secure Internet contributions via an electronic funds transfer. This was already the widely used norm for e-commerce and seen as a safe way to do business online. In fact, according to Visa USA's New Market Development Division, the majority of all businesses that ran websites in 1998 were accepting secure credit card transactions online (T. Attinger, Personal Communication, July 14, 2003). This is significantly higher than the 29.9% of campaign websites doing so at that time.

▓ Table 2

Methods of Soliciting Campaign Contributions

Requests for mail-in contributions	53.7%
Requests that the donor print-off a form and send it in via mail, fax or e-mail as a pledge	47.8%
Campaign requires that a donor request a campaign pledge form online which is then sent to them by regular mail	32.8%
Online secure credit card donations	29.9%

68 Senate Candidates and 65 House Candidates (n = 133)
Websites used by candidates in the 1998 election (n =111)

Table 2 adapted from Dulio, David A., Donald L. Goff, and James A. Thurber. "Untangled Web: Internet Use during the 1998 Election" *PS: Political Science and Politics,* March 1999, vol. 32 (1), p. 53-59. Table title: "Types of Web Site Solicitation Techniques" p. 55.

(Lack Of) Effects

At first glance, technology, in the form of Internet campaigning for Congress, does not appear to alter the campaign process very much. Thus far, traditional techniques have been adapted to the newest technology. We have yet to see the type of web-based, grassroots support generated for a congressional campaign that is similar to Howard Dean's bid for the Presidency. The Dean campaign has effectively used the Internet to raise money and organize a group of supporters that is unparalleled in campaign history.

Congressional campaigns and elections appear to be adhering to our theoretical understanding of them despite emerging technologies. (see Tufte, Jacobson and Kernell, and Campbell for a complete discussion of congressional elections theory). The Internet will not alter the outcome of elections, and will therefore not alter the way MOC go about their duties. Thus, the effects of technology on congressional elections are not yet as interesting as they may become. Campaigns are made more accessible, and donating money is easier than ever before. Again, though, these elections are not fundamentally altered by technology.

Communicating with Constituents

MOC fully realize that listening to citizen concerns and communicating their successes is important to their careers. If constituents feel a representative is out of touch with their needs, the right challenger can make this an issue and ride the sentiment of an angry electorate to a victory. Just ask Gray Davis in California who lost to an actor with no political experience. At the congressional level, communicating with constituents once was very limited. Before telephones, an in-person meeting or communication by mail constituted the bulk of contact MOC had with their constituents. Modern technologies such as faxes, cell phones, and e-mail make it possible to get in touch with a MOC at any time and from any place. Along with the ease of communication comes a heightened urgency to respond through casework and correspondence.

Casework requires a MOC to act. He or she will largely delegate casework to a staffer, but in some cases the MOC may intervene personally if the right resistance is met while resolving a constituent's problem. Casework may involve anything from tracking down a lost Social Security check to arranging a tour of the Capitol. Regardless of the issue, MOC take casework seriously. Given that this attention is important for success, technology has changed the way casework requests are communicated.

Representative John Boozman (AR-3) maintains a model website that embodies all of our current discussion. His website recently garnered the Golden Mouse Award from the Congressional Management Foundation's Congress Online Project (2003). Figure 1 is the homepage of Rep. Boozman. In the center of the page, users are drawn to a story about the Arkansas congressional delegation's success in steering funding for defense projects in the state of Arkansas. To the left of the story, Rep. Boozman makes it easy to request services through the various links under *Constituent Services. Other News* touts the accomplishments of Rep. Boozman.

Rep. Boozman's website is not only important because of its ability to help citizens get assistance with particular problems, but also for conveying Mr. Boozman's record of accomplishment and service. His recent votes are listed and explained under the *Recent Votes* section of the website. Users can sign up for e-mail updates by simply entering their e-mail address connected to a listserv. Contact information and Rep. Boozman's upcoming schedule give citizens an indication of what exactly is going on with their Representative in Washington.

In addition to Boozman, several other MOC effectively use the Internet to discharge their duties and communicate with constituents. Rep. Earl Blumenauer effectively uses the Internet. His site actually prepares citizens to interact with elected officials by giving tips for effective communication. Rep. Chaka Fattah uniquely targets messages to special groups through an *Education Resource Center* link. This makes it easier to find information for particular groups.

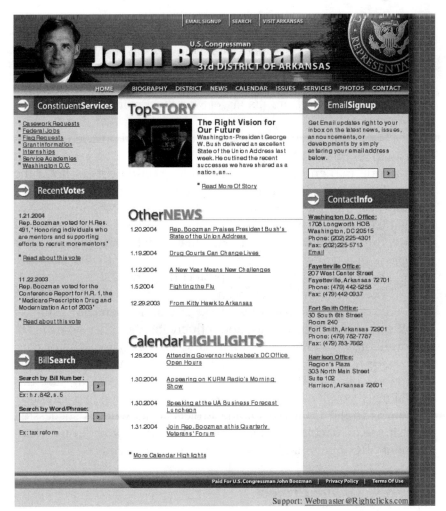

Figure 1

Rep. Kay Granger interestingly lists her staff and their responsibilities within her office. Her site also includes a Spanish version, and reflects the characteristics of her congressional district. These examples illustrate a desire by the Representatives to accomplish two things: serve their constituents and communicate their successes to those who wish to listen.

Interacting with Other Branches

Congress certainly attends to the many needs of their constituents. In most instances, attention to casework requires a MOC or member of the staff to interact with other branches of government. Since the vast government bureaucracy is organizationally situated within the executive branch, this is where MOC must go to resolve problems. An interesting method of working on behalf of constituents recently occurred when Senator Debbie Stabenow (MI), routed an online petition through her website. Its target was the Environmental Protection Agency (EPA).

Stabenow's issue with the EPA dealt with the issue of dumping Canadian trash in Michigan. Her ire translated a "don't dump on me" attitude into an online mechanism for constituents to flood the EPA with their position on trash dumping in the north. The online petition accomplishes several things for Senator Stabenow. As we have already demonstrated, MOC desire to serve their constituents. Clearly, through the online petition, Senator Stabenow demonstrates that she is in touch with her constituents, cares about what they care about, and that she is working to protect their interests.

These examples demonstrate how technology has been adapted to the traditional roles of congressional behavior: running for office, serving constituents, and influencing the other branches of government. We mentioned earlier that Congress is in a state of transition with regard to harnessing new technology that improves the institution's quality. There are groups interested in making sure this transition is positive for both citizens and Congress. Our attention now turns to the Congress Online Project. If its work is successful, we will see an accelerated incorporation of technology in the management of Congress and how it interacts with citizens.

Congress Online Project

The Pew Charitable Trusts supported an initial project by the Congressional Management Foundation to "examine the use of Web sites and other forms of online communications by congressional offices" with a two-year program beginning in 2001. The Foundation's first task was to determine what is expected of Congress in terms of online communication and Web access. Researchers interacted with MOC, their staff, and those who manage the information technology to gauge their expectations of technology for the purpose of carrying out their duties. The foundation also sought out the best practices of Internet usage and how they could be applied to Congress (Congress Online Project, 2003).

Armed with a clear purpose, the Foundation carved out four goals for the Congress Online Project (Congress Online Project, 2003b):

1. Determine the Best Practices for Internet operation on Capital Hill, with particular focus on Member-constituent, Member-press, and Member-interest group communications.
2. Encourage Member offices, leadership offices, and committees to adopt the Best Practices in their online communications.
3. Educate the public and public policy organizations about how to effectively communicate with Congress online.
4. Help Congress as an institution to create and implement a vision for truly effectively online communications practices.

These primary goals reflect the need for MOC to interact with citizens, interest groups, and the media. We have discussed the need for MOC to effectively communicate their positions, respond to citizen requests, and discharge their duties. Each of these tasks is made easier through the effective adaptation of technology to Congress Members' operations.

Results of the Congress Online Project are available, appropriately enough, online. The Best Practices Annual Report is a yearly report detailing how Congress uses online communication tools, how Member websites can be improved, and which Members in Congress are using the Internet better than other Members. We mentioned some of the best sites earlier. The Project also issues briefs concerning timely innovations of importance to MOC. Monthly newsletters discuss best websites, ideas for Web improvement, and trends in the usage of technology in the public sector. Most importantly, the Project maintains a website that reflects the aspects of a quality website (Congress Online Project, 2003c).

The work of the Congress Online Project has created some noticeable reforms. The web presence of MOC has improved. As the websites continue to improve, the communication with constituents, casework attention, and credit claiming will undergo changes. The prospects for technology improving the work of MOC in discharging their duties give us some hope. Our enthusiasm for the influence technology appears to have on our court system is significantly less than for Congress. Our attention now turns to the courts.

The Courts

The judicial process is an enigma to most citizens. Most people, we believe, understand the notion of the courts' role in judging disputes but the structure, methods, and nuances of the justice process are a mystery. For example, we have rarely met an advocate of tort reform who had a firm grasp on what needed changing. Moreover, many folks would be surprised to know that the court system, while slow and seemingly bogged down at times, rarely uses a full-blown trial for deciding innocence and guilt. These examples are not meant as an indictment of the knowledge people have about our court system. Rather, these examples indicate our prevailing assumption: technological advances will not change the court system drastically, particularly at the federal level. Most of the influence will take place in the administration of justice. Beyond the federal courts, state and local governments are experimenting with new technologies in the courtroom, such as better audio and visual presentations. Thus, we contend that the changes that technology has on the demonstrative procedures of justice are worth exploring.

Technology is influencing the court system in three primary ways: administering the work of the courts, proving new areas of laws, and increasing access to judicial proceedings. All of these are important, but they don't fundamentally alter the nature of judicial decisions. In a normative sense, we desire that judges be free from outside influences. Judges, though, are human beings with the experience and bias that comes from every day life experiences. That being said, we don't envision technology technology altering the way judges discharge their duties in the same manner as say a Member of Congress or bureaucrat working in a government agency. The potential lack of influence is grounded in the way judges are selected, particularly at the federal level, whereby all of them are appointed.

State courts operate differently. Judges at the state and local level are politicians with party affiliation and are subjected to popular election. Due to these structural differences, we would expect technology to be more influential at the state and local level than the federal level. Anecdotal evidence confirms this intuitive hunch.

Before we move on to the ways that technology is influencing our court system, it is important to briefly look at the structure of federal and state courts. We contend that an organization's behavior can not be separated from its overarching structural component. Our approach is not new. Just about any discussion of organizations, their membership, and their susceptibility to influences, such as technology, are conditioned by the context in which the individual organization operates. For example, it is a priori assumption that government workers who are appointed have different allegiances than their career counterparts. If they did not have different pressures and we didn't have public personnel history on our side, we would ask why the Pendleton Act is needed.

The Federal Courts

As one of the three branches of government, the judicial branch has become an important force in American politics. The Supreme Court regularly issues opinions that have far-reaching policy importance. This power was not originally recognized, however. Alexander Hamilton, in the *Federalist Papers,* argued that the judiciary would be the least dangerous branch. As a symbol of the Supreme Court's supposed impotence, it had no regular building assignment in the very beginning of its operation. This lack of stature led early justices such as John Jay, a Federalist author, to resign in order to seek the governorship of New York. Can you envision a contemporary justice resigning to become a governor? The idea is also remote to observers of politics.

Article III of the Constitution deemed that the Supreme Court would be created as Congress would see fit. The blueprint of the tiered court system, practiced by the federal government today, began with the Judiciary Act of 1789 and has evolved over time. In fact, the development of the federal court system can be characterized as one that has responded to change. The changes in the number of courts, justices, and specialized courts have been in response to increases in population, the growth of territories, and to enhanced complexities of trade, commerce, and globalization.

Box 1 sketches the relationship within the federal court system. At the pinnacle of the United States' court system is the Supreme Court. Nine justices, including a chief, hear cases from the lower federal courts. The bulk of federal cases are handled by a three-tiered system. The lowest rung of the federal courts system is occupied by district courts. Most cases involving infractions of federal law enter the court system at the district level. Cases not involving Constitutional issues, if appealed, are moved to the appellate or circuit court level. There are 12 circuit courts, in addition to a special court created by Congress in 1982, which handle cases arising from specialized courts such as the U.S. Tax Court and Court of International Trade.

The State Courts

Due to the system of shared power between the federal and state governments, the United States has a dual system of justice. Like the

BOX 1
The Federal Court System (2002)

The Regular Courts
The Supreme Court of the United States
    9 justices
United States courts of appeals
    12 circuit courts (plus 1 special court of appeals)
    179 judges
United States district courts
    94 courts
    672 judges
United States magistrates
    Created by the Federal Magistrates Act (1968)
    471 full-time, 59 part-time, 3 combination clerk/magistrate
    Assist in processing of cases
Specialized Courts
United States Court of Federal Claims*
    Created in 1855
    Primarily concerned with claims arising out of public contracts
    16 judges
United States Court of International Trade
    Created in 1956
    Primarily concerned with disputes about customs duties and the
        value of imported goods
    9 judges
United States Court for the Federal Circuit
    Created in 1909
    Reviews the decisions of the U,.S. Court of International Trade, the
        U.S. Court of Federal Claims, the U. S. Court of Veterans Appeals,
        and U. S. Patent Office
    12 judges
United States Tax Court*
    Created in 1924
    Considers citizen challenges to Internal Revenue Service tax decisions
    19 judges
United States Court for the Armed Forces*
    Created in 1950
    Reviews appeals from courts-martial
    3 judges with fifteen-year terms
United States Court of Appeals for Veterans Claims
    Created in 1988
    Reviews decisions of Board of Veterans Appeals
    3 to 7 judges with fifteen-year terms

* A court created under Article I of the Constitution. The decisions of these courts are not directly reviewable by other federal courts.

federal court structure, states maintain courts where cases are initially heard. These courts hold original and local jurisdiction. This simply means that they are the courts where cases enter the judicial system, and they handle cases within a legally created boundary or area. Beyond these courts are appellate courts. These courts serve as the first level of appeal for cases beginning at the local level. Most importantly, states maintain a high or Supreme Court that represents the court of last resort for most state issues.

      This structural sketch of the court system is meant to reinforce some things you already know about the courts. We also wished to cover some familiar things in order to make a subtle point. It is unlikely that technology will change the structure of the U.S. court system. Unlike the legislative and executive branches use of technology, the courts' structure and judicial behavior seem impervious to change because of technological advances. Some of the areas in which courts are adapting technology are important for understanding how the courts work and how to access court information. Coincidentally enough, technology serves as an emerging area of work to be wrestled with by the courts.

The Supreme Court

Our highest court has a modest website (see Figure 2). Users find links to information such as the court's docket, information about the court, and opinions handed down by the judges. Most importantly, the Supreme Court's website makes available recent decisions and links to cases of national importance, such as campaign finance reform. We mentioned earlier that the Supreme Court renders legal decisions that reverberate throughout the U.S. political spectrum. These "important" links to relevant cases are a direct acknowledgement of the Court's stature within our Constitutional system of governance.

      The Supreme Court, as its name implies, can be viewed as a form of imperial judiciary. Insulated from the rigors of elections and accountable only to the law they promise to uphold, justices are not required to adhere to any prevailing decision model when carrying out their duties. They don't have to sign pledges to be a strict constructionist or judicial activist. Supreme Court justices are driven by their sense of legacy and policy (see Segal and Spaeth for discussion of judicial decision making).

      Due to the Court's structure and its historical role, the website reflects the machinations of an august body. You will not find

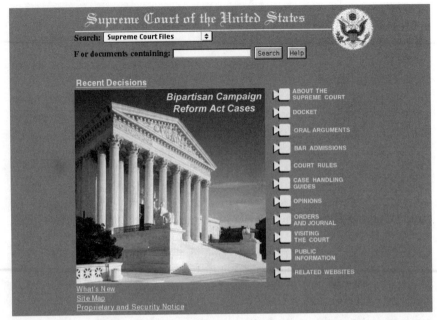

Figure 2   Supreme Court of the United States

justice's e-mail addresses on the website. Those seeking a justice's phone number will be disappointed, as they are not on the website. These examples of inaccessibility further exemplify the fact that judges at the federal level are left to their own sense of right and wrong. Technology cannot help them deliver "good" judging.

Inferior Courts

All courts below the Supreme Court are inferior courts. Therefore, the Supreme Court is a court of last resort. Once you have exhausted the Supreme Court as a legal option, legal remedies are virtually extinct. Below the Supreme Court are district and circuit courts. From a technological perspective, they seem more inviting to queries from officers of the court, as well as citizens. Unlike the Supreme Court, the website for the 11th circuit court of appeals openly advertises ways to reach the offices of the court. They also pay tribute to a former judge through biographical sketches and special features. Current judges have biographical data readily available on the website. Phone and e-mail addresses for sitting judges are not published. See Figure 3 for the main web page for the 11th circuit.

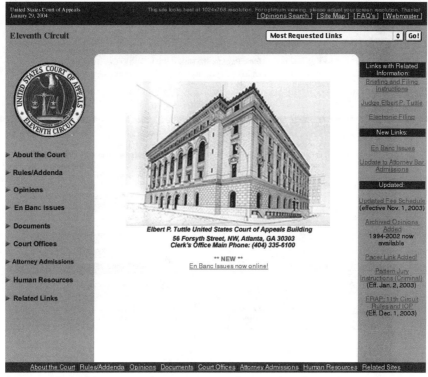

Figure 3   United States Court of Appeals, Eleventh Circuit

District courts such as the Western District Court of Virginia also seem hospitable to electronic interaction. See Figure 4 for the district's main page. Through the Clerk's office, web users can get filing information, fee schedules, and directions to the court. The court's jurisdiction covers a wide geographic area (according to the website, the area encompasses 51 counties and includes 7 offices). Finding out where they are is important. Missing a court date due to ignorance is embarrassing. Nevertheless, the district court's web page is fairly adequate. An electronic case filing system is scheduled to be online in Spring 2004 (Western District of Virginia, 2004).

Online Filing of Cases

New Case Management and Electronic Case Files systems (CM/ECF) are making the management of cases flowing through the federal court system easier to handle. As the number of users continues to grow, we should see substantial improvement in the filing of cases, sharing of information, and growth of access to court records by

U.S. District Court
Western District of Virginia

Home
CM/ECF
PACER
Court Schedule
Clerks Office
Jury
Forms
Standing Orders
Opinions
Employment
Other Courts

13 online now

Email Webmaster

*W*elcome to the Home Page for the United States District Court Western District of Virginia. This district has 4 District judges, 4 Senior District judges, and 3 Magistrate judges. It covers 52 counties with 7 divisional offices.

The Office of the Clerk of the United States District Court for the Western District of Virginia is dedicated to providing the administrative support, within the bounds of the law, necessary to ensure the effective administration of justice within the United States District Court of the Western District of Virginia. This mission includes developing financial, information and document management systems to establish, maintain and retrieve official case records, to oversee information processing during sessions of the Court, and to respond to orders of the Court. In conjunction with this mission, the Office of the Clerk provides assistance with and informs members of the public and the bar of procedures observed by the Court and of the status of cases maintained by the Office of the Clerk.

New Standing Order

Redaction of Personal Data Identifiers from All Pleadings 1/5/04

Case Management
CM/ECF
Electronic Case Files

Warning! Unauthorized attempts to upload information or change information on this web site is strictly prohibited and may be punishable under the Computer Fraud and Abuse Act of 1986 and the National Information Infrastructure Protection Act.

Home		CM/ECF		Pacer		Court Schedule
Clerks Office		Jury		Forms		Standing Orders
Opinions		Employment		Other Courts

Figure 4   U.S. District Court, Western District of Virginia

those who are interested in them. These technological adaptations can positively benefit the courts.

Under the current system, the CM/ECF process begins by receiving a case from an attorney's office. The system sends an e-mail confirmation to the sender, as well as to the parties of the case. Any subsequent information can be uploaded to the system and easily accessed by participants. There are no additional fees beyond the normal filing fee. The current rate for accessing documents is meager. It is the judiciary's intent to make electronic access and filing commonplace. Usage at the appellate level is set to begin in late 2004 (Case Management, 2004).

PACER
PACER is an acronym that stands for Public Access to Court Electronic Records. It works in conjunction with electronic case filing. Parties to a case can easily access information for a small fee. The ease of the information flow is important for several obvious reasons. Informed litigants hopefully make better advocates. That the

quality of legal representation varies from attorney to attorney is not a secret. Access to easy information can improve the quality of representation. Aside from being better represented in court, public users can research cases that are similar to legal problems they may be experiencing. Armed with this information, citizens can be emboldened to use the legal system for their protection. Without access, they are likely to let their legal problems fade away.

State Court Administration

Both the federal and state courts are keenly aware of how technology can help improve court operations. Through the work of the National Center for the State Courts, for example, court officers benefit from the attention paid to the nature of court administration. The NCSC's work is best summarized in their own words:

> "For more than 30 years, court leaders have called on the National Center for State Courts (NCSC) for up-to-date information and hands-on assistance that helps them better serve the public. Through original research, consulting services, publications, and national educational programs, NCSC offers solutions that enhance court operations with the latest technology; collects and interprets the latest data on court operations nationwide; and provides information on proven "best practices" for improving court operations in many areas, such as civil case management. NCSC is an independent, nonprofit, tax-exempt organization in accordance with Section 501(c)(3) (NCSC, 2003)."

Important for our discussion is the NCSC's work in the area of technology. Administering the work of the courtroom has been the most influenced area of judicial process. The information age we are in allows court officials to use technology for managing dockets, contacting parties to a case, filing electronic briefs, displaying better evidence in the courtroom, and increasing dissemination of court proceedings. Technology has the potential to be a pervasive part of the judicial process. There are a few issues related to technology and its usage in the courts

Access

How much access should citizens have to court records? The simple and quick answer is that unlimited access to court records is ideal. The Constitution of the United States, as amended, guarantees a speedy and public trial. Therefore, the proceedings of the court are a matter of public record. As such, there are times when cases are ongoing and working documents may jeopardize justice. Arguing for complete and open access that hinders justice is a difficult position. The courts have sought a compromise between the positions of open access while protecting basic individual rights to privacy and the pursuit of justice.

Technology, when used, allows for the widespread dissemination of judicial proceedings. Some argue there is a difference between access to court records and the essence of mass publication and access that technology allows (Stekettee and Carlson, 2004). The availability of public records in an information age subjects sensitive information to those who may be interested in the information for motives other than pure justice-oriented interests. Thus, a scenario does exist for limiting the availability of information.

Many people are attempting to create a balance of the courts' responsibilities and functions within an open government system. This work is fueled by a desire to balance the needs for open judicial proceedings, the status of the cases, and court findings with that of protecting the integrity of the justice system. At the federal level, the Judicial Conference of the United States worked for two years on developing, vetting, and adopting guidelines for privacy of court records (Steketee and Carlson, 2004). Similar work has been conducted at the state level.

The status of access to court documents is evolving. Ultimately, court officers will need to balance open access to court records with how this widespread availability can affect such access. They will also need to work toward uniform access to court records. This task is the most difficult as jurisdictions across the country are not equally endowed with resources that allow them to develop and implement access plans. Important attention to this issue will help make the realization of access a reality for everyone, not just a few.

Technology and the Law

Technological advances, development of new knowledge, and their interactions with our court system have a very interesting history. As the interactions of businesses and individuals become more complex—if not scientifically based—can our court system understand the nature of legal problems and efficiently apply the law? When Microsoft appealed its antitrust ruling, part of their appeal was founded on judicial incompetence (New York Times, 2000). Their case may have been bolstered when the judge in the case, Judge

Thomas Penfield Jackson, ceded that his knowledge of the technology case was limited. This issue is not isolated to Judge Jackson, or to federal courts. Technology is posing special problems in most courts everywhere.

States have created special courts to hear business cases. It wasn't until the state of Maryland created a task force to look into technology and its effect on business cases that any court had studied the idea of creating a specialized court that would handle the complex nature of technology cases. Maryland's work in this area raises serious questions. Can judges handle complex technology cases? Is technology a special consideration? Even those in charge of looking at the issues are, and it is unsurprising, not in agreement about the need for a special court.

The major tenets of the law are malleable enough that they can be applied to any case. The law is not the problem. Technology cases bring up age-old issues of rapid change, jurisdiction, and property rights. In cases involving music sharing, for example, these offenses occur within states, but federal courts handle patent and trade infringements. Where should the case be heard? Why isn't sharing music like sharing a book? The only difference is the method of sharing. How do we protect intellectual property and privacy, and encourage free trade within a technological climate that is changing rapidly? The rapid rate of change requires quick response. Our courts are notoriously slow. In the music sharing example, a year's worth of looting and illegal sharing of music files occurred before the courts closed down websites such as Napster. Circumstances may come to dictate a specialized court.

Summary

Technology is just beginning to influence the legislative and judicial branches of government. We have not seen the fundamental influence of technology upon judges in the same manner as we have seen with Members of Congress and government bureaucrats. There are good reasons why each branch of government has been influenced differently. The executive and legislative branches are proactive branches of government. This does not mean the judicial branches are passive in their duties. We only mean to imply that the judicial branch of government reacts when cases are filed. They owe no allegiance to staying in the good graces of citizens except when they too are elected officials.

Members of Congress desire to stay in office. We believe they will use all the tools available to discharge their duties and communicate with their constituents and benefactors. Technology helps them accomplish the main goals they set to do. We predict that Members of Congress will only increase their usage of technology. The courts will also enhance their usage, but the adaptation will not be as visible as it is in Congress or the Executive branches.

Court administrators are facing interesting careers. Technology has only begun to alter the administration of the courts' activities. While this balancing act may be, as some have called it, a conundrum, it is a worthwhile endeavor. We look forward to how technology shapes the courts and court administration. Our discussion of technology, the courts, and Congress is as brief as the history of technology's influence upon their operations. Our intent was to lay the groundwork by providing an overview of what Congress and the Courts do within a system of shared power both vertically and horizontally. Armed with this understanding, perhaps it will be easier to place the true effects technology potentially has upon our core branches of government.

Political Participation and Voting

6

Democratic Political Participation in America

The potential impact of new technologies on political participation in America is a topic that has, from one perspective, provided great hope to those desiring a more robust participatory form of democracy, and from another perspective, provided further proof that trends in individual political participation in America are not easily altered by mechanical, technological or procedural enhancements.

The purpose of this chapter is two-fold: first, to investigate the ways in which new technology has been used to facilitate individual political participation in America, and second, to discuss the potential importance of those developments. In order to do that, however, it is necessary to first briefly asses the importance of political participation in democracies and what is known about political participation in America. The first two sections of this chapter will be devoted to these topics.

The Importance of Political Participation

Individual political participation in America has been a topic that has long befuddled political scientists. On one hand, it appears to be the true glue of democratic governance. The physical act of citizens expressing their opinion to their government is assumed to be the *sine qua non* of a democratic system, and being so, is a necessary fuel required to keep the engine of state the operational. On the other hand, levels of political participation in the United States have been much lower than expected, specifically with regard to voting. One

123

might expect high levels of citizen participation in strong, stable democracies. These levels are not seen in the United States.

Generally defined, political participation can simply be regarded as actions by which ordinary citizens attempt to influence the structure, activity or staffing of government. This activity, regardless of its level, is a key element in democratic governance. Its inclusion appears to be an understood element when we discuss the topic. Indeed, even school children in America will likely tell you that a democracy is "government by the people." This simple definition underscores the implicit assumption that democracies should exhibit robust levels of citizen input and governmental responsiveness.

In much more sophisticated terminology, classic democratic theory suggests the same basic thing. Supporters of this theory assume that citizens are interested in politics, knowledgeable of politics, and participate in government by applying political information to whatever set of values to which they subscribe. Regardless of how one classifies, expresses or defines the importance of citizen input in democracy, the fact remains that it *is important* and continues to be a defining characteristic between democratic and non-democratic forms of government.

Types and Trends: Political Participation in America

It is inaccurate to refer to participation as if all forms of it were the same. Political participation in America, as in other democracies, can take a variety of forms. We generally refer to political participation strictly in terms of voting, largely because it is one of the most fundamental, low-cost, and institutionalized forms that exist. However, an accurate discussion must also include other forms, including, but no limited to, signing petitions, attending public meetings, contacting a representative, wearing a politically-oriented button on your clothes or simply putting a campaign sticker on your car. While the potential types of participation with which one could be involved are quite numerous, the trends involved are not.

Since the early 1950s the percentage of eligible voters who actually turned out to vote has generally declined. While there have been temporary counter-trends to this, most notably in 1992 during Ross Perot's candidacy, turnout rates at the polls for presidential elections have been slowly sinking. Voter turnout rates have generally dropped about 10% from 1952-2000. Voter turnout, while in the low-60s during some presidential elections in the 1950s and 60s, has generally dropped to the low-50s in the late 90s (Federal Election

Commission [FEC], 2003; Center for Voting and Democracy, [CVD], 2003).

Compared to other democracies, this figure is even more striking. Voter turnout in America consistently ranks far behind most other developed western democracies. In comparison, since 1945 The United Kingdom, Germany, and Sweden exhibit average voting rates of approximately 74-83% (The International Institute for Democracy and Electoral Assistance [IIDEA], 2003). This is substantially higher than the 48% average that is currently found in America (Ibid.). While these figures lose some of their gravity when one takes into account mandatory voting laws, voting holidays, and government sponsored registration drives found in many of these European democracies, there is still a notable difference between America and other established democracies.[1]

When other forms of participation are assessed, Americans have shown little movement or improvement. Since the 1950s, participation rates for other non-voting forms have remained low. When Americans were asked if they attended party meetings, worked on a campaign or donated money to a candidate, fewer than 10% on average responded affirmatively (Conway, 2000). That number rises above 10% only when less costly forms were suggested, such as wearing a button or discussing politics with a friend. These rates, however, while low, have remained fairly constant since the 1950s.

In general terms, Americans don't vote in high numbers. Even in high-profile national races voter turnout typically involves only about 50% of all those who are eligible to vote. With regard to presidential elections in particular, we have also seen that number slowly decline since the 1950s. 50% appears to presently be our approximate vote ceiling. In addition, the number of citizens turning out to vote has been shown to drop further when races are in off- (non-presidential election) years (Ibid.). Levels of participation in other forms of activity also tend to be quite low, even though those levels have remained somewhat consistent over time. In these instances, participation rates tend to be below 10%, while that

---

[1]There remains some debate between the negative effect of voter registration laws, however. Please see Frances Fox Piven and Richard Cloward, "Government Statistics and Conflicting Explanations of Nonvoting," PS: Political Science and Politics 22 (Sept. 1989) as well as Stephen Earl Bennet's "The Uses and Abuses of Registration and Turnout Data: An analysis of Piven and Cloward's studies of non-voting in America," PS: Political Science and Politics 23 (June 1990).

percentage will increase somewhat as the form of activity declines in cost and the amount of effort required.

Who Participates and Why?

In assessing the potential impact of new technologies on participation, it is also important to know which individuals in our society choose to participate. We know that the numbers of individuals who chose to be politically active are lower than one would expect given the importance of participation in democracies, but within those who are politically active, what characteristics are found? What do those people who vote have in common?

In the abstract, it seems very easy to ascertain who is politically active. A hypothetical study would involve a person simply describing the types of people who actually do a certain activity on a fairly regular basis. For instance, you may very well measure that the people who voted in a given set of presidential elections were generally older, relatively well-dressed individuals who seemed to be fairly perceptive and articulate about matters (political and otherwise) who all arrived driving transportation that they appeared to own. While that study may be accurate, it fails to offer a satisfactory explanation as to who chooses to vote. You obviously cannot conclude that everyone who exhibits the previously observed characteristics will likely be voters. Being older doesn't necessarily *cause* you to vote. However, something about those attributes does shed some light on voting levels.

Studies that have assessed which of us are politically active, have sought to understand what it is that may actually *cause* us to be more likely to participate. These research efforts have sought to discover what characteristics are more likely to cause one to participate. The most accepted approach in explaining who participates and who does not focuses on socioeconomic characteristics (SES) (Verba & Nie, 1972).

In the example above, the people seen at the voting booth may have shared some outward similarities, however, these similarities are more accurately seen as manifestations of shared socioeconomic status. It is a person's education, occupation, and income which tend to indicate the type and frequency of participation that is attempted.

It is the socioeconomic, or SES model, that most accurately provides us with an explanation of *who* votes. Put in its most basic form, the socioeconomic explanation argues that those with more education and higher status will be more likely to frequently engage in various types of conventional participation. Of all the elements in the model, education is seen as being the most influential (Verba, Schlozman, & Henry E. Brady, 1995). Education, for instance, tends to lead to a variety of other positive developments. First, those with higher levels of education will most likely have the skills required for more prestigious and high-paying jobs. Second, there is reason to believe that those with higher levels of education may think more broadly and abstractly about politics, thereby placing a higher value on political participation. In that sense, not only does education play a key role in one's socioeconomic status, but it plays a key role in determining a number of other things in a person's life as well.

While socioeconomic status provides a helpful cue in determining *who* participates, other research has expanded upon this idea and provided more insight as to *why* these characteristics are important (Brady, Verba, & Schlozman, 1995; Verba, et al., 1995). For instance, why do more educated and wealthy people tend to vote at higher levels than others? What specific thing about these attributes makes people participate the way that they do?

Some argue that socioeconomic status works as an explanation because people of a certain SES status have the time, the money, and the skills to become politically active (Verba, et al., 1995). Also, they likely have had a desire to participate in some form and have probably been asked to participate as well. This expansion of the SES model is referred to as the Civic Volunteerism Model. In a very real sense, the Civic Volunteerism Model suggests that these traits tend to be the currency with which citizens barter for a "say so" in government. The more currency, the more likely one is to engage in having their "say."

Of course, SES characteristics do not account for all the differences among those who tend to participate. Age, race and gender also have had an impact. However, as certain legal barriers have been removed over the years, some of these explanations have lost their potency. When SES status is controlled for, participation rates between blacks and whites are very similar (Murray & Vedlitz, 1977; Verba & Nie, 1972).Other races, however, such as Hispanics, still exhibit a lag (U.S. Bureau of the Census, 1998). Gender differences are also diminishing. With the creation of the 19th Amendment in 1920, gender differences in participation rates between males and females have largely disappeared (Flanigan & Zingale, 1998).

As a final point of discussion, age does prove to be a significant factor (Conway, 2000). While the SES and Civic Volunteerism models still provide a strong explanation for who participates in America, age has proven to be an important element as well. Generally speaking, participation rates for individuals who are 18-25 are very low. That rate rises as one's age progresses (as SES status changes). Obviously, the old adage about old people voting in large numbers bears some significance. However, as citizens past the age of 65, participation rates quickly decline, largely due to health and mobility issues of those who are over that age.

The Internet . . . a Solution to the Puzzle?

Given what we know about participation, one would expect participation levels in America to increase over time, particularly with regard to voting. As registration burdens and voting impediments are removed, and education levels generally rise, one would expect an increase in citizen involvement. However, this has not been the case. Political participation in America remains somewhat of a puzzle, particularly with regard to voting. Large percentages of the voting public seem unwilling to actively participate in their own governance, even after impediments to participation *have been removed*. This is, as one political scientist has stated, the true "puzzle of participation", particularly with regard to education (Brody, 1978). Indeed, there seems to be a counter-intuitive trend, whereby increases in the sheer number of American citizens with characteristics believed to be necessary for participation are coinciding with diminishing numbers of those who choose to do exactly that. The answer to this puzzle is unclear, however, one can speculate in two directions: one positive and one negative.

The positive explanation proposes that citizens in this country tend to participate in low numbers because they are relatively satisfied with the political process. In essence, they tend to subscribe the old adage, "if it isn't broke, don't fix it." In other words, a lack of participation may be interpreted as a *non-vote of confidence*. Conversely, citizens may be refraining because it is still too costly or difficult. They may also be refraining in response to some perceived lack of efficacy, sense of alienation, or mistrust of government. Regardless of explanation, low levels of participation continue to be a concern.

A great deal of research has been done to assess the impact of new technologies on this puzzle of participation. As some have suggested, the Internet will empower citizens and cause participation levels in America to rise (Morris, 1999). Others, however, have suggested that the Internet is nothing more than a political tool

which will prove be used in ways and at levels similar to other political tools (Margolis & Resnick, 2000). The next section of this chapter will not directly address this question, but will begin to assemble
some explanation by investigating the ways in which new technology has been used to facilitate individual political participation in
America. While the jury may still be out on the true impact of the Internet on the political participation, an accurate and thorough account of its uses and potential is definitely in order.

Democratic Political Participation in America and the Internet

Prospects and Predictions in General (great change vs. more of the same)

The growth in the use of the Internet since the 1990s has caused
many to investigate the true nature of its relationship to participation. For many, the Internet is seen as a revolutionary political tool.
Dick Morris, for instance, has aggressively proposed that this new
technology will, in fact, cause a drastic change in the way people relate to their governments. The title of his book, *Vote.com,* is sugges-
tive of his position. In it, he proposes that the Internet will have a
substantially positive effect on democracy. He claims that, indeed,
"There has been a quiet but radical revolution shaking the very
foundation of our politics" (p. xvii). This revolution, he argues, will
empower the voter and put power directly back into their hands. Implicit in this argument is a shifting of power away from institutions
and special interests to a waiting public. This perspective is quite optimistic with regard to the transformative power of the Internet.

There are others, however, who are quick to draw a distinction between possibility and reality (Margolis & Resnick, 2000). The
suggestion that the Internet can be classified as a "revolutionary" element in American politics may be premature, if not simply inaccurate. In this regard, cyberspace is just another extension of the existing political arena where politics will continue to play out as it
always has. There are those who participate and those who do not.
Cyberspace will likely exhibit the same division, if not reinforce it.
The Internet may further prove that those who do not participate,
fail to do so for reasons that new technologies cannot remedy. It is
very possible that cyberspace will also be dominated by those with
the time, money and civic skills to do so. In this sense, one may simply see new technology as further reinforcing what we already know
about political participation, leaving its puzzle unsolved.

Affecting the Type and Volume of Political Participation

Initial discussion on the impact of the Internet on participation has focused on two areas: type and volume. First, what new forms of participation may new technologies create? Is it possible that they will transform or alter existing types that are seen? Second, will the Internet cause an alteration in the volume of citizens who choose to participate? Will the Internet increase the number of those who choose to involve themselves in democratic processes?

Types of Participation

The most fundamental form of political participation for a citizen is the act of casting a ballot in an election. Online voting has been seen as the most obvious and simple new form of participation on the horizon. With paper ballots falling under some scrutiny as a result of the 2000 presidential debacle, "hanging chads" and misaligned hole punches are problems some hope that new voting technology will correct. Following the 2000 election, there has been more support for more accurate voting methods. While no national general election in the United States has yet to use Internet voting, there have been electronic devices used to record votes at local polling centers. However, Internet voting *from home* seems a long way off. Forms of electronic voting are gaining more momentum, but Internet voting is far from being commonplace.

In this regard, electronic voting, has been the most successful technological development in voting thus far. This specifically refers to the use of electronic machines to register the votes placed by citizens. It does not mean that Internet voting has occurred. In fact, in terms of electronic voting, Internet voting appears to be third in a line of technological developments on the horizon (The Center for the Study of Technology and Society, 2001).

They are as follows:

- ⊛ Electronic voting at traditional polling sites (touch screens)
- ⊛ Internet voting at traditional polling sites (or at alternate manned kiosks).
- ⊛ Internet voting from any location

While electronic voting can be seen as beginning with optical/scan-style systems from decades ago, this chapter's use of the term will imply the installation of systems that use no pencil or pen to make a mark. Of the states who have used electronic voting, Georgia was the first to implement this method state-wide. In the 2002 elections, the state of Georgia went to great expense to make a state-wide effort to replace all older voting machines with electronic voting stations which used touch screens to register vote preferences, hoping that this method of registering votes eliminated vote loss or inaccuracy in vote tallies. The idea behind these systems was that new technologically advanced voting stations will insure total accuracy, even in the face of hardware failure or power outages where battery back-ups, external memory devices and CDROMs insure no loss of information.

In 2003 Georgia's Secretary of State Cathy Cox expressed some satisfaction over the electronic voting machines, implying that this system will prevent Georgia from experiencing the ballot nightmare that Florida endured in the 2000 presidential election (Cox, 2002). This project was successful, but its implementation came at a cost of $53,950,000. It was the largest state contract of its kind (Georgia Department of State, 2002).

While Georgia is the first state to implement the system state-wide, there is some evidence of wider patterns of use. In 2002 the Federal Election Commission reported that 19.6% of votes nationwide were cast on electronic devices with touch screens and 31.6% were recorded using optical scanning equipment. With regard to touch-screen equipment alone, this is an increase from rates of use measuring 3.9% in 1992 (Lubell, 2003). As time progresses, some have predicted 75% of voters will cast their ballots electronically by 2010 (Legon, 2003). Currently, however, the presence of electronic voting machines is not commonplace.

As with most forms of voting, electronic voting systems must be concerned with fraud. A recent study at Johns Hopkins University found that the electronic voting machines built by Diebold Election Systems and used in some states exhibit "significant security flaws" ("Study: E-voting Flaws", 2003). While this does not mean that nationwide vote manipulation will easily occur, it does raise questions about the caution needed in implementing these new systems. In March of 2002, a precinct in Palm Beach County, Florida that used electronic voting machines was reported to have 78 unrecorded ballots in a local city government election (Lubell, 2003) While this was likely an electronic error, rather than vote fraud, it does provide an example of why these concerns may be warranted.

Internet voting appears to be much less frequently in use. Currently, very few states have even experimented with this option. The hesitancy tends to resolve around two issues: access and security/fraud. First, Internet voting will likely only be of benefit to those who have access to computers. Attempts to facilitate Internet voting are helpful only to those who already use the Internet and have access to it. Understandably, the push to use the Internet as a device for voting is tempered with a desire for fairness of access. Second, security is a vital concern. There needs to be absolute certainly that people can freely and anonymously cast ballots and that those voters are real, eligible and who they say they are.

In response to these fears, Internet polling at the polling location has been seen as a compromise, as well as a way to test the viability of Internet voting in an environment that is much easier to control and police. However, currently, there are few states that have experimented with this method. Some of the lack of activity on this front is obviously rooted in the fact that Internet polling *at the polling facility* fundamentally robs the idea of its immediate attractiveness.

Only in exceptionally rare instances has Internet voting been used in an election. In January of 2000 the Republican Party in Alaska executed a very small presidential straw poll via the Internet. In April of that year, the Washington State Republican Party used the Internet to select delegates to one county convention, using the same method to select delegates to their party's state convention later that year (The Center for the Study of Technology and Society, 2001).

The first binding Internet election that applied for a federal office occurred in Arizona over four days in March of 2000. During this period the Arizona Democratic Party conducted its presidential primary, and indeed, the first binding Internet election in the country for a federal office. 39,942 votes were cast via the Internet with only 10% of those votes coming from Internet kiosks located at polling places (Ibid.). This is the first time a true at-home binding Internet vote has occurred.

There is significant interest in developing this technology further. Of the groups interested in developing Internet voting strategies, the Department of Defense has expressed some of the strongest support. It is their hope that voting in this fashion will greatly lighten the voting burden of U.S. military personnel overseas. Traditionally, these individuals have had to send in absentee ballots from their current location, which had to be tallied in a separate process from the votes cast domestically. To further investigate the possibility of this option being widely used in the future, the DOD Federal Voting Assistance Office conducted a voting pilot program in the 2000 election for military personnel in Florida, Utah, Texas and South Carolina (Vote Here, 2001). The successful completion of the pilot study is hoped to be the beginning of a much larger effort to facilitate voting efforts of all military personnel deployed overseas.

The viability of Internet voting has also been the subject of a great deal of research by other groups. One such study in California in 2000 by the California Department of State was not so hopeful. In that report The California Internet Voting Task Force clearly stated that the technology exists to make Internet voting at least as secure as absentee voting, but a total replacement of the vote recording systems currently in place would not be feasible at this time (California Department of State, 2000). The security and privacy problems that would exist simply do not have good solutions at this point.

A second study by the National Science Foundation was also requested by the White House under the Clinton administration. It concluded that there is tremendous work to be done in order to make at-home Internet voting a reality. Both the NSF (National Science Foundation, 2001) and California studies have concluded that at-home Internet voting is a long way off. They both suggest that polling site Internet voting via browsers be the first step since voter identification can be best secured. In sum, remote Internet voting still poses a much greater risk than any of its benefits can outweigh.

At Home vs. Home Voting: Another Perspective

In general, the technology in voting debate can be couched in terms of either voting "at home" or "away from home." In America there has always been a need to leave home to vote. Citizens traditionally have had to leave their homesteads to convene at a third location to cast votes in an election. When this was not an option, for those, for instance, who might be out of the country or traveling within it, absentee ballots were used. This, however, requires more significant levels of forethought and effort. Voting from home was simply never a realistic option on a large scale. The advent of the Internet has changed that situation somewhat.

Of course, low-tech "at-home" voting techniques have been used in the past. The most used format would likely be the absentee ballot whereby a voter pre-arranges to have their vote mailed in advance. This method of "armchair voting" has been used by the state of Oregon for some time (Southwell and Burchett, 1998). Usually used for state and local elections in Oregon, the vote-by-mail option was first applied to federal (Senate) elections in 1996. There was, however, some debate even over the appropriateness of this method. Supporters argued that it would save money, increase turnout, and simplify the process for busy voters; in essence making everyone an absentee voter and alleviating the need to trek to the polling place to cast one's vote. Critics claimed that security could not be maintained and the identity of the voter would always be in question, particularly if ballots were mis-delivered or duplicated. With mail-delivered ballots it is obviously much harder to verify to whom the ballot is delivered. At a polling location this is easier to track. In addition there is some concern over voter privacy and the influence of third parties on vote choice, such as a neighbor, spouse or family member pressuring you to vote a certain way. Vote-by-mail options compromise anonymity to a certain degree.[2] Interestingly, the same basic arguments have been made over Internet voting.

The ability to vote from home is now technically possible and definitely desirable. All along, however, the issues of voter fraud and security have been serious problems. For this reason, Internet voting seems to be at the end of very long continuum of voting options: first, the option to vote electronically; second, the option to vote via the Internet, but only in areas where there are security officials present to certify identities; and a distant third, remote Internet voting.

The overwhelming majority of researchers currently feel as if "at-home" voting on a large scale is simply too risky. In fact, Internet voting can actually be exclusionary if other forms of "at-home" voting such as mail-in ballots are not explored as vigorously.[3] It would be undesirable for at home online voting to become an immediate reality, since it would tend to ease the costs of voting for those who

---

[2]Survey results, however, indicate that some of these concerns were unfounded (Southwell, Patricia L. and Justin Burchett, *Armchair Voting: The Vote-by-Mail Experiment in the State of Oregon,* p.175-183 in *Engaging the Public,* Thomas J. Johnson, Carol E. Hays and Scott P. Hays, eds., Rowan & Littlefield Publishers, Inc., Lanham, MD, 1998). Evidence of undue influence or pressure was nonexistent. In addition, vote-by-mail voters tended to resemble the traditional voter in terms of information levels. Overall, the Oregon experiment seemed quite successful.

[3]Please see *The E-democracy E-Book: Democracy is Online 2.0* for a lengthy discussion on this matter http://www.publicus.net/ebook/edemebook.html.

are already overrepresented: those of higher SES status. As some have quipped, Internet voting may eventually become an updated Motor Voter push . . . for luxury car drivers only (Alvarez & Nagler, 2000). To avoid the exclusionary impact of an intense national Internet voting push, other forms of at-home voting must also be tested, safe, and available.

Arguments for and against Internet Voting

For individual citizens, it has been argued so far that new technologies will have their most obvious attractiveness in voting. This idea appears to have the simplest and most direct appeal for those who participate. The advantages to this idea are very attractive. First, Internet voting greatly eases the burden of casting a ballot. One could conceivably vote in one's pajamas. This is of particular value to the elderly, or those who are disabled. Second, the reduction in transaction costs may increase the likelihood that more would vote. Internet voting could be seen as a method for mobilizing larger numbers of citizens to participate in elections and hopefully strengthen the democratic process. Third, the transaction costs for states would be reduced as the number of polling centers, voting machines and poll workers diminished. This would be a welcome relief to state budgets which are perpetually tight. Fourth, electronic voting methods will introduce a new level of accuracy in vote tabulation. The risk of misinterpreting one's mark on the ballot is greatly decreased when the method of casting a vote is done electronically. The box is marked yes or no; there are no dimpled chads. Also, there is no need for a recount or to wait for a manual tally. Results are immediate and accurate. Finally, the security risks that do exist can be solved through research and investment. This is simply a logistical matter. Large segments of corporate America trust the Internet to aid in conducting their business transactions. Undergraduate students who plan on going to graduate school now take entrance exams electronically and receive their results instantaneously. There is no reason that the same levels of success and security could not be found elsewhere in the public sphere.

However, convenience may not be the best rationale on which to alter a core element to a country's democratic existence. First, to lighten the burden of simply casting a vote may further encourage thoughtless participation. It is somewhat unsettling to possibly vote for the president through the same basic procedure that one may order a pizza. Disabled or truly inconvenienced voters can easily request an absentee ballot or arrange for transportation and voting assistance. After all, we are talking about something that occurs on a fairly rare basis, albeit a regular one. Second, if voter registration efforts like the Motor Voter Bill (as it is popularly called), and the lengthening of polling hours, etc. fail to increase turnout, why would Internet voting succeed?[4] There is actually a risk of weakening the democratic process if voters are driven by convenience rather than a concern for themselves and their government. Third, the burden that would be lifted from the states in the long run would require substantial investment up front to develop and maintain the software needed to execute the election. The saving may be outweighed by maintenance issues and security needs. In essence, states may be jumping out of one budgetary frying pan and into another. Fourth, advantages in accuracy would likely be offset by problems with hackers and/or data or system failure. Even with back-up systems in place, if any votes are lost, they are forever vanished. There would be no easy way to verify for whom someone voted, unless paper records were also kept (which defeats the purpose). The Internet may simply not be a safe environment to conduct the affairs of state. Fifth, not everyone has a computer or feels at ease using one. Online voting is unfair to those without computers. Finally, Internet voting weakens the privacy and the anonymity of the process. At the voting booth, workers are there to insure the voter has an unencumbered and private space in which to cast a vote. This environment cannot be secured in a private living space, where spouses, friends, or family members may attempt to influence one's vote as it is being cast.

The Internet and Information Gathering

In addition to an increase in the variety of ways in which votes may be cast, the Internet has also increased the ease with which a citizen

---

[4]There is research that suggests that Internet use is generally not predictive of voting or other forms of political participation, for that matter. Please see: Bimber, Bruce. 2001. Information and Political Engagement in America: The Search for Effects of Information Technology at the Individual Level; *Political Research Quarterly*, 54:1, March 2001, for an extended discussion of this topic. Conversely, other research suggests that Internet use does increase the chance of one casting a vote. For more information on this please see Tolbert, Caroline, and Ramona McNeal, *Does the Internet Increase Voter Participation in Elections?* A paper presented at the 2001 annual meeting of the American Political Science Association.

can access government information. It has also made it easier to contact elected officials by multiplying the options by which one can engage and express opinions to public officials.

In this regard, perhaps keeping up with public affairs and being knowledgeable about politics is a participatory element that precedes even the fundamental task of voting. Citizens obviously (or hopefully) should know what they are voting about! Here, the increasing ease with which information about government is acquired has quite simply been astounding. Prior to the growth of the Internet, citizens had to invest much more time in acquiring information about their government. If a citizen wanted to know much more than what the evening news offered, he/she had to seek other sources which were usually acquired at some cost. Something as simple as buying a newspaper would require extra expenditures of income. Something as simple as going to the library to access more information also came at the expense of other important things in one's daily life (assuming that person's job was not that of a librarian or college professor). In a very real sense, there is a cost associated with political participation, whether it is time or money. Depending on the activity one or both have to be expended in order to become politically active.

The Internet allows the access of almost any information a citizen would require without substantial cost and without substantial effort.[5] Imagine the following example: If a person in 1990 wanted to access a transcript of a president's recent speech, find recent executive orders issued, or find list of recent appointments made to certain executive branch agencies or departments, this information hunt would likely have to be delayed until they were published in hardcopy by the Government Printing Office and then sought out in a university or public library who chose to carry them; obviously a daunting task for someone with a busy life and demands on his or her time. Even a more common task, such as learning about the issues and candidates in the 1992 presidential race would, at the time, be quite costly if you desired more information than the mainstream media outlets chose to offer.

Those same quests currently can be satisfied within minutes once one has access to the Internet. Information on recent presidential speeches, executive orders, or appointments, for instance, can be quickly found on The White House website (http://www.white-

---

[5]There is obviously a cost to owning a computer with Internet access. This issue will be discussed in the next section.

house.gov). There you can access information on activity in the White House in two languages, and in a condensed, well-organized, manner that would otherwise be nearly impossible for the average citizen to compile in any reasonable amount of time. In addition, The White House website currently offers a new feature entitled "Ask the White House." This feature takes advantage of the interactive potential of the Internet to provide citizens a chance to ask the featured White House or executive official questions regarding important issues. Questions are e-mailed an hour before the online discussion begins and responses are almost immediate. One excerpt from Chief of Staff Andrew Card on the segment's inaugural "broadcast" follows:

Secretary Card:

Good evening, I'm Andy Card—Chief of Staff to President George W. Bush. I welcome you to the inaugural "Ask the White House" online discussion. I am pleased to be here tonight to answer your questions. The Internet is an important communications medium. We have witnessed, especially during Operation Iraqi Freedom, a substantial increase in the amount of traffic to Internet sites as more and more people—worldwide—are relying on the Internet for information.

We see the "Ask the White House" series as another way for our citizens to interact with the White House. I look forward to hearing your thoughts and answering your questions during tonight's online discussion.

With that, I'm happy to begin . . .

Russ, from **Cookeville TN** writes:

Please step us through how you learned about the second plane hitting the World Trade Center on 911, your informing the President of this, and the seconds and minutes immediately following. Thanks.

Secretary Card:

I was with the President in Sarasota, FL on 9/11. Just as The President was entering a room with elementary students, we were informed about a single plane hitting one of the World Trade Center Towers. The President and I thought it was a horrible accident—a pilot heart attack or something. Once the President was in the room with the students, I received a call from the Situation Room that another plane had hit the second tower. I gathered my thoughts, deciding that the President

should know, and succinctly—two facts one editorial comment. I walked into the room, trying not to be disruptive to the young students and whispered in the President's right ear, "A second plane hit the second tower. America is under attack!" I then stepped back so as not to invite a discussion. The President waited for an appropriate moment to excuse himself from the room. We then gathered in an adjoining room to learn more about the situation. It was an unbelievable day.
    (http://www.whitehouse.gov/ask/20030416.html)

Contact of this type and with this amount of ease and immediacy has practically been impossible before. Information on the Senate and House of Representative sites carry similar features whereby citizens can find out what is currently being discussed in committee. They can simultaneously discover the partisan make-up and membership of each committee as well. The House of Representatives and Senate both maintain detailed websites for these purposes at http://www.house.gov and http://www.senate.gov, respectively. Additional information on party platforms and party events is also readily available online. A full text version of the Republican Party's current platform, for instance, can be found at http://www.rnc.org/.

In fact, as mentioned in previous chapters, there are large well-run websites for most federal institutions. These sites allow citizens to gather information on almost all government non-classified activity. The Environmental Protection Agency website, for instance, is an effective resource for investigating government attempts to secure clean air and water in your area. The Food and Drug Administration site provides a quick reference guide for new food recalls or new drug or medical procedure approvals. This information is easily accessible and provided at no cost.

New technologies have also provided new ways to contact elected officials. Congresspersons' websites almost always have links so that you can e-mail your representative with praise or criticism regarding any topic on your mind. These sites also provide more traditional contact information so that phone calls and letters can be sent if so desired.

New technologies have, at this point, been shown to profoundly increase the ease with which a citizen in a democratic society can involve him/herself. It also greatly adds to the variety of options one has in pursuing traditional avenues of participation. The real question remains, however: Will new technologies cause an increase in the *number* of people participating? Given the potential ease with which one may soon participate, will that cause more people to become involved?

Volume of Participation

It is arguable that the impact of the Internet not only affects the *type* of participation seen but also the *volume*. As previously mentioned, new technologies increase the convenience of being politically active. The Internet has the potential to make it much easier to participate in politics, whether you are voting or trying to find friends with whom to start a new political party. The reduction of these transaction costs can cause an increase in the number of those who participate. However, there are those who argue that new communication technology will further solidify the patterns of behavior that are already seen. This has been a defining element in the study of technology and democracy. Will the Internet increase "the pool of those who participate in politics," or will it, "reinforce the existing participation gap between the engaged and the apathetic?" (Norris, 1999, p.71).

This debate has been defined by two distinguishable sides: mobilization theorists and reinforcement theorists. Mobilization theorists argue that the Internet will be a great asset to democratic deliberation. They propose that this technological development will reduce barriers to civic engagement, and increase access to information, particularly among resource-poor groups (Greenberg, 1999). This new medium will empower citizens in new ways and strengthen social connectedness. It may even facilitate the growth and proliferation of direct democracy. Generally seen as a positive development for mobilization theorists, the Internet is argued to be somewhat of a catalyst whose presence has the potential to change the political environment significantly.[6]

---

[6]For a survey of research supporting the mobilization position please see: Budge. *The New Challenge of Direct Democracy,* Oxford: Polity Press 1996; Grossman. *The Electronic Commonwealth,* New York: Penguin, 1995; Rheingold. *The Virtual Community: Homesteading on the Electronic Frontier.* Reading, MA: Addison-Wesley, 1993; Schwartz. *Netactivism: How Citizens Use the Internet.* Sebastapol, CA: Songline Studios, 1996; Dertouzos. *What Will Be: How the Information Marketplace Will Change Our Lives.* San Francisco: Harper, 1997; Negroponte. *Being Digital.* New York: Knopf, 1995.

Reinforcement theorists suggest that existing patterns of political behavior will remain intact, even with the presence of the Internet. The Internet *may* even widen the participation gap between those who are resource-rich and those who are resource-poor.[7] Access issues may, in fact, be a serious impediment to the Internet's transformative potential. The Internet is simply a tool, whose use will be dominated by those same people who have the time, money and civic skills to do so. In this sense, the Internet will reinforce what we already know about political participation in America.[8]

Affecting Who Participates

The debate regarding new technologies and participation so far has proceeded from one basic assumption, and that is that the Internet's impact on participation is important because everyone is using it! However, the debate thus far has to be qualified by a discussion of who has access to the Internet and what those people do when they use the Internet. Everyone does not have equal access to cyberspace, and it is false to assume that they do. It is also false to assume that everyone uses the Internet for political reasons.

Those who participate in politics in America tend to be older, better educated, and wealthier than the average citizen. If, for instance, Internet access is found to be most prevalent among this group, there will be a need to revise some of our grander hopes for this medium. Conversely, we know that poorer, less educated individuals tend not to participate in politics. For the Internet to live up to its potential, we should see robust patterns of use among this group. Therefore, before any thoughtful speculation can occur, with regard to the impact of the Internet, it is necessary to understand who uses it, and for what they use it.

To begin with, not everyone has access to the latest digital communication technology. This issue of Internet access is referred

---

[7]For a more thorough discussion of this topic, please refer to the following section on the Digital Divide.

[8]For a survey of research supporting the reinforcement position please see: Davis and Owen. 1998. *New Media and American Politics;* New York: Oxford UP p. 185; Murdock and Golding. 1989. Information Poverty and Political Inequality: Citizenship in the Age of Privatized Communications, *Journal of Communication;* 39:180-193; Hill and Hughes. 1998. *Cyberpolitics: Citizen Activism in the Age of the Internet.* Lanham, MD: Rowan & Littlefield; Davis, Richard. 1999. *The Web of Politics: The Internet's Impact on the American Political System.* New York: Oxford UP.

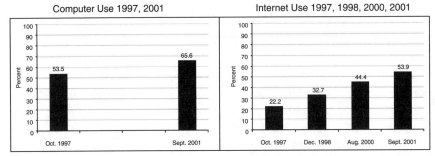

Figure 1 Computer and Internet Use from Any Location, Percent of Persons Age 3+

Source: NTIA and ESA, U.S. Department of Commerce, using U.S. Census Bureau Current Population Survey Supplements

to as the digital divide.[9] The digital divide is generally referred to as the gap in access between those who are "wired-in" and those who are not; between those who are computer literate and those who are not. However, its use is somewhat changing and more often refers to the spectrum of technological access and information disparity between groups in society. If the Internet and new technological developments are to be discussed as democratic, there must be universal accessibility by all qualified citizens. With regard to the political impact of the Internet, the issue of access is a critical one. If the net is to be a tool of democracy, there needs to be serious attempts to make this tool available to those who have yet been able to gain access.

Most research on Internet usage has been somewhat consistent. There are distinct trends with regard to Internet use in America. To begin with, the number of Americans who use the Internet has grown substantially. Current federal figures show that Internet usage grows by 2 million new users a month (National Telecommunications and Information Administration [NTIA], 2002). Presently, more than 50% of the nation is online. That includes general increases in numbers for all races, incomes, ages, education levels, and genders. As can be seen in Figure 1, overall computer and Internet usage in America has been continually growing in recent years (Ibid.).

---

[9]While this discussion focuses on the digital divide in America, there is substantial concern about its effect worldwide, specifically between countries who are more or less industrially developed. Pippa Norris's *Digital Divide: Civic Engagement, Information Poverty, and the Internet Worldwide;* Cambridge UP, Cambridge, UK, 2001.

Internet use figures in 2002 have been reported to be as high as 71.1% (The UCLA Internet Report [UCLA], 2003). Not only have these percentages continued to grow over time, but the amount of time spent online has continued to increase (Ibid.). The 71.1% who reported Internet usage in 2002 also reported using it 11.1 hours/week (Ibid.). This is compared to reported levels 9.4 hours/week in 2000. Data in 2002 also suggests that more people have Internet access at home. This number is currently at 59.3%, as compared to 46.9% who had home access in 2000 (Ibid.).

Research also shows important trends as it applies to age and Internet use. Recall that with regard to voting, the likelihood of one casting a vote increased with age. Applied to Internet usage, age currently displays a reversed trend. The older one is, the less likely he/she is to use the Internet (and possibly new technologies in general). As Figure 2 shows, usage is highest among those 12-35.

Usage rates generally decline as age increases. However, even for 65+ in age, the figures were approximately 30% (Ibid.). Age, therefore, is a strong indicator of Internet usage.[10] This trend will likely be temporary. As high usage groups advance in age there will likely be a leveling off of this decline with age. When gender is taken into account, very few differences emerge. Recent studies show that there is very little difference between men and women when it comes to Internet usage (NTIA, 2002; UCLA, 2003). There is a difference when race is controlled for; however, this is generally explained as a disparity in resources. More on this will be discussed in the proceeding sections.

Of those that do use the Internet, what do they do when they use it? This is an important question because if new technologies are to have an impact on political participation, there should be some visible sign of them being used for just that. However, there is some evidence that cyberspace is only occasionally used for political purposes. While there has been a growth in the number of those who turn to the Internet for political news (Pew Research Center: Institute for Politics, Democracy and the Internet, 2003), most users report news gathering to be quite low on their priority list. Figure 3 shows the ranking of online activity.

---

[10]NTIA data from 2002 indicates slightly lower levels in usage by age, however, the trends and general inferences are the same. The full report can be found at http://www.ntia.doc.gov/ntiahome/dn/nationonline_020502.htm.

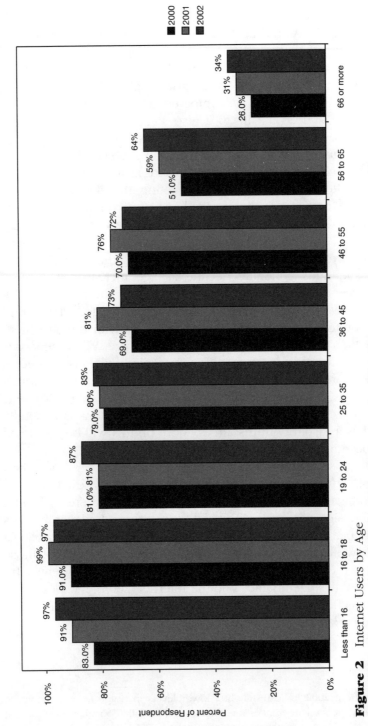

Figure 2 Internet Users by Age

Source: The UCLA Internet Report—"Surveying the Digital Future" (Year Three)
UCLA Center for Communication Policy
January 2003

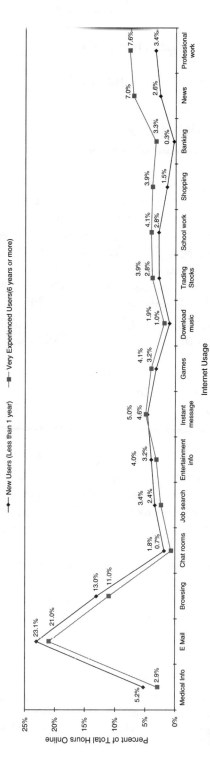

Figure 3 Internet Usage by Activity

Source: The UCLA Internet Report—"Surveying the Digital Future" (Year Three) UCLA Center for Communication Policy January 2003

Online Activity as a Percentage of Users

- e-mail and instant messaging: 87.9%
- web browsing: 76.0%
- reading news: 51.9%
- entertainment information: 46.4%
- shopping and buying online: 44.5%

Of the users reporting these activities, an overwhelming majority thought the net helped them understand politics better, but they did not feel strongly that the net would give them more say about what the government does. There is no clear consensus as to whether or not the Internet gives "people like me" more political power, though the data shows some significant skepticism as to that fact (UCLA, 2003). There is also significant skepticism as to the likelihood of the Internet being an effective tool in influencing the decisions made by government. These findings suggest that the Internet is not generally seen as being a radical new political tool in the life of the average citizen.

In terms of equal access, there remain some significant disparities between those who are on and those who are off line. Those who are online tend to be more affluent and have higher education levels than those who are off line. Of these two variables, education has been suggested to be the most important factor in predicting Internet use (The Stanford Institute for the Quantitative Study of Society [SIQSS], 2000). Encouragingly enough, usage is up over all income categories, and is growing faster among those in lower income brackets (NTIA, 2002). Put more simply, there is an SES issue with regard to Internet use. Cyberspace appears to be more the domain of the wealthier and better educated, and currently, to some degree, the young. There is though, a growing equilibrium in the Internet population. The digital divide appears to be shrinking.[11]

There does appear to be a diminishing chasm in the digital divide. The Clinton-Gore administration in February of 2000 issued a statement stressing the importance of eliminating this digital divide in the interest of American society in general (The White House,

---

[11]It is interesting to note that some research suggests 1 in 5 Americans have no plans to go online. There appears to be an "Internet resistant strain" within the American population. This data is based on a recent Pew Internet and American Life Project and quoted on CNN.com (http://www.cnn.com/2003/TECH/Internet/04/17/offline. americans.reut/).

2000). Vice President Al Gore, in particular, has been a strong proponent of Internet use in schools. It was the hope of that administration that access to computers in the future would be as universal as telephone access is today (Ibid.). This effort was supported by 2 billion dollars in tax incentive proposals to encourage private sector computer donations as well as 380 million dollars in federal funding (Ibid.).

In fact, the Internet population had begun to reflect America's population as early as 1998. Web users are simply looking more like America, rather than being the predominantly white, male contingent seen in the early to middle 1990s (Birdsell, Muzzio, Krane, & Cottreau, 1998). There are, however, differences with regard to where people have access and the ease and speed at which they can do that. This remains an area of concern ("Internet Access Gap Closing," 2002).

There is no doubt, though, that the Internet population is becoming more and more typical of the general population. This has prompted the obvious question as to whether or not the divide is on its way to being closed. While the jury on this issue is officially still out, the Bush administration in 2002 expressed relief in the divide's apparent closing. Evidence of their confidence was seen in 100 million dollars in proposed cuts to two programs charged with bridging the divide: The Technology Opportunities Program within the Department of Commerce and the Community Technology Centers Program within the Department of Education (Oder, 2002).

It is entirely possible that an assessment of the digital divide may very well be seen through partisan lenses. Democrats may see a divide where republicans do not! In fact, this partisan assessment of the digital divide is interestingly seen in the titles of the two major reports on the matter, one by the Clinton and the other by the Bush Administrations entitled, *Falling Through the Net: Toward Digital Inclusion* and *A Nation Online: How Americans are Expanding Their Use of the Internet,* respectively.

The Bush administration's report does, however, show some encouraging figures on the growth of Internet usage. Thus, the title may very well be warranted.

Summary

Given what is known about political participation in America and the trends that we see within Internet usage in America, there is a need to moderate the enthusiasm one may feel toward the Internet revolution. The evidence suggests that there is still an equilibrium being established between traditional political endeavors and new options being introduced through new technological developments. There appears to be a substantial potential for new development and considerable impact, but that effect has yet to be seen. Internet usage is certainly becoming more commonplace among all ages and races, but their application of this new tool may not be what many political scientists have hoped for.

There are some things that can be said to support the claims of the mobilization theorists. First, the Internet is drawing closer to becoming a true mass medium. This is an absolute prerequisite to the Internet having the political impact its potential allows. Second, the digital divide does appear to be shrinking. This is an important step to the Internet being more than a tool of the elites in American society. More have access to the Internet, and more are using it from home.

However, there are still some serious impediments to overcome. Reinforcement theorists are not wrong in their skepticism. First, there are still a large number who don't take advantage of new technology in our society. One in five say that they have no plans to go online any time soon. Second, the digital divide is not closing for the extremely poor. They will not likely even gain access at work since most work-related computer/Internet usage involves jobs that the poor in our society do not have and cannot get. Third, the Internet is not being used for political purposes 100% of the time. Its most frequent use is for e-mail and instant messaging for personal communication.

One thing that the Internet has done for the individual citizen is greatly ease the difficulty with which one can access political information about government activities. Will easing the access to information about our political system or its elected officials increase participation? That answer is unclear. One qualification can be stated, however. The Internet solves problems of time and convenience, but it does not address the issues of cynicism, alienation, or mistrust.

New technologies decrease impediments to participation and decrease transaction costs. However, technology does not necessarily alleviate the cynicism one feels. The Internet does not necessarily instill a desire to participate as a mere result of its presence. The Internet does, however, carry with it more political potential than any other recent technological development.

So far, this chapter has been largely concerned with the impact that new technologies will have on participation as it applies to individual citizens. In essence, how will the Internet change the way we as single citizens try to impact the operation of our political system? This chapter has purposefully excluded the attempts of groups to participate in the political process. The next chapter will address this issue. Chapter 7 will discuss interest groups and political movements and assess how these groups have used new technology in their effort to influence public policy in America.

Political Parties, Interest Groups, and Social Movements

7

Introduction

Outline and Plan of Chapter

The previous chapter discussed efforts of individual citizens to impact the political process. In that chapter, there was a lengthy discussion about what we know about individual political participation in America and how new technologies may affect what we know. It was generally assumed that as cyberspace becomes more normalized, that is, as its population begins to reflect more accurately the population of the United States, traditional trends in participation will likely develop there too. That is, of course, an opinion based on what we know about Internet usage so far.

This chapter will take a similar approach, although its focus is different. Rather than continue to focus on individual patterns of participation, the discussion will now emphasize group activity in America. Our level of analysis will shift from the individual citizen, to the group, specifically, interest groups, political parties and social/political movements.

Interest groups, political parties and certain social movements are all involved in some sort of political activity at any given point in time. These are groups, not individuals, and are potentially more worrisome because they typically have the resources and numbers to make their voice heard above the voice of the individual citizen. In gaining the ear of the government, the clarity and force with which these voices exist is an issue. This concern is rooted in the basic fact that different groups in society generally have their own interests in mind, and not the interests of the whole. This idea simply echoes the sentiments of James Madison in *Federalist Paper #10,* in which he addresses the concern over competing special interest groups, or as he calls them, *factions,* in a democratic republic. These groups are definitely nothing new, but their role needs to be reassessed in the light of new technological developments.

In general, new computer-mediated technology should affect group activism in America significantly. First, electronic mail will allow for an ease of communication between group members that has not existed in the past. Second, new communication technology will allow for discussion groups and information flows that are more dynamic than in the past. Communication has the potential to evolve from a top-down flow to a bottom-up or side-to-side process, thereby encouraging interaction for all members of a political group rather than simply messages from leader to follower. Third, the Internet allows for easy dissemination of information that can be of benefit for all members via a group's websites 24 hours a day (Diani, 2001). These things should enable an increase in speed and a reduction of transaction costs for groups across the board. It also allows for total accuracy in information delivery as well as an opportunity to bolster group identity and enhance mobilization efforts (Ibid.).

Madison on Faction

The study of these groups is important because their existence is not necessarily a worthwhile development. Chief architect of the Constitution, James Madison, was quick to point this out. In *Federalist Paper #10* he clearly states that certain groups in a free society may organize into what he refers to as a "faction". Madison defines faction as "a number of citizens, whether amounting to a majority or minority of the whole, who are united and actuated by some common impulse of passion, or of interest, adverse to the rights of other citizens, or to the permanent and aggregate interests of the community." Put more simply, a faction is a group whose political designs further their own agenda, rather than that of the country. For instance, an interest group composed of big pharmaceutical companies would fight any legislation that would put a cap on drug prices. It is in their interest to maximize their profit and sell their goods at the highest price the market will bear. However, with health care costs rising to extraordinary levels, poorer and uninsured citizens around the country would very much benefit from a cap on what they would have to pay for very expensive drugs. The interest of the single group in question is fundamentally at odds with the best interests of the community.

Madison states that this is a serious problem for democratic societies. If, as he claims, liberty is to faction as air is to fire, there is little that can be done to eliminate the causes of faction. In a free society factions are natural and expected.[1] The solution for this dilemma, according to Madison, lies in two areas: the fact that we have a democratic republic, and the fact that our republic is so large.

First, he argues that in a republic, or put differently, a system of government where there is a scheme of representation, there will be a body of elected officials who are able to moderate and interpret the long term needs of the country and neutralize the rash impulses of politically zealous groups. Second, since we have such an extended territory with so many citizens, there will more likely be a variety of interests and parties so that it would be more difficult for a majority faction to assemble under one idea. If by a chance it does, Madison argues, "it will be more difficult for all who feel it to discover their own strength, and to act in unison with each other (paragraph 20)."

It is this second check on the effects of faction that is of direct concern in this chapter.[2] New advances in communication technology have greatly limited the importance of geographical distance for those needing to contact one another. For interest groups, political parties, and social movements, this is of particular importance since one half (if not the whole) of Madison's argument may be weakened by the development of e-mail, the Internet, and cellular phone technology, among other advancements in communication. The Internet, for instance, may provide a level and ease of communication that will greatly advantage politically active groups in America, particularly those who are resource poor. Technological developments may force us to reevaluate some of Madison's claims.

---

[1]Admittedly, this same freedom also allows for the creation of other groups that can be very concerned about the whole. Public interest groups such as Common Cause and environmental groups such as the Sierra Club are fed by the same liberty, but act on behalf of the interests of others. They, obviously would not be as problematic, though their interests are certainly not shared by the whole of society. In that sense, they still fit Madison's description.

[2]For an in depth discussion of what problems new technology may cause Madison's first remedy, please see the discussion of direct versus indirect democracy earlier in this text.

The remainder of this chapter will assess each of the three political groups in turn. Each of the subsequent three sections will assess what we know about these groups, what potential implications may exist for these groups, and what ways they have embraced new technology in furthering their cause. The chapter will conclude with a brief discussion of these implications as they relate to the potential strengthening or weakening of group political activity in America in general.

Political Parties

What Do We Know about Political Parties?

It is difficult to think of modern democracies without political parties.[3] They provide sponsorship for candidates who in turn run for political office under that organization's name. It is during these elections that citizens most directly determine who will literally be their government. In sponsoring candidates, parties assist the voter in a number of ways. First, parties help to structure vote choice. They winnow down the list of hopefuls within their party to the strongest candidate and present that person to the voters during the election. Second, they also help the voter make sense of the political environment by providing an easier way to evaluate candidates and assess the political problems of the day. They propose comprehensive plans for what the government should be doing, and hopefully will do, when their candidate gets into office. Once in office, a party's candidates use party identification as a means for doing business, such as drafting laws and voting. Parties manage government, stimulate debate, and encourage participation. All of these things inextricably tie parties to the political process and bind people to government.

As political organizations, parties have struggled. Their ability to fulfill their basic functions have been somewhat undermined by other forces. As organizers of campaigns, their role has been weakened by private campaign management firms. Their ability to act as conduits for candidate to voter exchanges has been replaced by new media. Their ability to determine the candidate for their party's nomination has been weakened by the introduc-

---

[3]For a more erudite assessment of this claim, please see EE Schattschneider's *Party Government,* New York: Rinehart, p. 1; 1942.

tion of primary systems. As a result, party discipline is often weak and unpredictable.

Perhaps more significantly, American citizens have also become less inclined to strongly identify with political parties. That psychological attachment, known as party identification, has been weakening in past decades. More American citizens than ever before have been identifying themselves as independents rather than committed members of a well established party. All of these things, while not necessarily a phenomenon exclusive to the United States, cause us to give pause when we discuss political parties in this country. Parties in a democracy are of vital importance, but they are facing serious problems that may impact the functioning of our political system. The question is, what role will new technologies play with regard to this scenario? Will they serve to further weaken parties or will they supply new resources to parties who can use them for strengthening their position in the political system? Perhaps they will have no impact at all. To this topic we now turn our attention.

Affecting the Strength of Political Parties

There are those that argue that the Internet will further weaken parties. Specifically, the Internet may further weaken party discipline. Elected officials have often been satirized as caring too much for what the voters back home think of them. The Internet has the potential of diminishing the distance between voter and representative. What happens when a representative's stance in Congress contradicts the will of one's constituents? What happens when voters can instantly access a representative's voting record and recent speeches? The willingness of a representative to fall in line with the party leadership may diminish even further if the Internet allows for an even more rapid account of a representative's activity in Washington. The same can be said of the opposite instance when the Internet might allow a Congressman an immediate opportunity to cheaply assess constituent opinion on a frequent basis. In essence, the Internet has the potential of "cutting out the middle man" (i.e. the party), by bringing the voter and the person voted for in closer, albeit virtual, proximity to one another.

This idea is based on the concept that the elected official is indeed a delegate, in the strictest sense of the word. They are there to strictly convey the wishes of their constituents and thereby fulfill their duty within the republic. If the Internet is used as an immediate method of issue preference delivery from voters, party discipline may very well take a back seat to immediate constituent needs back home, largely due to the elected official's desire to endear themselves to the voter for the next election (Morris, 1999). This idea is merely an amplification of what telephone polling has already done for the decision making process in Washington. Put more simply, the Internet may be a more useful linkage between government and citizen than the party.

It is argued that this same arrangement reduces the reliance on campaign donations from special interest groups (Ibid.). The Internet has the potential to reinvigorate the relationship between voter and government by easing the exchange of information between them and emphasizing the need of the elected official to respond to voter interests rather than those necessarily of the party or of special interests.

Parties may also be weakened by the fact that the Internet provides candidates with a mass medium that is completely under their control. The need of the candidate to rely on the party for assistance in disseminating candidate information on issues is further diminished. This medium is relatively cost free in comparison to television or radio, and is free of third party interference. Due to this, the party's role in campaigns may further deteriorate. A more thorough discussion of this topic in particular can be seen in Chapter 8.

This, of course, is a set of ideas that assume political parties will necessarily suffer from the development of new communication technologies and fail to use them on their own for their own benefit. Candidates are not the only ones who stand to gain. Parties are not likely to quietly stand for an erosion of their power and influence. While new communication technologies have the possibility of further eroding the ties between party and candidate, there is an equal opportunity for parties to seize this opportunity and reestablish their role as a democratic linkage between government and citizen.

There is the possibility of parties seizing the Internet as a medium through which they can reinvigorate their role. The interactive nature of the Internet allows for an ease of communication in not only a quantitative way, but a qualitative way as well. Cyberspace provides parties with an environment where information transference is relatively cheap, fluid, and easily controllable. It allows them a chance to regain control of their message and mobilize (and recruit) members in a way that the radio, phone and television have not allowed. The question remains: How have parties taken advantage of this development and how has it served to strengthen their role as political linkages between citizen and government?

The Use of the Internet by Political Parties

Historically speaking, political parties have made use of new technologies. They have adapted their operational strategies to accommodate the use of the telephone, television, and new digital forms of communication as well. To a certain degree, the environment in which parties exist will determine how they will conduct their business. This is true for any entity which strives to maintain its existence. If the water is now only found on top of the mountain, it well suits one to ascend the incline. Parties are not necessarily victims of change, but are participants in it. In this regard, political parties have adapted their activity to incorporate new methods of communicating with their supporters in hopes of strengthening their position.

The Internet is unique in its ability to give control over data delivery. School children (and perhaps university students) have the same control when they pass notes to one another in class. They can exactly dictate the text and pinpoint its audience. Parties now have the same ability in a way that is far more effective. Parties may now have complete control over the issues and positions that are dear to them without fear of manipulation or distortion by third party media outlets (Nixon & Johansson, 1999). To invoke the previous comparison, parties may now pass notes to millions of people with as many bells and whistles as their web servers will allow without the fear of a third party commandeering the message and intentionally or unintentionally changing it as when they rely on mainstream media outlets for delivery (Ibid.). The Internet simply improves the ability of parties to contact voters directly and more cheaply. As two political scientists have put it, the Internet allows for a 24 hour a day "party" store for the latest information (Ibid.).

Recent research has assessed parties' use of the Internet around the world and found that political parties have been somewhat successful in using cyberspace for their advantage. In this regard, an analysis of party websites can be driven by two ideas: information transparency and communication interactivity (Norris, 2001a). This dichotomy will more easily help us understand how parties are functioning online. Information transparency is defined as the quality of having thorough information about the party's history, platform, organization, etc. Most parties have exhibited fairly high levels of this type of information on their websites (Ibid.). Communication interactivity is defined as "web-enabled donating, volunteering, e-mailing party officials, joining discussion groups, etc." Worldwide, research finds these qualities less prevalent than the ones previously described (Ibid.).

A cursory examination of the websites maintained by America's most active political parties finds both elements fairly well developed. These sites are listed below:

> http://www.rnc.org (The Republican Party)
> http://www.democrats.org (The Democratic Party)
> http://www.lp.org (The Libertarian Party)
> http://www.reformparty.org (The Reform Party)

All of these sites give the basic information that one would expect, such as platforms, party constitutions, etc. It is interesting to note differences in the more interactive elements, however. Democratic, Libertarian and Republican sites currently maintain modest links to secure pages that accept immediate credit card donations. The Reform Party website currently solicits donations only by check. All sites offer chances to be added to e-mail lists for regular party information, but they do somewhat vary on the degree to which they offer contact information. The interactive element to all four of these sites seems adequate for the average citizen, and should be generally satisfying for the activist. In many of these instances not only is national party contact information given, but state party contacts are also available through easy-to-navigate menus.

However, these websites offer information in a way that has been described as being "top-down". They are not necessarily designed to solicit grassroots, "bottom-up" participation and feedback (Norris, 2001b). There are no overt features, for instance, asking what you think of the site or how the party could change to best meet your interests as a citizen. They are mainly electronic pamphlets designed primarily for information delivery rather than interactive forums whereby party affairs are discussed.

The degree to which American parties are online is, however, somewhat impressive. Major and minor parties have appeared to adapt to the use of the Internet quite well. In a recent study, America had 67 digital parties (Ibid.). This is particularly noteworthy since America is a two-party system, where third parties are at a serious electoral disadvantage.[4] Parties in America have gravitated to

---

[4]In this chapter we refer to third parties in such a way as to mean all parties who are not the Democrats or Republicans. Since America has a two-party system, it is common to refer to all other parties as "third." This term is not unlike the use of the term "third world" during the Cold War to refer to all other nations that do not fall into the first (democratic/non-communist) and second world (non-democratic/communist) countries.

the Internet to disseminate their message and to mobilize support. All of these 67 party sites, however, fail to show the presence and sophistication that the Republican and Democratic sites do. This is likely the result of the financial and organizational prowess larger parties in the U.S enjoy over other smaller parties.

Use of the Internet by Third Parties

One of the overriding advantages to recent communication-driven technological developments has been the ease of mobilization afforded those who have been politically disadvantaged. The Internet allows small parties the luxury of quick and effective information dissemination as well as more cost-effective opportunities to mobilize potential support. These opportunities may impact the strength of third parties in America by lessening the disadvantages small parties face from America's single member plurality electoral system.

Originally, when the Internet was in its infancy, third parties generally had a more pronounced presence on the web. Particularly through the Usenet newsgroups and list-serv mailing lists, they were very quick to seize its cost-saving and mobilizing potential (possibly because they were the most in need of relief from these limitations) (Margolis & Resnick, 2000).

There is evidence that that advantage is no longer held. In recent years, the Democrats and Republicans have developed a dominant party presence on the Internet. The superior resources and organization that these parties have always enjoyed, enabled them to digitally outshine the less well-funded, less well-organized third parties in America. By 1996, for instance, Democratic and Republican websites had outnumbered other third party websites on the Internet (Ibid.). As the Internet population grew, so did the presence of America's two major parties.

Minor party sites currently command a less noticeable presence on the web and are somewhat more difficult to find. They have fewer links exchanged with similar sites and are less integrated into the web of interconnected political sites than the major two parties.[5] Their websites often lack the more expensive interactive and

---

[5]These links are often referred to as "backpointers," which are hotlinks from other sites. For a more thorough discussion on this topic, please see Margolis, Michael, David Resnick, and J. Wolfe. 1999. Fall. Party Competition on the Internet: Minor Versus Major Parties in the UK and USA. Harvard International Journal of Press/Politics, 4(3), pp. 24-47.

animation features that require much more money to produce, post, and maintain. Most third party sites also lack the volume of new information and new features that attract visitors for repeated visits. These are things that the larger parties are more able to provide. They also happen to be the type of things that the average citizen likes to see. GOP-TV, for instance, gives visitors to the Republican Party website chances to view video footage of important party events and political issues. This information is easily obtained and updated frequently. Things of this nature greatly increase the appeal of the site, but also require significant resources to maintain. In this regard, small parties have failed to keep pace with what the Republicans and Democrats have done in cyberspace. This has caused their impressive strides during the early days of the World Wide Web to wane in importance.

While the Internet has been somewhat effective in helping to level the playing field to a certain degree, it appears that all parties have not been as successful in taking advantage of this. Equal access does not necessarily equal success. Third parties, while aided by their presence on the Internet, still look like they are "marginal political operations" as compared to major party sites (Margolis & Resnick, 2000). This is consistent with the general idea that the reinforcement theorist (in chapter 6) suggest. For whatever level of potential exists within cyberspace for parties, the actual environment for them appears to be mimicking the real world.

The Future for Digital Parties

We know that political parties continually struggle. They attempt to control government by sponsoring candidates in a political environment that is always changing, sometimes in ways that undermine their very efforts. Parties in America have always used new technological developments to their advantage, and this discussion reflects nothing new in that sense. What is new is that recent technological developments have given parties one of the best chances for new political gain in modern times. This applies to parties in democratic as well as in non-democratic states (Norris, 2001a). Digital communications, including cell phones, beepers, e-mail, etc., all facilitate organizational cohesion within parties. E-mail, in particular, can be a very cost-effective tool in linking people within organizations (Neu, Anderson, & Bikson, 1999). These advantages have been so profound, there has been a need to debate whether or not they will change the political landscape for political parties. From the evidence seen so far, that does not appear likely. In fact, it is possible that this new media will simply provide a means to further entrench the domination of the Democrats and Republicans in American politics.

So far, those parties with the money and organizational support that have tended to dominate politics in real-life, have been able to recreate that effect on the web. Party politics on the web appears very much to be "business as usual." With regard to the Internet causing the relationship between candidate and party to splinter further, evidence for this has also not been seen. As will be discussed in Chapter 8, party candidates are also using digital communications, but there is little evidence to suggest that they will be abandoning parties any time soon. Candidates still need parties and parties still need candidates. Many of the possibilities discussed earlier in this section have remained just that, possibilities. What has been seen is not necessarily a strengthening or a weakening of the players, but simply an adaptation and a change in the way the game is played. There has been a re-shuffling of positioning and tactics, but not a change in the power structures involved.

Major parties have adapted to the Internet and third parties have remained marginalized. There has been no leveling of the playing field in this regard. The major political parties in America have also failed to use the web to aggressively reach out to members or reinvigorate their support base. Their communication on the web at this point remains largely "top down" in nature with little importance placed on member input or feedback.

Interest Groups

What Do We Know about Interest Groups?

The Frenchman Alexis de Tocqueville traveled to America in 1831 and recorded his observations on American government and society, which were later published in two volumes entitled *Democracy in America*. In those volumes he remarked on a variety of social and political characteristics he saw, one of which involves American's tendency to form associations, or groups. In it he states that "Americans of all ages, all conditions, and all dispositions, constantly form associations" (Tocqueville, 1956, p.79). This is noteworthy because he is implying that this characteristic reflects our strong democratic culture.

According to Tocqueville, Americans like to get together and join groups at particularly high rates.[6] We like, as most humans do, to associate with like-minded individuals for social or political benefit, material or otherwise. When we gather with like-minded individuals for political benefit, we sometimes form interest groups in order to advance our wishes more effectively.

While there are many varieties of definitions applied to interest groups, we will define an interest group as a formal organization of individuals whose primary purpose is to influence public policy on behalf of its members. Interest groups are vehicles for participation who also educate government and citizens about issues, bring new issues to the forefront, and often provide additional benefits to their members. In a free and democratic society interest groups are natural. They help make up the political environment where competing interests vie for the attention of policymakers.

Interest groups are much like political parties. Interest groups, too, provide a linkage between the citizen and government. They provide a medium by which one can more effectively pressure the government to respond to the individual's concerns. They do not, however, run candidates for office or wish to directly control government through the election of its members.

While political parties are almost universally seen as a good thing in democracies, interest groups sometimes are not. The very term "interest group" connotes a quality that parties do not share. Political parties, while ideologically driven, have the good of the whole in mind when they act. Interest groups usually have only a small section of the whole in mind when they pressure Congress for action on a particular issue. Political parties also care about a wide variety of issues, ranging from military expenditures to welfare reform. Interest groups typically have only a small number, if not a single issue, that drives their activity, such as gun control, or the rights of the unborn.

The question remains, though: Are they good or bad? James Madison definitely thought they could be an undesirable element. Interest groups, or factions as he uses the term, seek to use government authority for their own benefit, rather than that of the commu-

---

[6]Robert Putnam's *Bowling Alone* asserts that Tocqueville's observations are in need of reassessment. His data suggests that Americans are becoming less civically engaged.

nity. A paper industry interest group, for instance, may desire that Congress allow them to cut down trees within certain protected national forests. This is obviously at the expense of other interests who may desire that area left undeveloped for public use. In this sense, interest groups are somewhat undesirable, especially if they can use their clout to dominate the policy making process at the expense of the public good.[7]

They do however, fulfill a role in democracies that some argue is quite healthy. They give substance to a pluralistic society. That is, a variety of politically active groups in society contribute to a wide mixture of competing voices. This provides a positive and stabilizing outlet for variations in public opinion and issue stances.[8] Interest groups provide another means by which to pressure government to respond to one's concerns, particularly if the existing avenues fail to respond to what pressure is brought to bear.

While our purpose here is not to resolve any debate over the destructive or productive tendencies of interest groups, it is our duty to take what is known about them and assess the state of interest groups in America as they relate to new technological developments. Interest groups do play a large role in the political process in America. Their activity as an organization will be affected by changes in information delivery. An assessment of the change in their status is the topic of this section.

Affecting the Strength of Interest Groups

Assessing the strength of interest groups in terms of new technology is important for two reasons. First, interest groups are powerful. They have an effect on what laws are made in America and how these laws are drafted. Second, these groups are not necessarily interested in the common good and often times are simply at odds

---

[7]Theodore J. Lowi is highly critical of the negative effects of interest group activity. Please see *The End of Liberalism,* NY: Norton 1969 for a thorough analysis of this issue.

[8]For two seminal works on this topic, please see: Arthur Bentley, (*The Process of Government;* Bloomington, Ind., Principia Press, 1949) who argues that all political phenomenon can be understood in terms of group activity; and David B. Truman (*The Governmental Process,* New York, Knopf, 1951.), who argues that group participation in society helps to stabilize it.

with it. This is of particular concern since these groups are not accountable to the voter through elections.

One of the themes that recurs in debating technology and democracy is the lowering of the costs that result from forming associations. Maintaining an organization is very expensive and demands significant resources. Even something as fundamental as keeping up with membership dues, or mailing lists, requires people, paper, postage, and a variety of other things just to sustain minimal operations. This can be a particular problem for large groups such as American Association of Retired Persons who have over 30 million members (American Association of Retired Persons [AARP], 2003). The Internet has been a significant development in the administration of group activity. As one author has noted, the Internet may be the best thing since the postal system or the telephone for interest groups (Hill & Hughes, 1998). The amount of cash required to mobilize, inform, or recruit is greatly decreased when new technologies are employed. Paper supplies or newsletters, for example, are not needed in the quantity they once were for a group wanting to do something as simple as send out updates to its members. That can now be done at far less cost through e-mail. Another theme often seen is not only the ease, but the speed with which information can be delivered. Near instantaneous delivery of group news, issues, or directives, can potentially mobilize interest groups at rates rarely seen in the past.

If these things greatly increase their strength, this may be of concern, particularly if you are a Madisonian. If you are more of a pluralist, this may be good news. It is not our concern to assess the effectiveness of interest groups. We do, however, have an interest in assessing interest group's use of new technology and the advantages it offers them. By looking at what methods interest groups employ to reach their goals, it is easier to see how technology might be effectively used to increase or decrease their strength.

The Use of the Internet by Interest Groups

Much like political parties, interest groups have adapted to computer mediated communication and have incorporated its advantages into their political strategy. Almost all of these groups, particularly ones that are well financed, have been able to use the Internet to fortify almost every aspect of their operation. Most of these efforts can be categorized by constituency: the mass public, group members, and government (Davis, 1999). All three of these groups are objects of interest group activity; the mass public because they are potential supporters, existing members because they are already converts and in need of mobilization and education, and the government, since they obviously are the ultimate object of the group's efforts. Tactics aimed at each of these constituencies provide a framework within which to begin an analysis. Each will be addressed in turn.

First, interest groups have extended and updated their efforts to educate and persuade the mass public to their cause. The many interest groups' websites have detailed information on the group's mission and history. The Sierra Club, for example, clearly states its purpose and identifies the issues with which it is currently most concerned on the main page of their website at http://www.sierraclub.org. Much like the tactics of political parties in the previous section, the Internet gives these groups absolute control over the text and tone of "their message." This can be of particular importance for press coverage whereby television networks and reporters can use official websites in research for stories. The AARP, for instance, has an area on their main page which contains information for the press who may be doing research on the organization or its concerns. This "Press Center" located at http://www.aarp.org/press/home.html has links to useful data on issues important to senior citizens as well as organizational information on the mission and activity of the AARP. The general public can also be given a carefully tailored mission statement that corrects or sidesteps certain undesirable notions about the group's goals or purpose. A good example of this is the People for the Ethical Treatment of Animals site (http://www.peta.org) where their often aggressive and unorthodox stances on animal rights and cruelty can be presented in a way that is free of third party interference or manipulation.

Additionally, in educating and persuading the mass public to their cause, interest group sites often have features for joining and donating. This recruitment and solicitation mimics the attempts of political parties. Joined with the tactic above, both provide for a way to send a finely tuned message to a wide variety of individuals who, if they choose, can immediately become affiliated with the organization as they see fit. Both the ability to educate and persuade are certainly strengthened by an Internet presence.

Second, the Internet allows interest groups the ability to more easily educate those who are already members and can more easily mobilize those members who are prone to activism. The

National Rifle Association (http://www.nra.org) website provides an extraordinary example of the effectiveness that can be achieved in this area. The NRA website offers tips on communicating with those in Congress, information on where to find them, a "politics and legislation" area for the latest on legislative efforts on gun control, as well as links of interest on gun safety, sports, headlines, and stock quotes. As a major interest group in American politics, the NRA website extends past simply providing information for members and encouraging activism. It provides a portal by which one has access to expanded member information and services such as one's own e-mail account hosted by the NRA.

Third, and maybe most importantly, electronic communication has strengthened interest groups' ability to lobby. It has greatly enabled interest groups to do what they are primarily there to do: influence government activity. The Internet allows for interest groups to identify potential activists cheaply and easily. Furthermore, it allows for their rapid deployment in grassroots lobbying efforts. This is what some research has suggested as being a most significant source of strength for interest groups activity (Ibid.). Through the Internet a group can very cheaply and very quickly deploy significant numbers of individuals to pressure key Congressmen for some action to be taken. Prior efforts would have had to involve mass mailings via the United States Postal Service or phone calls simply to make a call for action. This would be done at great expense as well as be quite time consuming. Present calls for action can be made via e-mail at minimal cost and at maximum speed.

In 2003, an intense grassroots effort on behalf of Common Cause, Moveon.org, and the Future of Music Coalition showcased the potential activity that could be mobilized in a very short period of time. Beginning on Wednesday May 21, 2003, at 3:00 pm,[9] these interest groups launched a campaign to get the Federal Communications Commission to postpone a meeting date during which they had intended to further relax the ownership restrictions on corporate acquisitions of media outlets. Within weeks, these groups had launched a widespread e-mail and e-petition campaign aimed at the FCC and Congress. The speed and aggressiveness of this lobbying effort would have been impossible a decade ago.

---

[9]The press release stating the campaign start date and other facts can be found at http://www.moveon.org/press/pr/release51903.html.

CASE STUDY *Common Cause, Moveon.org and the Future of Music Coalition vs. the FCC*

The Problem

On June 2, 2003, the FCC had plans to meet in order to assess the rules governing media ownership in the United States. It was generally thought that the commission was intent on loosening the restrictions, allowing large communication corporations to own more television and radio stations than was previously allowed.[10] Specifically, they were believed to have plans to:

For newspaper-television/radio cross ownership:
⊛ Lift the ban on one company owning a newspaper and a television or radio station in the same city (except in the smallest cities).

For national television station ownership:
⊛ Raise the broadcast cap from 35% to 45% (currently one company is not allowed to own television stations that combine to reach more than 35% of the national audience).

For multiple local television station ownership:
⊛ In large cities, raise the number of stations a company may own in a city from 2 to 3 (currently a company may own 2 stations in the same city if at least 8 independently owned stations remain).

For television/radio cross ownership:
⊛ In markets with 20 or more media voices (radio, television, newspapers), lift or greatly loosen the cap on one company owning one television station and 7 radio stations in all but small cities (Ahrens, 2003).

---

[10]For more information on this topic, please see the Common Cause and Moveon.org websites as well as an interesting article in *The Nation* by Robert McChesney and John Nichols entitled "Media Democracy's Moment" found at http://www.thenation.com/doc.mhtml?i=20030224&s=mcchesney. Additionally, the U.S. Senate Committee on Commerce Science and Transportation has partial transcripts of its hearing on May 22, 2003, regarding the matter located at http://commerce.senate.gov/hearings/witnesslist.cfm?id=770.

This Man Wants to Control the News in America.

The FCC Wants to Help Him.

Rupert Murdoch, the Australian media mogul, already owns the Fox TV network, eight cable networks, and local TV stations in 34 U.S. cities. He owns American newspapers, movie studios, publishing houses, and record companies.

But Murdoch wants more. Much more. And to get it, he needs to repeal the last laws that protect the public from monopoly control of the news media.

Unless we act now, Rupert Murdoch is going to get his way.

Next week, the Federal Communications Commission plans to sweep away ownership restrictions that, for three decades, have guaranteed at least minimal competition and diversity of opinions on the public airwaves.

What will it mean? For Murdoch and his fellow moguls, it means swallowing up independent broadcasters and affiliates, and gaining further control over news content, advertising revenue and cable rates. The new rules will allow them to own several "competing" TV stations in most cities. And they'll be permitted to control the largest newspapers, radio and TV outlets in a single market.

For the public, it means higher cable bills, fewer choices, "canned" programming and reduced coverage of community issues.

Rupert Murdoch's News Corporation, together with four other conglomerates (Disney, Viacom, GE, and AOLTimeWarner), already control 75 percent of the total U.S. television audience and 90 percent of the TV news audience. That's local and national, broadcast and cable. Isn't that enough? Isn't that too much?

You Can Help Stop Them.

Of the thousands of public comments filed with the FCC on this issue, *more than 97 percent* oppose increased ownership of local TV by media conglomerates.

Public outrage is perhaps our only chance to stop or reverse these changes. Let the Commissioners and Congress know what you think. Visit **www.MoveOn.org** to send an instant, personalized comment.

□ **YES!** **I Want to Help Protect Media Diversity in My Community.**

Your contribution will be used to fund additional efforts to get the word out through more advertising and other means.

NAME

ADDRESS

CITY   STATE   ZIP

EMAIL ADDRESS

Because Common Cause lobbies, your contribution is not deductible for income tax purposes.
Make checks payable to Common Cause. Mail to: Common Cause FCC Campaign, 1250 Connecticut Ave. NW, Washington, DC 20036.
www.commoncause.org

MoveOn.ORG
Democracy in Action.
www.moveon.org

Common Cause
www.commoncause.org

FREE PRESS
mediareform.network
www.mediareform.net

Copyright © 2003 by Common Cause, www.commmon cause.org. Reprinted by permission.

The Debate

For deregulation: The old regulations have been made obsolete by the proliferation of Internet websites and cable television channels. The old rules are outdated and made in an era when there were fewer broadcast networks and mediums. Additionally, anti-trust laws exist to deal with potential monopolies in the marketplace, so fears of domination by one company are unfounded. There remains little to no evidence that media diversity is related to opinion diversity and visa versa.[11]

Those for it: The FCC's three Republican members and large media corporations.

Against deregulation: More consolidation will lead to problems of a free exchange of ideas. Fewer independently owned voices will lead to a homogenization of news and programming that will tend to disadvantage minority opinion. Fewer independently owned media outlets practically guarantee less diversity of opinion. Our democracy's health may be at stake since this issue involves the control and dissemination of information.

Those against it: The two Democratic members of the FCC, and several interest groups such as Moveon.org and Common Cause.[12]

The Lobbying Effort

- The FCC received hundreds of thousands of e-mails and e-petitions (Ahrens, 2003).
- Moveon.org, a public interest organization, claims to have collected 170,000 signatures on a petition to keep the rules in place (Ibid.).
- Upon launching a petition to postpone the vote, Moveon.org received 150,000 signatures in five days (Common Cause, 2003).

---

[11]Please see Mr. Kent W. Mikkelsen's comments before the U.S. Senate Committee on Commerce, Science and Transportation found at http://commerce.senate.gov/hearings/testimony.cfm?id=770&wit_id=2119 .

[12]Common Cause is a 200,000 member interest group who works for open, accountable government. Moveon.org is an online outlet for democratic participation who boasts a membership of more than 2 million online activists. Both have allied with Stone Gossard of Pearl Jam and Mike Mills of REM.

- Common Cause launched a $250,000 TV and ad campaign against the changes (Ahrens, 2003).
- The FCC website claims to have gotten over 9,000 e-mail comments over recent months from individuals that claim no affiliation to either group . . . all but 11 of those e-mails were critical of the proposed changes (Ibid.).
- Congressional offices have reported substantial e-mail traffic as well (Ibid.).

The open meeting of the five member FCC commission, which occurred on June 2, 2003, evolved into a fairly high profile event given the general apathy most hold toward bureaucratic decision making. By 9:30am EDT that day, the movement to delay the decision had, within weeks, generated widespread media coverage along with a deluge of postcards, e-mails, and e-petitions sent to various government officials. It was reported that the FCC alone received over half a million e-mails and pieces of traditional mail (Stone, 2003). The volume of e-mail and voicemail alone was so substantial, it caused the FCC's computer and voicemail systems to crash. During the meeting, some of the FCC members acknowledged the volume of correspondence and publicly stated that it had an impact on the commission.

Regardless of the effect that deregulation of the media industry may or may not have, the controversy over the issue illustrates the speed and momentum that can be gained through interest group activity whose strategy employs new digital communication. Lauren Coletta, Director of Field Operations for Common Cause, has stated that with regard to the FCC case in particular, digital communication allowed for extreme speed in mobilizing district meetings as well as establishing local leadership and protest guidelines (L. Coletta, personal communication, June 18, 2003). A sizeable response was mounted in days as opposed to weeks or months, which, with regard to the FCC decision, was vital to the movement's success.

The Future for Interest Groups Online

While there has been substantial evidence of the Internet providing effective and efficient new tools for interest groups, it does not provide them with a magic bullet that will always find its target. It also does not provide a new level playing field for all interest groups in American society. The Internet helps interest groups much the same way it helps parties. It offers both groups organizational benefits including advantages in administration cohesiveness, mobilization, member updates, and fundraising. However, it has not been the great equalizer, nor has it been the great leveler for those interest groups who are resource poor.

First, there is some evidence that suggests that mass e-mails are becoming less and less useful. It is possible that they, in fact, are seen more often as high-tech junk mail that takes little to no time to send and whose contents might not be of great value. Representative Tom Campbell was quoted as saying "When it [e-mail] came out it was great . . . And then I began to get unsolicited e-mails, then the majority are unsolicited, then the majority are blasted to a hundred people. And so it becomes less and less useful" (Davis, 1999, p. 81). There is some concern that e-mails, as primary mode of interest strategy, will deflate in importance, particularly when questions of fraud and identity are assessed. Electronic communications certainly does not appear to be the magic bullet, although its use does appear to strengthen and expedite certain efforts for those who are engaged.

Second, there are still significant levels of disparity between interest groups. The advantages that money and organizational strength offer tend to be replicated in the adaptation of new technologies as well. The ability to seize the advantages offered by new technologies varies by group. Groups with better funding tend to have websites that are richer in content, layout, and innovation (Ibid.). This more thoroughly increases their ability to inform and to persuade than if they had a more moderate site with only the most basic information that rarely changes.

Finally, interest groups online appear to be encouraging only traditional forms of participation. They do not seem to be encouraging new ones (Margolis & Resnick 2000). There is a definite lack of any request for feedback or input. The web presence of interest groups very much appears to be "top down" rather than "bottom up." This is of particular interest since the medium which we are investigating is tailor made for interactive and immediate communication.

There is, however, a rough ideological parity in the Internet. There is not a significant difference in the volume of those websites belonging to those groups who are right or left leaning (Hill & Hughes, 1998). However, when all political websites are taken into account, research has identified 21% of political groups with websites could be identified as "fringe" (Ibid.). While these groups cannot necessarily be called interest groups, they are an important element to the political landscape. They are of particular importance because the Internet's egalitarian character also adds a new facet to their operational capabilities as well as to other movements which are categorized differently.

Social Movements

What Do We Know about Social Movements?

The previous section began by describing how interest groups differ from political parties. A clarification that remains to be stated is the difference between interest groups and social movements. Admittedly, there is very fine line between the two groups. However, there are important differences. Interest groups are formal organizations with distinct organizational features and generally have quite narrow policy goals. This is not true for social movements.

Social movements do not have a well defined organizational structure and fail to exhibit the formal membership criteria that interest groups do. They tend to consist of loosely associated groups who share some common goal. In this sense they often have the effect of mobilizing quite large sections of society under an umbrella topic with which many groups, regardless of agenda, can identify. A widely recognized example of a recent and quite effective social movement was found in America during the civil rights era of the 1960s. The Civil Rights Movement was composed of a wide variety of groups all working for the common purpose of changing the way The United States treated African-American citizens. Another example would be the women's rights movement in the 70s (Norris, 2001a).

Social movements obviously have political goals, but their concern largely focuses on changing people's perception on particular topics and altering the prevailing attitude that exists on a given topic. The Civil Rights Movement was undoubtedly a political movement, but its goals ran far deeper than simply enacting legislation. The movement wanted to bring to light injustice and to revise many Americans' notion of equality. Additionally, it is also appropriate for our purposes to identify mass protests and demonstrations as features to our discussion. While their function and purpose can vary greatly from what would be seen in a social movement, the benefits they may receive from improvements to communication technology are much the same. In that regard, both are informal organizations who could potentially be greatly impacted by computer mediated communication. For this purpose both activists and social movements will be discussed in this section and referred to as one general group, if nothing more than out of a need for convenience.

Affecting the Strength of Social Movements

Given the loose nature of social movements and protests, this category of group political participation stands the most to gain from the Internet and e-mail. Unlike well organized interest groups or political parties, social movements do not have a well defined membership or internal structure from which they can draw support. This means that communication issues provide a real challenge, particularly to large movements. These groups rarely maintain a "hub" or headquarters where decision making can be formally carried out. They lack the significant organizational structure required to carry out precise and well organized efforts.

The widespread use of computers in America allows for social movements and protests to possibly gain the most from the speed of communication and reduction in transaction costs offered by the Internet and e-mail. From a pessimistic standpoint, some of these movements have no where to go but up. Any advantage of this nature is likely to cause resource poor movements to mobilize and act in more effective ways than ever before. It is possible that it is here one will see a more authentic "bottom-up" use of technology rather than the "top-down" strategy argued to be employed by political parties and interest groups.

The Use of the Internet by Social Movements

The overriding advantage the Internet has offered to social movements and protest groups has been the general ease it has provided in mobilization efforts. Since these groups usually have looser organizational structures and are typically less well funded than traditional interest groups or political parties, it is argued that they stand the potential to gain the most from the use of computer mediated communication.

It has been said that the Internet is the most effective tool ever created in organizing people (Foundation for Public Affairs, 2000). If this is true, social movements will be able to mobilize and act at a speed and with an effectiveness not seen before. Much of the literature on the Internet and social movements suggest that computer mediated communication helps create 'virtual communities' that benefit from the Internet's ability to compress space and time. Digital communications allow for things to be done in a far shorter period of time. They also reduce the impediment of distance that hinders mass movements.[13] This is true of international as well as localized efforts. In this regard, there have been numerous examples of groups taking advantage of this new development.

On a most basic level, under-funded and loosely organized groups have been able to use new communication technology in very effective ways. On Mother's Day, May 11, 2000, gun control advocate Donna Dees-Thomases organized a "Million Mom March" which was a demonstration in Washington, D.C. by mothers who supported more aggressive gun control measures. Organized through a website, the promoters of the event claim the Internet was a vital tool in the success of the demonstration. Communications Director Kathy Moore was quoted as saying that the group could not ". . . Imagine using snail mail and telephone to accomplish what we did as we organized . . . because many of the people involved were mothers, much of our work was late at night after the kids were in bed and the e-mails went flying" (Anonymous, 2001, p.15).

From the website there was an opportunity to register for the march, as well as chances to get additional information on transportation options and general information on organizing and public relations. Images, merchandise, and donation opportunities were there as well, with each state having its own site so that local coordination could be facilitated.

Events such as this can happen on an international scale as well. In 1997 a group known as Citizens Against Police Brutality (CAPB) in Canada learned of a Swiss group's plan to stage an International Day Against Police Violence. In contacting the Swiss group, CAPB was able to assist in contacting other human rights activist groups and acted as an electronic intermediary between groups who wanted to have the same type of demonstration in their home country or community. After months of organization, CAPB had a substantial hand in extending the Swiss-initiated demonstration across the globe. The International Day Against Police Violence on March 14th and 15th of that year included fundraisers, rallies, and concerts on six continents (Krause, 1997). While the Million Mom March em-

---

[13]For a thorough discussion of this topic and a debate involving the true nature of "space", please see Capling, Ann and Kim Richard Nossal, "Death of Distance or Tyranny of Distance? The Internet, Deterritorialization, and the Anti-Globalization Movement in Australia", *The Pacific Review*, vol. 14, #3, 2001: 443-465.

ployed a broader use of the Internet, CAPB's efforts were based largely on e-mail exchanges worldwide.

Similar demonstrations were seen in February of 2003 when the "Virtual March on Washington" focused a coalition of 32 organizations (claiming more than 400,000 registered participants) on a call-in campaign to demonstrate opposition to the war in Iraq ("Activists Hold 'Virtual March'," 2003; "Anti-war Protesters Go Digital," 2003). Here as well, the "virtual world" made the plans of activists much easier to execute at minimal cost. Other real world anti-war demonstrations earlier that spring also claimed excessive use of the Internet and other digital communications in mobilizing the millions of activist who participated in street demonstrations worldwide (Ibid.).

Perhaps the most illustrative example of this are "flash mobs." Typically non-political in nature, flash mobs are smaller numbers of people who are rapidly organized by e-mail to simultaneously "mob" an area at a specific time, and then immediately disperse. One recent event in August of 2003 involved approximately 300 people simultaneously meeting in front of a Times Square toy store to confront a large dinosaur. The mob was instructed in advance (by e-mail) to assemble at a specific location at a specific time. From there, they received further instructions and moved *en masse* to the toy store, where they froze in front of the dinosaur, stared silently, then suddenly fell to the ground, screaming and flailing their arms in mock terror. When security was called, the mob quickly dispersed and blended into the normal Times Square crowd ("E-mail brings together flash mob," 2003). While the gravity of this example may be in question, the organizational impact it illustrates is not.

The Future for Social Movements Online

The great boost that social movements and demonstrations get from new digital communication has to do with the easing of organizational impediments. As access to computer mediated communication becomes more widespread, it is likely that this will continue to advantage these groups even further in the future. Activists typically lack resources. They are almost always working from the outside, hoping to impact those who are within. The Internet and e-mail, while not addressing all of the needs of the activist, make their time and efforts reverberate more clearly and easily.

The quickness and immediacy of communication and its effects on mobilization efforts are equally distributed. All groups have the potential to benefit in the same way, as long as their members and supporters have computer access. This is also true for groups who mobilize for less than desirable purposes, such as extremist groups or hate groups. For example, the benefits of digital communication enjoyed by protesters at the World Trade Organization meetings in November and December of 1999, in Seattle, or at the Multilateral Agreement on Investment (Capling & Nossal, 2001; Deibert, 2000) event a few years earlier are also shared by far right militia groups and white supremacy groups campaigning for their cause.

The future, then, for social movements and protest groups is a bright spot as far as group participation in politics is concerned. The "cyber-diffusion" of information significantly enhances a group's ability to assemble resources. The only negative element to this, however, is that this forum allows for the rapid and effective dissemination of information and mobilization of support for all groups, regardless of intent or positive social value, and certainly without concern for the *accuracy or reliability* of that information (Ayers, 1999).

Summary

This chapter has attempted to address the impact of new communication technology on the political participation of groups in American society. Reminiscent of the conclusions in the previous chapter, it is again likely that new developments in technology will *not* substantially change the political environment for these groups. The Internet has not been shown to necessarily level the playing field or to completely "democratize" the way resource-rich and resource-poor groups interact with the government or operate.

At this point, it seems that a group's success in cyberspace directly reflects its success in "real world" politics. Those with the resources and organizational skills to succeed in traditional political environments appear to be using those same resources to succeed on the Internet. Those with fewer resources and those who are less organized in the real world appear to be much the same in the virtual world. In other words, those who are already politically active and influential will likely remain that way. The Internet will not substantially change that.

However, the Internet arguably impacts the *way* business is conducted for these groups, particularly for social movements and protest groups. By compressing both space and time, so that distance becomes less of an issue and time is more effectively used, the Internet can accelerate group activity, allowing for a speed of activism that has not been seen before. According to political scientist Bruce Bimber, this activity of political groups, or linkages, will not wither, but accelerate (Bimber, 1998). For all of the groups discussed in this chapter, particularly social movement and protest groups, the Internet allows an ease of mobilization that is unprecedented. In fact, the groups that stand to benefit the most tend to be the ones that lack a well-established infrastructure; the Internet allows less bureaucratic and hierarchically structured groups to work at a level they likely could not have achieved using traditional resources. In that sense, the activities of major political parties are impacted the least.

In sum, the evidence seems to suggest that the groups who will benefit the most from the Internet are those who already exist in real life. Cyberspace is not expected to create a plethora of new politically active groups who exist exclusively online. This is because the Internet is said to be incapable of creating new groups because it does not create community out of thin air (Diani, 2001). It is an extension of it. Virtual networks work best when they have real networks of people behind them (Ibid.). New communication technology will allow these real networks, regardless of size or purpose, the added advantage of being able to quickly and accurately disseminate information and mobilize members to a common purpose in a way that is very different from in the past. The players are not changing, but what *is* changing is the rate at which they play and the cost at which they play the game.

Campaigns
and Elections

Introduction

From Television to the Internet

Since the 1996 presidential campaigns, the Internet has been used more and more widely for campaign purposes. Like the buttons, bumper stickers, yard signs, and television ads of past campaign strategies, the Internet is just another tool used to market a political candidate to the public. But as an emerging new mass medium which has the potential to engage voters in new ways, its importance is greater than if it was merely a new twist on an old tactic. This point is evident by the introduction of the last new mass medium into politics: television.

There is no doubt that television has profoundly affected the way campaigns and political strategies are executed. Television has developed into a core element of any campaign strategy. The 1960 televised presidential debate between Nixon and Kennedy showed an example of how important a new mass medium can be for politicians. Much to Nixon's dismay, it also showed the dangers of underestimating new media developments as well.

The emergence of television was significant because it was a new medium that offered things previous media formats did not: it combined the sound of radio with a revolutionary visual component. Today, political campaigns are inextricably linked to televised media. Campaign flashpoints such as primary races and debates have not only become televised media events, but the way these events develop very often dictate the pace, tone and volume of television coverage that may come later. Television has become a key element to modern campaign strategy, and a *very* expensive one at that.

Though it clearly mimics the audio and visual components of television, the Internet offers something that television does not: interaction and direct dissemination. Through chat rooms, discussion lists, and other features, the Internet allows users to immediately respond to an audio-visual message from a candidate, thereby allowing for a dialogue between candidate and voter, regardless of locale. Additionally, campaign messages are directly sent to recipients without going first through privately owned radio or television stations and without the licensing and expensive hardware such stations require. There is no fear of messages being altered or filtered as they move from party A (the candidate) to party B (the voter), as often occurs in more traditional media formats. Not only is two-way communication more likely, but the messages involved are completely controllable.

It is still too early to say that the Internet will change campaigns the way television has. However, the differences between television and the Internet are significant enough that there is a need to assess the impact of this medium on campaigns. This chapter will address this issue by first, stating what we know about modern campaigns, and then determining how new communication technologies may change what we know. In essence, what can be expected? Has there been any evidence of the Internet impacting campaign strategy or election results?

What Do We Know about Political Campaigns?

Campaigns in America have been proceeding in a direction that many feel is not all together desirable. Since the 1950s the role of the political party in elections has diminished. Campaigns now are driven by the candidates themselves, with the help of professional political consultants. Political parties may aid the campaign, but they do not wholly control or direct the candidate. There has also been a rise in the use of primaries, and an extension of the campaign season, which has no official start date. Particularly for the presidency, the campaigns begin not just months but sometimes years before the election date. This means that while campaigning in earnest is most visible the months before an election, there are preparations made and fundraising initiated long before then.

Predictably, campaigns have become very expensive affairs, with many hundreds of thousands, if not millions, of dollars usually needed to effectively compete, especially if one's opponent is an incumbent. These dollar figures tend to rise along with the prestige of the seat for which one runs; in other words, the higher the office, the more money needed to run for it. In sum, campaigns have become longer, candidate-driven affairs, which have become more and more expensive over time.

Comparatively speaking, the Internet as a campaign tool is dirt cheap. It, like television in the 1950s, shows potential for becoming a mass medium. In retrospect, we are able to see the impact that television has had on campaigning. First, it has contributed to the rising cost of running for office. Second, it has also focused our attention on more personal, if not superficial, qualities of those running for office, such as one's dress, haircut, or demeanor.

The purpose of this chapter is to assess how new developments in communication technology may be changing what we know about how campaigns are executed. It is very doubtful that they will cause a tremendous change, but there is evidence that there will be some measurable impact. The following sections will assess how candidates are using digital communications and what consequences those actions will have for the direction and effectiveness of political campaigns in America.

Campaigns

What Can the Internet Offer a Campaign that Other Mediums Do Not?

New digital communications will not necessarily alter the shape of elections completely, but they will likely change the way things are done and provide new advantages to campaigners that other mediums fail to offer. First, the Internet is a prime source of information for people at work. Because office workers have widespread access to computer terminals, there is a very large "online public" at the workplace who heavily rely on the Internet as an information medium. Second, a candidate's website can be very effective at crucial moments. After a candidate makes the televised news or engages in a high profile appearance, a well constructed website can seize upon the spike in interest and immediately convert that interest into contributions, mailing list additions, and supporters. The website can act as a clearinghouse for information and as a mass mobilizer when a candidate's interest is at its peak. Finally, a candidate website simply saves money and time while increasing accuracy in campaign messages. For instance, a candidate's response to a frequently asked, and sometimes delicate, question can be readily available for reference online. A website can act as a permanent record of a candidate's stance on issues and a document attesting to the campaign's success. This can be particularly valuable as a research source for writers and reporters in the more traditional media. This can greatly save on labor cost and confusion, increase the level of consistency in messages, and minimize backtracking and corrections (The Institute for Policy, Democracy and the Internet [IPDI], 2002a).

Moreover, digital communications, as a new medium, are suggested to offer additional benefits that other mediums do not:

⊛ A greater volume of available information.
⊛ Faster gathering, retrieving, and transmitting of information.
⊛ More control over the media by consumers.
⊛ Greater ability of senders to target their messages to specific audiences.
⊛ Greater decentralization of the media.
⊛ Greater interactive capacity (Abramson, Arterton, & Orren, 1988; Lewicki & Ziaukas, 2000).

The key to this discussion is the extent to which modern campaigns have utilized these potential advantages. There is, however, a need to separate potential from reality by describing what exactly has been done by candidates in the Internet age. Indeed, the whole topic of the Internet in politics has been framed along two lines: what is possible and what is actually occurring. This approach will be followed here as well.

The Evolution of the Internet and Campaigns

Interviewer: It seems as though the Internet has come of age during this campaign. How has the Internet or technology changed the way you run your campaign?

Gov. George W. Bush: It certainly makes it a lot easier to communicate. We're constantly passing back and forth information, ideas and talking points, and other things that happen in a campaign that require much more tedious communications than in the past. I think the great thing about the Internet is going to be able to connect with voters, and this is just the beginning of maybe a new style of campaigning, where much of it will happen over the Internet. After all, this is a conversation related to the Internet. Four years ago, I don't think campaigns were even talking about it. But time is precious in the course of a campaign, and here I am spending 30 minutes with you, all because you're relevant and you're alive and you're real and you talk about a changing world (Knox, 2000, p.31).

In 2000, soon to be president Bush expressed significant interest in the use and potential of the Internet in campaigning. These types of claims tended to abound in the late 90s. However, campaign consultants were initially hesitant to invest serious campaign capital, be it time or money, into an Internet component to their campaign strategies. While the Internet was used in the 1992 elections by the Clinton-Gore campaign to post campaign-related information, it was not until 1996 that it was more widely used by candidates and seen by larger numbers of voters (Davis, 1999). The elections of 1996 were a testing ground for Internet strategies, with *few* candidates using the medium in their campaigns (Browning, 1996). Of those that did maintain campaign websites, they appeared to be somewhat of a campaign novelty rather than the serious strategic component that they would later become. There was, at the time, some speculation as to whether or not candidates were truly interested in embracing the possibilities of Internet campaigning or if they simply felt "obliged to demonstrate their commitment to the latest technology" (Margolis, Resnick & Tu, 1997, p. 73).

Campaign websites certainly provided some evidence for this. Most websites for national office seekers were, by "today's standards," quite traditional and uninventive if they existed at all. Some have observed that the Internet at that time appeared to be much like the television in the late 50s: a new medium in search of a purpose (Coleman, 2001). The appearance and functionality of campaign websites was largely limited to basic information and exhibited very little interactivity. However, by the next election cycle two years later some momentum was evident.

A sampling of Senate and House races in 1998 showed that by October of that year, more than two-thirds of the candidates for open seats in the U.S. Congress had a website (Dulio, Goff, & Thurber, 1999). Table 1 shows the '98 breakdown in more detail. Here widespread use is seen, except for the House elections in '98 (this is partly explained by the approximate 100 seats that were uncontested and resulted in minimal campaigning).

Additionally, both party's candidates appeared to use the web equally. In the 1998 races, just over 71% of Democratic candidates used the web in their campaigns, while a little over 68% of Republicans

📰 Table 1

Candidates with Campaign Sites on the Internet
(Major Party Candidates only)

	Percentage of Candidates with Sites in 1998	Percentage of Candidates with Sites in 2000
Candidates for U.S. Senate	72%	91%
Candidates for U.S. House	35%	66%
Candidates for Governor	95%	83%

Table adapted from: "Political Campaigning on the Internet: Business as Usual?", Elaine Ciulla Kamarck, p.88. In *Governance.com: Democracy in the Information Age*. Elaine Ciulla Kamarck and Joseph S. Nye Jr., eds. Brookings Institution Press: Washington, D.C., 2002.

did the same (Ibid.). Clearly, as a novelty or not, the Internet had, by 1998, become more widely used as a campaign resource.

A more significant point of discussion is the level of sophistication that these sights developed. A survey of candidate websites before '98 determined that the Internet provided candidates with little more than "digital yard signs" (Casey, 1996). This is certainly more a statement on the use of the Internet rather than its potential. It does, however, indicate the state of Internet campaigning in the mid-90s. The '98 election cycle showed a departure from this, albeit a modest one.

As businesses gravitated to the Internet as a potential source of new revenue and marketing, they developed more effective site designs and methods for enhancing their business. Political campaigns soon followed. In fact, these revenue and marketing strategies from the private sector eventually became elements in Internet campaign strategy. Site design was seen as a more critical element, especially as websites became proven portals for revenue. Taking cues from corporate success in this area, candidates in '98 used the Internet as a way to solicit contributions as well as a way to market themselves cheaply and directly.

By the election of '98, nearly 73% of candidate websites were being used to solicit campaign contributions, with both parties exhibiting approximately equal rates of activity in this regard (Dulio, et al., 1999). This did not, however, mean that all of these websites were soliciting secure "online" donations. As shown in Table 2, the majority of those websites who were soliciting contributions were doing so in a fairly traditional manner.

⬛ Table 2

Web Site Solicitation Techniques

Web site requests for mail-in contributions	53.7%
Solicitation requests that the donor print-off a form and send it in via mail, fax or e-mail as a pledge	47.8%
Campaign requires that a donor request a campaign pledge form online which is then sent to them by regular mail	32.8%
Online secure credit card donations	29.9%

68 Senate Candidates and 65 House Candidates (n = 133)

Web sites used by candidates in the 1998 election (n = 111)

(Table 2 adapted from Dulio, David A., Donald L. Goff, James A. Thurber. "Untangled Web: Internet Use during the 1998 Election" *PS: Political Science and Politics,* March 1999, vol. 32 (1), p. 53-59. Table title: "Types of Web Site Solicitation Techniques" p. 55.)

The '98 election cycle definitely shows an increase in use and sophistication, but this advance appears to be measured in inches, not yards. While more candidates were using the web, few of them were using it as a direct interface for secure Internet contributions via an electronic funds transfer. This was already the norm for e-commerce and was widely used and seen as a safe way to do business online. In fact, according to Visa USA's New Market Development Division, the majority of all businesses who ran websites in 1998 were accepting secure credit card transactions online (T. Attinger, personal communication, July 14, 2003). This is significantly higher than the 29.9% of campaign websites at the time.

There were still other problems. Campaign sites exhibited significant differences in their quality and content (IPDI, 2002b). Not only was online fundraising in its infancy, but key campaign issues such as engagement, recruitment, fundraising, and persuasion were not always reflected in candidate websites and were, in fact, conspicuously absent on occasion (Ibid.; Kamarck, 1999). In a certain sense, the candidates used "the new medium of the Internet to fight the same ground war they have in the past," (Dulio, et al., 1999, p. 57) similar to combatants in a gun duel using a new machine gun with the single shot rather than the rapid-fire option engaged. Campaigns simply failed to maximize the potential of the Internet in '98[1] and the potential impact of that medium was, in turn, diminished (Sadow & James, 1999).

---

[1]One significant exception to this statement is the Jesse Ventura campaign for governor in Minnesota. This is discussed in more detail later this chapter.

These websites can also be assessed from the demand-side. As mentioned in Chapter 6, only 32.7% of the U.S. population was "online" in 1998. This means that candidates likely knew what general importance should be given to web campaigning at that time. The candidates cannot be blamed for failing to have a fancy online party if they knew no one was going to attend. However, things were changing on both the demand and the supply side.

The number of Americans online increased dramatically in the following years. Given this fact, one would expect campaigning on the net to follow suit, much like television's role in politics gained momentum as more and more households owned television sets. This was seen in the elections of 2000.

The 2000 elections are a particularly interesting point in time to study because 2000 was a presidential election year. Also, unlike 1996, 2000 not only saw what, at that point, was a crescendo in e-commerce, but a high point in Internet use overall. In 2000, nearly 1 in 5 used the Internet for election news, making it a major news source, with 18% of Americans reporting going online for election news that year ("Survey: Internet established as major news source," 2000; U.S. Department of State, 2001). This was up from 4% in 1996. The presidential race of that year was somewhat pivotal for Internet campaign strategists because it was the first national election in which the Internet was widely seen and used as an effective campaign tool, rather than being merely a novelty or campaign accoutrement.

The election of 2000 was eagerly viewed by many as being the first national election in which the Internet may have been closest to playing a large role in national races. Many wondered whether or not Internet use in the presidential election of that year would provide Americans with a new "JFK moment," (Lewicki & Ziaukas, 2000), where the televised presidential debates of 1960 showcased the ability of John F. Kennedy to successfully manage the new televised medium for political gain. This not only helped his campaign that year, but it also marked the dawn of a new era in politics where television would play a vital role.

This prediction was somewhat overly optimistic, but not entirely. While not quite a "JFK Moment," the Republican primary race for the 2000 election proved to be a defining moment for Internet campaigning (Ibid.). It was during that primary season that Senator John McCain was credited with using the Internet in a way that would somewhat set the standard for online campaign strategies in the future. During this race McCain put Internet strategy on somewhat equal footing with other traditional campaign activities. He aggressively pushed the website in public speeches, constantly encouraging people to logon to the McCain website and become somehow involved in the campaign. McCain strategists were one of the first to thoroughly incorporate Internet use and advertisement into the larger media strategy. The McCain strategy was seen as unique because it made web browsing a form of political activity and made McCain's site, in particular, a portal for political activism (Ibid.). This proved to pay-off in a way that no presidential candidate had yet seen.

Following McCain's success in the New Hampshire primary, more than half of a million dollars was donated in 24 hours to his campaign via the McCain website. The following day $600,000 was raised the same way with upwards of 10 million dollars being raised online over all.[2] These efforts, for the first time, showed the capacity of the Internet to compliment traditional campaign strategies and greatly facilitate mobilization and fundraising maneuvers. While these successes failed to deliver McCain the Republican nomination that year, it did create an event that indicated the maturation and true potential of this new medium in campaigning. For the McCain campaign, alone, it was a "magic" moment, not only for his campaign, but for the Internet in campaigning.

> **Senator John McCain's "Magic Moment"**
> The magic moment for the McCain campaign arrived when the Arizona Senator defeated George W. Bush by 18 percentage points in the New Hampshire primary on February 1, 2000. As word of McCain's victory spread, money started gushing into the campaign Web coffers at a rate of $30,000 an hour—this according to the campaign, which cleverly fed the news media with e-mail bulletins on the phenomenon, which then reported it, which then generated more donations. After four days, the total topped $2 million, a rate of almost $21,000 an hour. In all, the McCain campaign said it raised $6.4 million through the Internet, representing 27 percent of its entire fund-raising take. Since much of this money came in amounts less than $250 (the

[2]There is some debate over the inflation of this exact number. Even if it was significantly inflated, it is still very impressive.

average was $112, according to the campaign), McCain reaped an additional $4 million in matching funds from the federal government. The McCain campaign also enjoyed a huge influx of volunteers. Its e-mail list rocketed from 60,000 to 142,000. As a result, it became easier for the campaign to advance and populate candidate appearances. (This utility of e-mail was first demonstrated by the 1998 Jesse Ventura campaign for governor of Minnesota.)

The McCain campaign had just about spent all of its money by the day of the New Hampshire primary. The online contributions, processed swiftly by the banks and government, came to the rescue. Together with the publicity and volunteers, the money enabled the campaign to convert its "momentum," a political asset akin to a mandate in that it exists primarily in rhetoric, into more concrete political resources. Over the next few weeks, the McCain campaign won primaries in Michigan and Arizona. This may well not have occurred (especially in Michigan, Arizona being the Senator's home state) had the McCain campaign not explored and embraced online campaigning during the previous year.

A year of Net work preceded the magic moment. Senator McCain and his communications chief Dan Schnur were willing to experiment with the Internet. Two McCain aides, Max Fose and Wes Gullett, devoted six weeks to planning, one month to programming, and then four to six hours a day to maintaining the online operation. Each day, Fose walked around campaign headquarters collecting information for the site. After he showed McCain how much their Web site traffic rose after the candidate gave out its address on CNN's Larry King Live on October 13, 1999, the Senator made such an invitation a standard feature of his stump speech. Visitors to the site would see underscored calls to action: send money so we can purchase air time for this ad (attached as an audio file); view the list of more than $13 billion in wasteful and low-priority congressional pork-barrel spending items; e-mail headquarters with your opinions of the new site navigation tools.

The two-way communication paid a big dividend for the first time in December 1999, when the campaign realized it needed help procuring signatures to get on the ballot for the Republican primary in Virginia. The campaign augmented its

Web site appeal for help with an online advertising buy that at-
tracted just under one hundred volunteers, and made the dead-
line. The next month, the campaign asked for volunteers to
make ten phone calls to registered Independents and Republicans in New Hampshire. Eleven hundred people enlisted
within six hours. After a week, 8,000 calls had been completed
and tabulated; the Interactive Phone Bank had been invented.
Cost of volunteer transportation, office rental, phone equipment, line leasing, supervisors, and donuts: zero. Value to
grass-roots politics: priceless. The magic moment actually began when the polls in New Hampshire opened, not when the
result first became apparent. New Hampshire (like Minnesota,
Jesse Ventura's state) permits same-day registration for voting.
More than 38,000 Granite Staters took advantage of that option
on the day of the 2000 primary. There is no telling how many
of them voted for McCain, but chances are that quite a few did.
There is also no telling how many McCain voters were moved
to show up and register by an online message or a personally
delivered turnout message logistically facilitated by the Net, but
again, chances are that quite a few were.

(Excerpt taken from: *The Net and the Nomination: Spring 2003,* Michael Cornfield and Jonah
Sieger, pp.10-12; published by the Institute for Politics, Democracy, & the Internet; The George
Washington University. Full text of this paper can be found at http://www.ipdi.org/net_nomi-
nation.pdf .)

While the Internet failed to produce a win in the Republican
primary of 1999 for John McCain, it did somewhat prove its worth
and found much more acceptance in the presidential race and general election of 2000. For the first time, the Internet in 2000 was
widely used as a campaign medium by all major candidates. While
there were differences in the way each candidate used the Internet,
there was a general sense that this medium was vital at best, and at
worst, too important to ignore. Table 3 shows site comparison statistics between the four major candidates.

As can be seen in Table 3, there were slight differences in
how each candidate used the Internet, but the use was thorough.
Each candidate used the web as a tool to reach supporters, and did
so more effectively than presidential candidates in 1996. In addition,
each of the candidates seemed to excel in different areas (Lewicki &
Ziaukas, 2000). Al Gore was credited with developing "warrior tools"

Table 3

Color scheme	Gore		Bush		Nader		Buchanan	
	7/4/00	11/7/00	7/4/00	11/7/00	7/4/00	11/7/00	7/4/00	11/7/00
	blue, white	red, white, blue, gold	red, white, blue	black, gold, white	blue, white, green, red	green and white	red, white, blue	red, white, blue, brown
Schedule	X	X	X	X	X		X	X
Issues	X	X	X	X	X	X	X	X
Search	X	X	X	X	X	X	X	X
Biography	X	X	X	X	X	X	X	X
Speeches	X	X	X	X	X	X	X	X
Press releases/News	X	X	X	X	X	X	X	X
Contributions	X	X	X	X	X	X	X	X
Volunteer	X	X	X	X	X	X	X	X
Contact/E-mail		X	X	X		X	X	X
E-mail list	X	X	X	X	X	X	X	X
Register to vote				X		X		
In Spanish	X	X	X	X		X		
List of contributors		X	X	X				
Kids' page	X	X	X	X				
Countdown clock	X		X					
Audio/Video of candidate	X	X	X	X		X		X
Petition					X		X	
Links page					X			

190

Feature							
Site map				X			
Q & A page	X				X		X
Merchandise (mail-order form)	X	X			X	X	X
Tax calculator			X				
Webcam	X				X		
Photo gallery	X				X		
Family resources	X						
Mobile option	X						
Spamming	X				X		X
Personalized page	X				X		
Downloadable files for campaigners	X				X		
Trivia	X				X		

This table originally appeared in the paper "The Digital Tea Leaves of Election 2000: The Internet and the Future of Presidential Politics" by Don Lewicki and Tim Ziaukas, First Monday, volume 5, number 12 (December 2000), at http://firstmonday.org/issues/issue5_12/lewicki/index.html. Copyright 2000, Don Lewicki, Tim Ziaukas, and First Monday. Reprinted with the kind permission of the authors and First Monday.

in so far as he used the campaign website as a virtual headquarters to connect avid supporters with one another. Similarly, each candidate showed strengths in different areas:

- Al Gore—warrior tools (the ability to connect avid supporters with one another for political action).
- Ralph Nader—clean and efficient design that downloads quickly and emphasizes key information without being too text heavy.
- Pat Buchanan—innovative presentation of candidate information allowing the user an ease of navigation that a series of pages, for instance, does not.
- George W. Bush—well written, regularly delivered e-mail, especially at critical moments in the campaign.

Presidential candidates in 2000, if only learning from Mc-Cain's primary race earlier, took their Internet campaigning seriously. There was, however, obvious room for improvement in the development of future campaign strategy. These successes only provided evidence of the effectiveness of the medium. The challenge that lies ahead of candidates in the future is attempting to synthesize the strengths of these aforementioned websites. This will likely become a defining characteristic between more successful and less successful candidates in the future.

The success of political campaigns' use of the Internet in 2000 was impressive, though not yet revolutionary, as some had predicted. These races were expected to be substantially impacted by Internet strategy, but this was not necessarily so. While Internet usage became more of a central issue than at any time before, it did not appear to be a deciding factor in any candidate's win or loss. However, one of the big lessons learned from the 2000 races was that the Internet mattered, and that campaigns stand to benefit from its effective use. Moreover, they could be hurt by its misuse or neglect.

The 2002 election cycle exhibited signs that the Internet was a usable and increasingly indispensable part of a candidate's media and organizational strategy. First, most campaign sites in 2002 had reached a level of sophistication not seen up until that point. Not only were site designs more savvy, but e-mail was used more effectively to target voters and to mobilize support. E-mail lists had become an important database. Second, Internet-based, password protected management tools for staff were more widely used. They not only allowed staffers to help manage sites, but also to manage data gathered through it. Third, online donations were becoming cheaper to process and their ability to get the money in the bank quickly has become more of an asset. The rapid availability of funds is critical and much less of a problem when a campaign does not have to wait for a check to clear before putting donations to use. This has encouraged more creative fundraising: online auctions, selling campaign merchandise in online stores, organizing online fundraising events, etc. There have also been efforts to seek out online money in more creative ways; not just letting them come to you, but finding potential donators online and soliciting their participation. Fourth, campaigns were realizing that websites are more than info-centers and donation portals. They are centers for coordination. The campaign of 2002 saw more volunteer efforts being assigned and managed via e-mail over long distances at low cost (Jalonick, 2002).

What all this amounts to is a change in campaigning where web strategists are being invited to high level strategy meetings more now than in past elections; the website question is now not *if* but *how*. While the Internet has not been proven to be a deciding factor in a national election, there seems to be near universal agreement among candidates that it is important and must be an element in a successful campaign effort. This does not, however, mean that Internet strategists are now playing a key role. There are many failures that they still see occurring.

First, although it's more cost-effective than radio and television, its value is overlooked. Given that money is such a precious commodity, there is less than expected importance given to the campaign website. Second, for all the discussion of online fundraising, soliciting donations via the Internet is often a weak link in campaign websites. The success of Senator John McCain in the 1999 Republican primary is a task few have been able to replicate. On average, about 1% of all visitors to sites donate money. That percentage needs to be raised and serious effort needs to be spent in order for this element to reach its potential. A third problem involves budgetary allocation. Webspace, etcetera, is generally not a very high budget priority. Many believe cheap sites can actually hurt a campaign. Internet strategists advocate the hiring of professional designers over amateur volunteers and suggest the allocation of 10-15% of budget for Internet strategy, not the 1-5% that is typically seen. Internet strategists suggest online efforts should be an integral part of communication and media budget, but admit it tends to be the first thing cut when money gets tight. Fourth, campaigns have not integrated the Internet well into their overall media strategy. They still

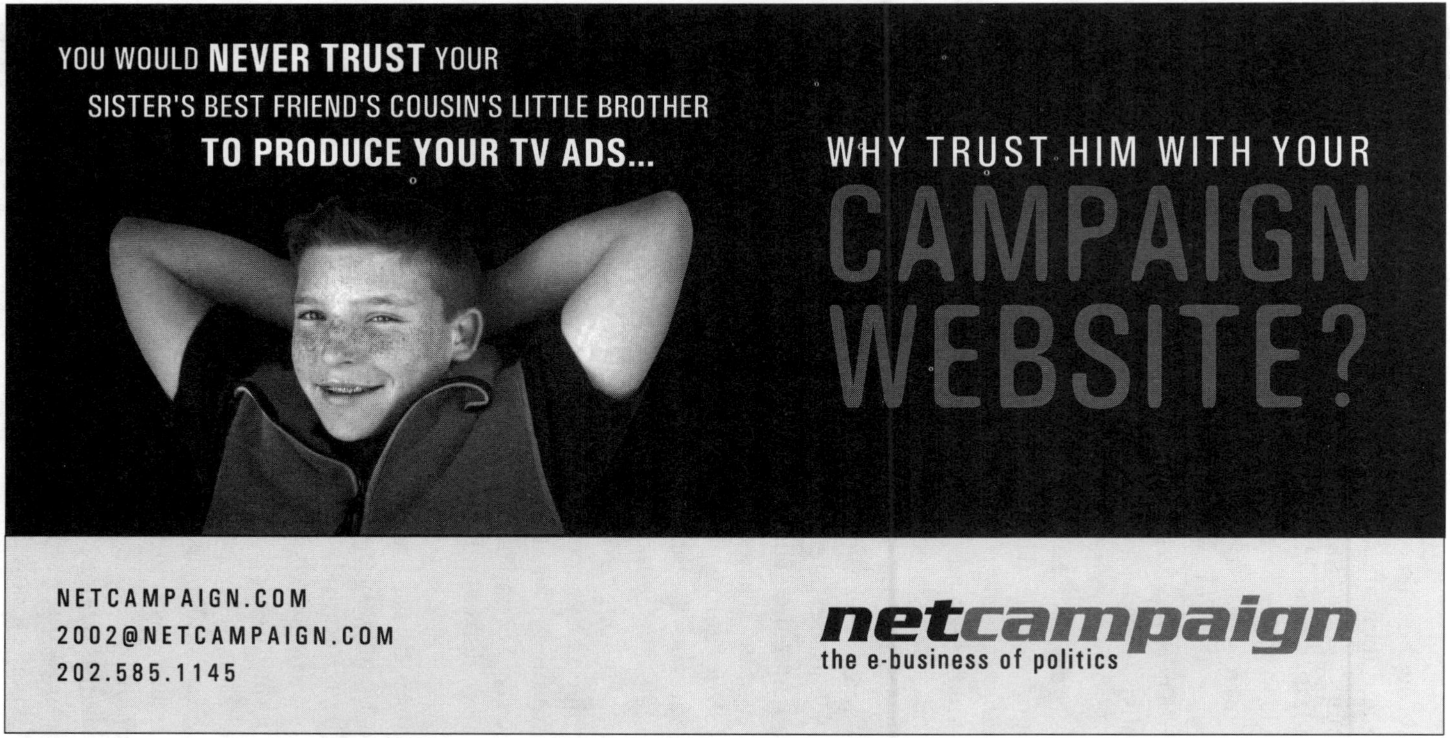

Reprinted by permission of www.netcampaign.com.

see it as a separate entity—a distant cousin to the television and radio—rather than a mass medium in and of itself.

Yes, Internet campaigning has moved from digital yard signs to virtual headquarters in a very short period of time, but its impact has yet to be fully understood.

With the discussion so far describing campaigns' use of new technology over time and the general successes and failures seen within that evolution, one vital topic remains to be examined more thoroughly. Does the use of the Internet have an impact on elections? If so, how can this impact best be described? Is it large or small, absolute or conditional? Does the use of the Internet by candidates increase voter turnout on election day? Does it mobilize or persuade voters? This is the topic of the next section of this chapter.

Impact on Elections

Are Campaigns Important?

The discussion of whether or not Internet campaigning has an appreciable impact on elections presupposes the fact that campaigns do matter. The way a campaign is run will affect the success or failure of a candidate regardless of incumbency or the sheer amount of money spent. While incumbency and money are significant predictors in determining electoral success, there is something to be said for strategy. There is something to be said for the old fashioned idea of connecting with voters and garnering support through thorough and meticulous campaign efforts.

The importance of campaign strategy becomes more pronounced when party identification is in decline. Over the past decades, more Americans have identified themselves as independent voters rather than declaring a loyalty to one or the other major parties. With fewer Americans identifying themselves as being a Republican or Democrat, campaigning becomes a more important conduit for voter-candidate interaction; candidate qualities rise in importance and their party identification somewhat decreases in importance.

This is similar to shopping for an item when brand names are removed. When a shopper looks for new tennis shoes without the aid of a Nike, Reebok, or Converse label, he or she is more likely to look at the stitching, appearance, sole strength, and comfort across items (as well price). When the value of party labels declines for voters, campaigns provide an important source for cues, giving shoppers information on leadership qualities, character strength, political experience and issue stances.

Therefore, the way a campaign is run does matter. While we do not know what exactly wins campaigns, a well run campaign is vital to a candidate's success. Many assumed that the 2000 presidential bid by democrat and Vice President Al Gore would be successful, particularly at a time when the economy was good and when the federal government was running a budget surplus. His failure to win the presidency was explained by some, in part, as the result of a poor campaign (and the "curse" of the electoral college). The 2002 governor and senate races in Georgia are other examples of predicted winners losing, even when vastly outspending their opponents. In these races hot-button topics such as the design of the state flag and school funding were big campaign issues that were successfully addressed by quality challengers with good campaign tactics.

The importance of campaigns is a point that has to be made. For if it is not, campaign strategy will be relegated to an electoral eccentricity rather than a core element to the democratic process. If incumbency is the only key to reelection, we degrade the electoral process. If money is the only key, we risk devolving into a plutocracy. Somewhere in the middle, campaigns play a role, a large role.

From this point, it is necessary to address the potential impact of digital communication on campaign strategy. As we know, the number of Americans online has been steadily increasing for most of the 1990s. In the elections of 1996, 1998, 2000 and 2002, the number of voters who went online for election news progressed from 4%, 6%, 18%, 13%, respectively (The Pew Research Center for the People and the Press [PRCPP], 2003). There has been a steady increase in this percentage in each consecutive election cycle since 1996. The 2000 figures, of course, show a spike since that was a presidential election year. This feature also somewhat mimics the spike in voter turnout in presidential election years as well. As an overall trend, these figures suggest that more and more people look to the Internet during elections to find out about candidates. Additionally, the online citizen, that is, the Internet user that gets general political news and information online, grew from 33 million to 46 million between the summer of 2000 and November of 2002, which is a 39% increase (IPDI, 2003). Citizens are online and looking for political information in larger numbers than in the past.

Campaigns obviously seek out voters. There is now evidence that a large number of them are online and can be reached through that medium. The million dollar question for those researching campaigns and the Internet is to determine how this interaction can best take place and what impact it has on elections. The first half of this chapter describes what the interaction has looked like over the majority of the past decade. The second half is concerned with the impact. Does the Internet impact a candidate's ability to win or lose an election as some say that the television does today? Does the Internet help or hurt a candidate in a more marginal way? Does it have any effect at all? These types of questions will be addressed in the rest of this chapter.

Impacting Who Wins: For Better and for Worse

There is definitely a mixed bag of evidence regarding the impact of Internet strategy on elections. Initial assessments of this impact were, in fact, quite bleak. In 1996 there was some sense, and accurately so, that major candidates felt obliged to use the "new" technology and that there was very little evidence to support the claim that campaign websites affected the outcome of elections (Margolis, et al., 1997). There were few voters online and resources were best spent elsewhere. As time progressed and as more Americans obtained Internet access, there were those, on one hand, like Dick Morris in *Vote.com* claiming that a "revolution" was underway and others like Michael Margolis and David Resnick in *Politics as Usual* claiming the opposite: that nothing unusual was occurring at the macro level. There would be no great change.

Indeed the evidence supporting the positive claim is anecdotal and sparse, and at times, has the flavor of late-1960s science fiction enthusiasts, who were so taken with the potential of the space program that some predicted lunar colonies and the like, prematurely. In both cases, their statements generally focused on the potential of the development in question, be it the Internet on politics or the space program on human settlements. In this sense, their claims were not false. The potential was certainly there, but the complete fulfillment of that potential was not.

For Internet enthusiasts, in particular, the evidence revealing the development of this potential has been slow to show itself. There has been no revolution seen. However, those individuals claiming a broad impact have not been completely let down. The Internet has become more widely used by candidates and has shown some potential in being an effective element in a campaign's media strategy. One of the first substantial pieces of evidence in this regard occurred in the 1998 race for governor in Minnesota.

©AFP/Corbis.

In that race, former professional wrestler and Reform Party candidate Jesse "the body," and later "the mind," Ventura beat Republican Norm Coleman and Democrat Hubert H. Humphrey III by 3 percentage points in the Minnesota governor's race. Ventura's campaign, which spent only $500,000 and employed only one paid staff member, won the election against opponents who collectively had an arsenal of $15 million (Raney, 1998). Many attribute the effectiveness of his campaign to the Internet and claim that this was the first major election in which the Internet made a difference.

This claim, however, was very cautiously applied by Phil Madsen, the webmaster for the Ventura campaign. Following the election he is quoted as saying, "The Internet did not win the election for us, but we could not have won without the Internet" (Kamarck, 2002, p. 100). His caution was warranted. The Internet's exact role was very difficult to measure. What is known is that Ventura's use of the campaign website and e-mail as a coordinating tool was very impressive. Lacking the resources and infrastructure of a major party candidate, Ventura's campaign was able to employ the

Internet as a way to mobilize and coordinate volunteer efforts. One such effort, for instance, involved the campaign's final 72 hour pre-vote tour of the state, which included a Friday night bar-hopping tour in key areas. This entire 72 hour event was coordinated through a 3,000 name e-mail list maintained by Madsen. Through this list, meetings were established and plans were made for how to best execute the tour, including warnings on overindulgence during the proceedings on that Friday night (Kamarck, 2002). In a sense, Ventura used the website as the campaign headquarters and coordinated efforts from that "locale." In fact, for a great deal of the campaign, Ventura's website appeared to fulfill the role of a surrogate headquarters where mobilization and coordination could occur in the absence of a traditional brick and mortar headquarters building.[3]

All of this was in direct opposition to the strategy employed by the major party candidates whose campaigns were more traditional in nature (Kamarck, 2002). In terms of web use alone, it was also very different from Coleman, in particular, who maintained a much less impressive website.[4] There was a qualitative difference in the types of campaigning seen between the Ventura campaign and that of the two major party candidates.

The Minnesota gubernatorial race in 1998 proved to be an eye opener for many analysts who watched the race from afar. Ventura's win was a tremendous upset, if not an all-out coup for traditional two-party politics in America. It set a precedent, whereby people began to take the Internet more seriously. The Internet began to be seen as a campaign component that had the ability to actually have an effect in elections. The proliferation of quality campaign sites by the 2000 elections certainly suggests that this was the case.

However, it may be premature to credit Ventura's victory entirely to his campaign's use of the Internet. There were other variables in the Ventura candidacy that could have had a major impact. First, Ventura's notoriety before the campaign as a professional wrestler and entertainment personality certainly played a role, particularly in getting out the young voters, who are notoriously apathetic

---

[3]The Ventura campaign did acquire a "brick and mortar" office space late in the campaign which they used more often for a storage facility for campaign paraphernalia than a strategy and planning outpost. See: http://www.jesseventura.org/Internet/netnotes.htm.

[4]It should be noted that Ventura's website was not particularly savvy and that the campaign website was the webmaster's first Internet creation. See: http://www.jesseventura.org/Internet/netnotes.htm.

when it comes to voting. And second, Minnesota's same-day registration laws likely added to his success by allowing late-comers and non-voters, who may have been purged from the rolls, to vote in the final days of the campaign.

These facts, of course, do not negate the Internet's effect on these election results, but it does force one to qualify those effects. Does the Internet only help ex-professional wrestlers who are poorly funded in states with same-day registration laws? There is evidence that suggests that this is not the case. Other, more traditional, races have been impacted by effective Internet campaign strategies as well. There is some proof that a well run candidate website may actually make a difference in the outcome of an election of major party candidates, too.

In 1996, Internet use by Senator John Kerry (D-MA) may have been effective in helping him in a close race. In that race, it was very effective in the mobilizing volunteers in the late stages of the game (Kamarck, 1999). In 1997 the same case can be made for the gubernatorial race of Christie Todd Whitman in New Jersey, who was the first female ever to hold that position (Whitman later went on to head the Environmental Protection Agency under the George W. Bush administration from 01/31/01 to 06/27/03). These candidates were not fringe candidates, nor third party candidates. They were fairly established politicians with significant ties to the establishment who used the Internet for electoral gain.

Not all candidates who employ the web use it successfully. The Internet, alone, has been the source of trouble for quite a few candidates and has caused some harm to their campaign, if only in the form of bad press. In 1998, Steve Langford, gubernatorial candidate for Georgia, attempted to solicit voters over the Internet using a mass e-mail program to help develop targeted mailing lists. The "target" audience responded angrily to the unwanted e-mail and prompted Langford to publicly apologize and to promise to not use the tactic again (Ibid.). This backlash from the use of mass e-mail was also seen in the elections of 2002 in Elizabeth Dole's campaign for the Senate in North Carolina as well as in Bill Jones' campaign in the Republican primary for the California gubernatorial race (Dunham, 2002).

Clearly, Internet use must be judicious and well directed. When this is the case, it can be a very effective campaign tool and can strengthen the overall media strategy that a candidate wishes to pursue. It is far too early in the medium's development to make any very broad statements about its influence on campaigning or elections. Research has, however, provided some initial findings that will help build a body of evidence towards this end. Is there potential? Definitely. Has it completely fulfilled that potential? No. While there has been no revolution, there have been serious changes in attitudes involving the Internet's use in campaigns, and a growing body of evidence supporting its effectiveness.

General Conclusions about Internet Use in Campaigns

It is too early to tell if the growth and development of this new medium will mimic that of television decades ago. What we do know is that the Internet has not yet revolutionized campaigning. The existence of a website and the proper use of digital communications may help a candidate win an election, but its exclusive use will not result in victory. In that sense, Internet campaigning is developing into simply another weapon in the campaign arsenal. However, we do not know at this point whether or not it will become a major or minor weapon.

No one actually knows what makes a person win an election. Campaign consultants claim to be able to ascertain what those things are, but no one knows for sure. We tend to think it involves money, but not always. We like to think it involves issues, but not always. One thing that we do know is that voters vote for who they know and who they like. The Internet can certainly affect that.

Based on the evidence presented in this chapter, there are a number of things that can be said about this topic with relative confidence. First, the Internet appears to be a new part of the campaign arsenal but has not been completely tested or fully utilized. Testing and development on this area is slow, partly because the risks are so high. There is no reward for second place in the American electoral system, so new strategies are applied slowly and cautiously until a positive return can be measured and assessed.

Second, candidate websites rarely convert non-supporters. Evidence from the 2000 campaign season indicates that these sites primarily reinforce the support that one may have toward a candidate. The voter, for instance, who intends to vote for candidate "A", will not be persuaded to vote for candidate "B" by viewing B's website. What is much more likely to occur is that the voter in mind will view their favorite candidate's site and have their opinions reinforced by that experience (Center for Information Technology and Society, 2002). This is likely the result of two things: one, the people who visit a candidate site are usually politically knowledgeable and already prefer the candidate in question; and two, candidate websites usually do not attempt to make voters out of non-voters and do not cater to the undecided voter. The evidence we have seen bears this out. Online fundraising, for instance, activates supporters; it does not create or convert them.

Third, candidates who are most likely to be helped by the Internet are those who lack a formal, well established infrastructure (Kamarck, 1999). The Internet is not a total replacement for "forces on the ground", but it does supplement, if not provide some substitute for a lack in party organization. Internet use during campaigns allows for certain "anti-establishment" candidates to succeed at higher rates. The Ventura and McCain campaigns are evidence of this. In both cases the creative use of the Internet allowed under-funded and somewhat underdog candidates to mount much more effective challenges to more well-funded candidates with more well-developed campaign infrastructures (Kamarck, 2002). In these instances, the Internet provides an advantage in the race to win, but has not been proven to win the race. No candidate is foolish enough to wage a campaign from their home computer through a 100% Internet-based effort.

Fourth, the Internet does not replace traditional campaign tactics. What it does is facilitate the coordination of those tactics. Issues are important. Therefore, the Internet will not turn a political fanatic into a winner. Large numbers of voters will not vote for a neo-Nazi candidate simply because they have been contacted via e-mail by that party. A party website will not replace the need for quality challengers who have well thought out campaign strategies and popular political messages. It will affect the game, not the players.

Fifth, the Internet can make a difference with regard to candidate coverage and issues. It can supplement a lack in coverage or a failure in coverage and, in a sense, make up for deficiencies in the mass media for the voter (Elberse, Hale, & Dutton, 2000). A well developed website can pick up where traditional media drops off, giving the campaign complete control over the message and assisting the voter in the process. The Internet allows voters a chance to have access to detailed information about issues that televised debates or advertisements might fail to give. In an age of attack ads and races to the middle, a well done web site can give a voter a chance to read a well written statement of intent on a variety of issues directly from the candidate. It can provide an immediate media resource whose content is likely to differ from that of radio, television and newsprint.

In conclusion, what has been seen in the area of the Internet and elections is growth: growth in the number of people seeking election news online and a growth in the number of political candidates using the medium as a campaign tool. Each subsequent national and large state election since 1996 has seen a general growth in the number of candidates using the web. Initially characterized for most of the 1990s by timid experimentation, its use in the elections of 2000 and 2002 was the most thorough to date. The 2004 election cycle has proven that this is continuing to be the case, particularly in dealing with the new fundraising limits in recent campaign finance legislation.

With its growth, we have seen increasing evidence of its importance in elections as a mobilizing, administrative and fundraising tool. Most importantly, we have also seen Internet use by candidates impact a number of national and state races for better and for worse. Clearly, this tool is of some importance.

However, Internet use in campaigns currently runs the risk of failing in its most appealing potential. Rather than engaging and impacting non-voters and undecided voters, the Internet has shown the tendency to activate those who are in least need of activation: those who are already engaged. Unless new uses and users are found, online campaigning risks preaching to the converted. Therefore, new traffic must be directed to websites for the purpose of evaluating candidates and learning about issue stances across the board. The fact that Internet users self-select their material is on one hand empowering, and on the other, a potential impediment to this technology having any transformative electoral effect.

The Media

Introduction

The Absence of Media Studies and the Renewal of Interest

If one considers all the sub-fields in American politics as a large extended family, media studies in American politics has been a distant cousin. Although the media has been the subject of substantial scholarship, compared to the study of the presidency, Congress, or voting behavior, for instance, it is an underdeveloped area of study. It is only in the last century that the media has received more thorough analysis. Even so, political scientists have been slow to grasp the issues of media influence on American politics. In fact, the widely used Ogg and Ray (1951) *Introduction to American Government* text in the 1950s failed to even have a chapter devoted to the topic. Why has this topic not received the same attention as other topics in Political Science?

This may be partly attributable to two factors. First, media studies fall under the purview of other disciplines, specifically, the fields of communication and psychology. Political Science simply has no established track record in studying how messages are sent and received from party to party. The cognitive processes involved and the nuances of communication between groups and individuals are not traditional concerns of political scientists. Second, because media were not always as prevalent as they are today, there was simply no significant need seen within the discipline to study these things. Radio, television, and digital communication mediums are fairly recent developments. Obviously, there was no need to study something that was not there. However, this does not mean that the media did not exist before the 20th century.

The printing press has existed for most of what we refer to as the modern political era, and the impact of the written word on the opinions of citizens has been assumed for some time. The efforts of James Madison, John Jay, and Alexander Hamilton in writing the Federalist Papers are a testament to this fact. The media's unavoidable presence in our 21st century society has caused a renewed interest in determining its role in American politics. This is the purpose of this chapter.[1]

The Importance of the Media in a Democracy

James Madison wrote in a letter to W. T. Barry that, "A popular government, without popular information or the means of acquiring it, is but a prologue to a farce or a tragedy, or perhaps both" (p. 103). This statement succinctly defines the need democracies have for a reliable media. Madison's underlying assumption is that information is of vital importance to a democratic society. The quality of information that the public receives will partly determine the quality of that public's discourse. Put more simply, in a government by the people, the people's input must be well informed.

The quality of public debate in a democracy results from two things. First, it is the result of *the information brought to the public marketplace.* That information must be detailed and accurate. Second, it also results from *the citizens' ability to use that information effectively* to make sense of the world around them and to comment on it for their benefit (Delli Carpini & Keeter, 1996).

Admittedly, we are assuming that the average citizen can and does willingly engage in thoughtful deliberation. There are differing opinions on this issue. One espouses a guardian theory of citizenship. This theory proposes that the people are not capable of prudent decision-making and are prone to rash, moody judgments on issues (Streich, 2000). In this case, the government exists to protect citizens from their own folly. An alternative to this theory is the participatory theory of citizenship. This Jeffersonian idea suggests that

---

[1]The placement of this chapter at the end of the book is particularly curious, considering this text's thesis is that digital communication technology is slowly impacting the way democracy in America works. In a way, it is like leaving the chapter on the automobile until the very end in a book describing the impact of the automobile on American society. Its placement, therefore, is not to undermine its importance.

citizens are very capable of engaging in quality debate and can be reasonably trusted in their ability to self govern. When provided with accurate information, citizens make sense of their world and decide on issues accordingly (Ibid.).

In either instance, the citizens deserve quality political information, even though their predicted ability to deal with it differs. The media provides the raw data that we use to form opinions on the political environment. Political information and the means to acquire it are vital for democratic forms of government. It is the responsibility of institutions in democratic systems to pursue this through education (Delli Carpini & Keeter, 1996). The media is the main institution charged with this responsibility.

The Importance of Media Studies

Interest in media studies has been driven by theoretical concerns over the strength of democracy in America and fears of its deterioration. The need to study the political effects of the mass media is justified substantially by this approach. A system of government that relies on the regular input of its citizens is likely to benefit more thoroughly from an informed polity. Therefore, the process by which this polity acquires and processes information is of primary interest.

Political and technological developments in the past fifty years have made the need to understand media effects more urgent. First, it is generally agreed that modern politics is essentially carried out not through the political party but through the mass media. The rise in the use of primaries, the diminishment of party strength, and the decline of party identification among voters have left a vacuum that has been filled by the news media (Arterton, 1984; Asher, 1984; Davis, 1992; Joslyn, 1984; Orren & Polsby, 1987; Wattenberg, 1994). Politicians no longer rely on the party for grassroots support and door-to-door vote gathering, as they did in the past. The media have provided a way for political aspirants to effectively bypass the party machinery and communicate their message directly to the voter. Coupled with the rise in popularity of the primary system, the media has become an important conduit between elected officials and citizens. Joining the ranks of interest groups and political parties, the press has become a key link in modern democracies (Davis, 1992), if not a political institution itself (Cook, 1998). Modern politics is therefore not party politics but media politics.

Second, most of what people know about the political world does not come through firsthand experience (Lang & Lang, 1981).

That news is largely filtered through second- and third-hand sources, which are largely comprised of some form of mass media (Ibid.). The ability of an individual to experience, firsthand, all the information needed to be sufficiently politically aware is an impossible task. The fact that people rely on secondary sources for their political information is very much a source of concern for political scientists and serves as the basis for political studies on media effects. The mass media's ability to "regularly and rapidly present politically crucial information to huge audiences" (Graber, 1997, p. 28) is an important function, particularly since the media are not government sponsored, nor are they run for the good of society (Schudson, 1995). Media outlets are private "active agents of transmission," which are run for profit and decide what information will or will not be made available to the general populous (Graber, 1989, p. 29).

Finally, the presence of the media in the daily life of the average citizen has grown to such an extent that some argue the media have actually become a powerful socializing element within society (Graber, 1997; Kraus & Davis, 1976). Their presence is strong and widespread. By the 1970s, for instance, ninety-five percent of America's sixty million homes had a television, which was watched on the average of six hours a day (Small, 1974). This is an impressive development considering that television itself did not even exist thirty years earlier. With regard to televised news in particular, the advent of cable television and the invention of videotape allowed news companies to spread political information more cheaply, quickly, and thoroughly than ever before (Brown, Brown, & Rivers, 1978). On average, fifty million people today watch one of the three major network news broadcasts on any given evening (Ansolabehere, Behr, & Iyengar, 1993). Of those that rely on only one media source, television is the medium of choice (Ibid.). The learning of political values and sociopolitical norms is no longer charged to parents and teachers exclusively. The media has taken on a major role in this process as well.

Given the media's important role in modern politics, research has been somewhat slow to accurately assess the nature of this influence. Unfortunately, much of the study in media effects has actually been marked by a failure to accurately describe this process. Only in the past few decades have studies generated somewhat consistent results on the nature of these effects.

The following sections of this chapter will break down the discussion of the media into two separate areas. First, we will discuss the traditional media. While we are primarily concerned with the new media, it is important that we first assess what we know about the old. Specifically, how has media developed in America over time? And what impacts has it been proven to have? Second, we will take what we know about the old media and assess what changes may be expected with the development of newer media.

Traditional Media

What Do We Know about the Traditional Media?

Our concern with traditional media is twofold. First, how has media developed in America over time? Specifically, how has the number of media outlets changed over time? How did America go from having one medium in 1900 to multiple mediums within the next 100 years? Second, given that proliferation, what impact has the media been shown to have in society? Is it a strong persuasive force, or is it a fairly weak and benign element? This second section will deal with the topic of media effects.

History of Media Development in America

Americans' access to political information was limited until fairly recently. During the first 100 years of America's history, there was no television, Internet, or instant messaging. For that reason political news spread slowly. Significant events (such as the end of The War of 1812) took some time to reach people in America, including the troops fighting the war. During this early period of American history, printed paper (especially newsprint) was the primary medium for disseminating information to the masses.

In the 1830s, the business of putting out a newspaper changed substantially. The development of the steam-driven printing press drastically diminished printing costs, making newspapers much more affordable (Grossman, 1995). "Penny presses" made the newspaper less an organ of a political party and more an independent news source whose content went beyond reporting basic political matters. Independent newspaper owners subsequently extended their coverage of political events to include social events and local affairs.

By the 1840s, the use of wire telegraphs also impacted the newspaper business in America by allowing news to be sent to different cities immediately. While facilitating the flow of information from paper to paper, the telegraph also shaped the style of news reporting. Wire stories were arduously tapped out in Morse code, which was time consuming and exceedingly tedious; as a result, wired stories were kept simple, without the flair or colloquial styling usually drafted into stories. This not only meant that news transmittal was becoming quicker, but the news itself was becoming more standardized in terms of format (Ibid.).

In the 1920s, the radio began exerting an influence on American society. In 1925 10% of all American families owned radios; by 1935, 66% of American families owned them (Davis, 1999). This is particularly striking given the impact of the Great Depression during that time. More significantly, the radio was a new medium of information transferal. Unlike the newspaper, it required no level of literacy to assimilate its content. It was a medium that relied on one's ability to hear, not read.

Television proved to be a new medium in its own right. In the 1940s, television blended the audio elements of the radio with the visual elements of the newspaper. As previously mentioned, the popularity of television grew at an impressive rate. By the 1970s, 95% of American homes owned at least one television set.

The introduction of the coaxial cable and satellite communication technology ushered in a tremendous change in the way television was used by media corporations. In the mid-70s, for instance, Home Box Office (HBO) gambled on cable television's ability to offer a wider selection of viewing options. HBO offered second-run movies to viewers for a fee. In the age of free network television, asking consumers to pay for something on television was tremendously adventurous, particularly when they could get network programming for free. The success of HBO, and the cable industry in general, opened a Pandora's box of niche programming on a national basis. Channels now exist for men (Spike TV), women (Lifetime Network), children (Nickelodeon), history buffs (The History Channel), music fans (MTV), political junkies (C-Span, CNN, Fox News Channel), and so on. Cable television succeeded so tremendously, today approximately 90% of American homes subscribe to it, compared to only 11% in the early 70s (Ibid.).

What has been seen in this evolution of the media in America is the rapid diversification and fragmentation of media outlets over a very short period of time. The variety and volume of information that we can now receive is unprecedented. However, all the media mentioned have one thing in common: they tend to be elite-controlled, and they all employ a one-way flow of communication from sender to receiver (Selnow, 1998).

Elite-controlled media are radio stations, television stations, and newspapers almost exclusively run by large media corporations. In today's media environment, local independent broadcasters are few and far between[2]. But both the independent broadcasters and the elite-controlled media engage in a one-way flow of information. With all of these forms of mass media, information is sent from one source to another without any possibility for feedback. The broadcasting mechanism offers no means of immediately responding to the information through the device from which it was disseminated.

In 1969 the Department of Defense developed a tool called the Arpanet that enabled local computer networks to connect with one another, rather than acting as autonomous, unrelated kiosks (Davis, 1999). The resulting commercial manifestation of that invention is today known as the Internet. Considering that radio and television both integrated previously existing media elements into a new medium, the Internet is the most integrative of all the media (Selnow, 1998). The Internet combines elements of newsprint, radio, and television, and adds interactivity. This new addition establishes a two-way exchange of information that previous formats did not have. With the Internet, the receiver can be an active participant in the flow of information rather than a mere consumer of it.

However, the theories that currently exist on media effects are based on traditional media and do not necessarily assess the interactive nature of newer media. This may make these theories somewhat obsolete, because with newer media we are now talking about interpersonal communication and not just the one-way flow of information from sender to receiver (Ibid.). Another problem with theorizing about new media is that it is simply evolving too fast to allow for any serious research into its persuasive power (Ibid.).

The following section, however, will discuss what we know about the traditional media's impact on the receiver. It lacks research involving new media, but it does provide a sense of what impacts have been seen over time. This will allow for a more informed speculation on the impact of new communication technology in the second half of the chapter.

Media Effects and the Traditional Media

The advent of media studies in politics is an interesting example of how society and subsequently the social sciences were changed by developments in technology. The need for research on how the media influence public opinion was far less an issue when a larger portion of an individual's political knowledge was acquired firsthand or

---

[2]Some have argued that this may limit the variety of opinions and the diversity of information that a citizen receives.

by personal contact. It was not until the growth of the newspaper industry, the invention of radio, and later the invention of television, that media studies developed into a formal field of interest.

The Hypodermic Model

Early work on media effects made broad and inclusive assessments of the media's impact on politics. As television, radio, and motion pictures joined the printed word as a source of political information, initial research hypothesized that these new sources of media would have a "hypodermic" effect by drastically changing opinions on political issues (Lasswell, 1927). Rooted in fears of wartime propaganda, it was thought that political communication through these new and varied sources would have a strong persuasive effect on the receiver.

These new mediums were an extra source of concern for one very important reason: by transmitting political information in such a way as to be heard and viewed as opposed to being only read, these new media outlets greatly expanded the potential size of their audience. There was some concern that this large audience could be easily manipulated by the persuasive use of mass media messages.

The hypodermic hypothesis, however, failed to explain media effects when tested empirically. The persuasion that had been anticipated was found to occur only rarely (Klapper, 1960). People not only failed to be automatically persuaded by new information, but they actually seemed to be quite immune to political persuasion in general. People do not seem to exhibit an unthinking response to events around them (Berkowitz, 1978). An individual's reaction to stimulus is, in part, determined by knowledge held prior to exposure (Ibid.). In other words, in terms of their beliefs, people are not clean slates upon which the media make a mark.

The Minimal Effects Model

Research in the late 1940s supported the theory of minimal effects (Barelson, Lazarsfeld, & McPhee, 1954; Hovland, Lumsdaine, & Sheffield, 1949; Lazarsfeld, Berelson, & Gaudet, 1948). Minimal effects supporters argue that, contrary to previous assumptions, the news media's effect on the public is quite small; mass persuasion through the media very rarely, if ever, occurs. The public may not know a lot about politics, but they do have opinions that are not easily swayed.

Lazarsfeld, Berelson, and Gaudet's work in *The People's Choice* (1948) found that, in general, the voters' minds are not easily manipulated by news. By doing a panel study in Erie County, Ohio, they found that most respondents maintained their vote preference throughout the study with only 5% showing evidence of being completely converted as a result of news coverage. The influx in candidate information over the duration of the campaign failed to result in a significant change in candidate preference over time.

In a similar study, Hovland, Lumsdaine, and Sheffield (1949) determined that exposure to certain propaganda films also failed to affect the general opinions and motivation of the viewers. While their results *did* show a change in the overall information levels held by the viewers, their data confirmed the minimal effects model as well.

With television's growth within the American home, studies in the 1950s and 60s continually confirmed the minimal effect of mass communications on the receiver. Barelson, Lazarsfeld, and McPhee (1954) found that even though candidates and politicians were going before the public more and more through televised media, a persuasive effect was still not found.

Additional post-war studies clarified these findings by discovering that not only was the American public not easily persuaded by media sources, but their pre-existing preferences were often found to be reinforced by such exposure (Katz & Feldman, 1962; Patterson & McClure, 1976; Sears & Chaffee, 1979). Applied strictly to campaigns, media effects have even been found to play a role in activating pre-existing vote preferences (Finkel, 1993). The media's ability to effect mass conversion was simply not found in high numbers.[3]

The Theory of Agenda Setting

Using a pendulum metaphor one can see the development of media studies literature as swaying between two poles. One pole represents the notion that, over the past hundred years, the media has

---

[3]In the face of consistently overwhelming evidence to the contrary, it is important to mention, however, that certain research still anticipated some larger effect. Barelson, Lazarsfeld, and McPhee (1954), for instance, concluded that while the media may not have an overwhelmingly persuasive effect, "mass communication entities play a decisive role in narrowing down, focusing, and defining what elections mean" (p. 251). This phrase is important in that it somewhat foreshadows the direction of media research over the next thirty years and expresses some initial doubts about the counterintuitive results published by those whose research conclusively supported the theory of minimal effects.

developed into a mass propaganda machine with the unique ability to change the way people think about political issues. The other pole represents the notion that people can develop ideas about political events separate from the media's direct influence; in other words, people are subsequently slow to be affected by new media information. More current research on agenda setting has struggled to move away from this tendency to polarize media effects.

In an attempt to more moderately and accurately explain mass media's impact, researchers began to alter their focus (Lemert, 1981; Zaller, 1996; Zucker, 1978). In arguing for an extreme effect in either direction, past media research failed to leave open the possibility of finding mid-range influences.

To use Walter Lippman's (1965) metaphor, the media acts very much like a searchlight. By moving about, it brings various events out of darkness and into the light. Because the average citizen simply cannot experience every political event that occurs, she relies on the media to convey not only the meaning and substance of the event, but the very fact that the event in question has actually occurred.

Media research returned to Lippmann's (1965) original assertion to explore the concept of agenda setting. Referring to Cohen's often cited assessment of media influence, modern media research generally concludes that "the mass media may not be successful much of the time in telling people what to think, but the media are stunningly successful in telling their audience what to think about" (1963, p. 16).[4]

The Theories of Priming and Framing

Recalling the tendency of early research in media effects to polarize the effects of media exposure, agenda setting was largely an attempt to moderate and more clearly define the exact nature of media influ-

---

[4]The agenda-setting research of McCombs and Shaw (1972) helped pioneer the effort of determining if and how the media determines what people actually think about. Using interviews with local residents in their Chapel Hill community, as well as content analyses of local newspaper and network television broadcasts during campaign time, they found an agenda-setting effect. By determining a story's length and position, they found that the mass media can alter the amount of importance a reader or a viewer attaches to a given issue; in a sense, the media set the agenda for the campaign.

ence. Following in this tradition, other theories developed out of the research on agenda-setting to further clarify this role. Bolstered by the data gathered with regard to issue salience, the theories of priming and framing offer two distinct looks at the agenda-setting ability of the media. As outgrowths of the concept of agenda-setting, priming and framing help refine the notion of media effects by introducing a way to understand how the media's ability to highlight certain issues may affect citizen assessments of presidential performance and issue responsibility.

In reassessing the impact of television news on issue salience, Iyengar, Peters, and Kinder (1982) simultaneously argue a "different though equally consequential version of agenda-setting" (p. 849). This different version of agenda-setting was referred to as priming. Priming suggests "that the criteria involved in presidential evaluations may be determined largely by the stories that television news programs choose to cover" (Iyengar, Kinder, Peters, & Krosnick, 1984, p. 779).

Priming is an important aspect of media studies for two reasons. First, people simply do not have the time or the energy to pay attention to all the news that is reported (Iyengar & Kinder, 1986). They will tend to absorb what they can, when they can, based on what information is most accessible (Iyengar, 1990). Secondly, people will tend to follow certain intuitive shortcuts to make sense of the news that they are given (Ibid.). In this regard, whatever issues the press decides to emphasize will be the raw materials people primarily use to assess the president's job performance. Emphasizing a positive foreign affairs issue, for instance, while ignoring a damaging domestic one, will alter the type of items available in assessing presidential job performance. The press's infatuation with presidential news makes this effect even more pronounced.

Further proof of priming was found during the Reagan administration (Krosnick & Kinder, 1990). Using data form the 1986 National Election Study, it was discovered that the "intervention in Central America loomed larger in the public's assessment of President Reagan's performance after the Iran-Contra disclosure than before" (p. 497). The public's evaluation of presidential job approval at that time seemed primed by the media's coverage of the event. This effect was also found with regard to approval ratings of President Bush during the Gulf War (Iyengar & Simon, 1993; Krosnick & Brannon, 1993).

Media's role in priming certain issues has been successfully applied to campaigns as well. Studies of modern and past elections have found strong relationships between media strategies used by candidates and voter preferences (Jacobs & Shapiro, 1994; Mendelsohn, 1996). Mendelsohn's (1996) work on the priming of candidate qualities further supports the theory of priming by showing that candidates indeed engage in priming certain elements within their campaign. Specifically, data suggests that as candidates highlight their own personal qualities more than the party's qualities, voters are more likely to ignore party identification and base their vote on candidate evaluations. It is argued that this effect partially accounts for voter instability during the campaign season.

Priming research, in general, has proven to be particularly fruitful. By refining the scope of media research, priming has greatly aided in the attainment of knowledge about the nebulous process that occurs between the news media and the news consumer. Research in this area has greatly defined the exact nature of agenda setting in mass publics.

The theory of framing "refers to changes in judgment engendered by subtle alterations in the definition of judgment or choice problems" (Iyengar, 1987, p. 816). Framing argues that the way the media present and define an issue affects the way citizens attribute responsibility for that issue (Iyengar & Simon, 1993). The way an issue is framed can also affect the way a citizen sees a political event. In contrast to its sister theory of priming, framing refers to content, while priming refers to volume.

In covering certain issues the news media are likely to affect the way one sees an issue. Specifically, media can structure the presentation of news stories in such a way as to suggest causal relationships within each issue. Iyengar (1987) argues that these causal beliefs are important elements in how people make sense of the political world around them. Apart from simply using partisan preferences and basic processes of information gathering, people naturally apply "issue responsibility" for certain events (Ibid.) The individual's application of that issue responsibility is affected by the media's framing of events.

In other words, news media can alter the way one sees an event by presenting a pre-fabricated frame of reference that biases one's judgment of that event (Iyengar, 1987). In framing stories on hate-group demonstrations, for instance, it was found that the way a demonstration was presented affected the degree of tolerance expressed for that group (Nelson, Clawson, & Oxley, 1997). Using an experimental design with manipulated news stories, Nelson, Clawson, and Oxley argue that an emphasis on free speech as opposed to civil unrest or public order affected the way respondents expressed tolerance for the group's demonstration. The issue was, in a sense, framed to elicit a certain response.

Using a different set of frames, Mendelsohn (1993) suggests that the 1988 Canadian election was presented using the frames of leadership and horse racing, in which the focus is on who is ahead rather than on what the important issues are. In presenting the campaign in these lights, Canadian journalists forced most viewers to struggle in order to grasp issue content; consequently, the media affected the political discourse and overall understanding that viewers had of the campaign. This is a substantial claim in that it makes the assertion that television viewers were led to vote on the basis of leadership and the horse-race characteristic of the campaign (rather than on ideology or issue content) because of the way television news framed its coverage.

In sum, we know a number of things at this point. First, the media's growth in America over the past 100 years has been substantial. There are more mediums through which we can get information than ever before. The Internet is very important in this regard not only because it is a new mass medium, but also because it is the first mass medium that allows for a two-way exchange of information between sender and receiver. The Internet is a hybrid of all the mediums that came before, yet it is substantially different than any of them. Second, due to the growth of media in our society, there has been an increasing interest in its effects on us. Rather than having a strong persuasive impact on us, the media appears to have very little power to convert our opinions. However, while the media may be poor at telling us what to think, it is very good at telling us what to think about.

The first half of this chapter describes the impact of technology on the evolution of the traditional media and its effect on individual citizens. The second half of this chapter addresses the state of the modern media in America, and its impact on democracy in America. In a sense, the first half of this chapter looked at the traditional media and the individual. The second half now looks at new media developments and their predicted impact on groups of citizens (and by extension, democracy in general).

New Media

The Current State of the Media in America

The mass media in America is currently in a state of tremendous change (Davis & Owen, 1998). This change is qualitative and quantitative in nature. It is qualitative because the media has begun to drastically change the types of things it broadcasts. With respect to news reporting, in particular, there has been great change in the way news is reported and the way it is generally presented. The change in the media is also quantitative because there are more channels, radio stations, newspapers, and websites than ever before. Not only are there more communication mediums now, but there is more variety within those mediums than ever before.

Very often we refer to the "new media." We can use this term in two ways. First, we can use it to describe new mediums of communication such as the Internet. This definition refers to new physical devices used in the dissemination of information. Second, we can also use the term "new media" (as it is defined by Davis & Owen, 1998) to indicate forms of mass communication with primarily non-political origins that have acquired political roles. This definition refers to content and programming, not computer networks or satellites, for instance. Examples of these "new" forms of media are talk-radio programs, television news magazines, television talk shows, and so forth. We will tend to focus on the second definition, although both are important to us.

The latter concept is particularly important because new media are fundamentally different from the mainstream press or the traditional news media (Ibid.). They are not established news services or news organizations, even though they often appear to be. They do not primarily exist to deliver political news and they do not subscribe to most journalistic norms. The new media are primarily entertainment driven and delve into politics only when giving time to current issues or politicians will increase their ratings and, in turn, their profits.

This trend began in the 1980s and developed into a full-fledged media movement in the 1990s. As talk shows occasionally adopted political topics, politicians and strategists eventually met them half way. The line between what is entertainment and what is politics began to blur. In the 2003 gubernatorial recall race in California, for instance, Arnold Schwarzenegger announced his entry into the race on The Tonight Show with Jay Leno, rather than holding a traditional press conference to announce that fact. His was only the most recent instance of this blurring of entertainment and politics. In 1995 Ross Perot, as a guest on Larry King Live, declared his intent to run as a third-party candidate in the presidential race the following year; Bill Clinton's appearances on The Arsenio Hall Show and on MTV are now almost legendary. Currently, most television talk shows are regular stops for candidates seeking national of-

©Reuters NewMedia Inc./CORBIS

fice. David Letterman, for instance, has hosted a variety of political figures during campaign season. This was unheard of decades ago.

This trend is not isolated to candidates and television talk shows. Many types of programming exist that blend entertainment and political news. Radio talk shows and television commentary programs regularly blend "soft," non-political news with more important political events. Moreover, there appears to be blending of what is entertainment, what is commentary, and what is news. The new media blurs the lines between these three functions. To make the situation more complex, new technology has allowed for an almost unlimited variety of programs to be nationally aired at all hours of the day.

The change we are seeing in the media is occurring at a very rapid pace and is resulting in a type of media that did not exist in the past. This new media has at its disposal varied methods of delivery, fragmented programming schedules, and an enormous amount of information. The quality and quantity of what is being broadcast is tremendously different from what was seen in the programming schedules of ABC, NBC, or CBS decades earlier.

How Does New Media Differ from Traditional Media?

In more formal terms, there are significant differences in how the new media and the old media operate. First, the new media vary in their approach to news. Since they have no primary interest in being a news outlet, per se, their presentation of the news will be inconsistent (Davis & Owen, 1998). Second, they often will not have the contact with politicians and newsmakers that quality news reporting requires. This negatively impacts the quality of the news they choose to report. Third, they have no sense of public service and are driven primarily to political news because of the viewing/listening audience that it may bring.

All of these cause new media to be quite distinct from the mainstream press. News wire services and professional news organizations are fairly consistent in their presentation of the news. They hire and promote based on quality news reporting that is structured through journalistic norms. They have established relationships with national figures to whom they can rely on for first-hand accounts of political events (Ibid.). In this sense, the old and new media are very different structures and produce very different things.

However, there is a problem. It has been argued that market forces have been blending what we have been calling new media and the old (Ibid.). The reason for this is very simple. Both the new media and the mainstream news media have to deal with the same economic pressures. Both are in an exhaustive race for the maximum viewers during the times at which they broadcast. More than ever, this is causing the entire media system to undergo a metamorphosis driven by the competition that a varied and advanced media environment brings.

While traditional journalism has always been credited with serving a "higher power" (i.e., fulfilling the public's need for accurate political information), it has been unable to avoid the pressures of corporate profit. Once seen as public service, journalism is now "big business," and the news corporations who employ journalists realize that there is money to be made in delivering the news. This puts traditional journalism at odds with ratings and profit. Stressed by these economic concerns, traditional media are moving closer in appearance to what we have disparagingly called the new media; what was originally assessed as two, appears to be now more accurately assessed as one.

The days of only 3 networks providing only 30 minutes of national news each evening are gone. Now there are a multitude of news outlets with news and news-like programming competing for the same audience. This drives each outlet to make their news more appealing than the news being carried by the next outlet.

The Negative Effect of Profit on News Delivery

Technological advancements in news delivery have caused an inadvertent fraying of traditional journalistic norms. This change in delivery is the direct result of private media companies' search for profit and subsequent competition for viewers. Traditionally, competition is good for the consumer because it brings lower prices and higher quality goods. In the media's delivery of political news, however, this benefit does not necessarily occur. In fact, this problem is exacerbated by the wave of media mergers that occurred in the wake of the Telecommunications Act of 1996.

Media outlets compete to provide news programs that audiences will find most appealing. In determining what we like to see, they are driven to prioritize two things in their presentation of the news. First, stories that are chosen for broadcast will likely be the ones that exhibit the most sensational qualities; in other words, stories will be selected partly for their emotional impact, rather than their ultimate political value. Second, stories chosen for broadcast will likely be more negative in quality. Happy stories fail to attract and hold viewers' attention. As a result, negative ones will almost always take precedence (see Figures 1, 2, and 3).

There is almost an unlimited supply of newsworthy stories that merit attention on any given day. There is, however, only a limited amount of time to deliver the news and a limited amount of attention that the news audience is willing to provide. Very often program length or other programming issues simply limit the stories that can effectively be told at that time. Given this restriction, only certain stories are selected for broadcast, and those stories are overwhelmingly sensationalistic and negative. This has serious ramifications for citizens and government.

For citizens, this means that they will get news that is high on fluff, and low on content. The news will be lacking in quality political information, and what quality information is provided will likely be negative and somewhat anti-government. For the government this is also an issue. In 2003, this was vividly seen by the Bush administration's concern over news reporting in Iraq.

After George W. Bush declared an end to major hostilities, major news outlets predominantly reported the daily attacks on U.S. soldiers and the continued failure to apprehend ex-president Saddam Hussein, not to mention the immense cost of the operation. The Bush administration became concerned that the successes of the U.S.

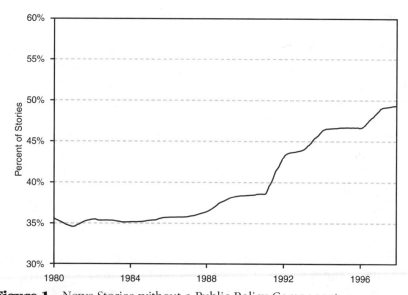

Figure 1 News Stories without a Public Policy Component

From *Doing Well and Doing Good: How Soft News and Critical Journalism are Shrinking the News Audience and Weakening Democracy—And What News Outlets Can Do About It* by Thomas Patterson. Copyright © 2000 by Thomas Patterson. Reprinted by permission of the author.

military in rebuilding the Iraqi infrastructure and in encouraging the further development of its civil society were going unnoticed.

This example is consistent with the media's preference for negative news that is high on emotional impact. The media seemed to realize that viewers are more likely to tune in to a story about a blast that kills 9 American soldiers than to a story on the printing and delivery of new schoolbooks which no longer display the image of the country's ex-dictator. Both stories are newsworthy, but if a news editor must pick one or the other, the choice is quite clear. Some stories simply attract more viewers than others, and programming decisions are often impacted by these concerns.

Taken to the extreme, this notion of profit and the news media results in what Robert McChesney (1999) refers to as hypercommercialism. This quality is driven by the absolute search for profit, resulting in giant media conglomerates placing a commercial rather than a social value on news delivery in America. The media in America once reported news as a public service, even though it was not terribly profitable to do so. When news reporting became more lucrative in the 1970s, the media began to think of the public as consumers, not as a polity (McChesney, 1999). The quality of the news

Figure 2   Sensationalism in News Stories

From *Doing Well and Doing Good: How Soft News and Critical Journalism are Shrinking the News Audience and Weakening Democracy—And What News Outlets Can Do About It* by Thomas Patterson. Copyright © 2000 by Thomas Patterson. Reprinted by permission of the author.

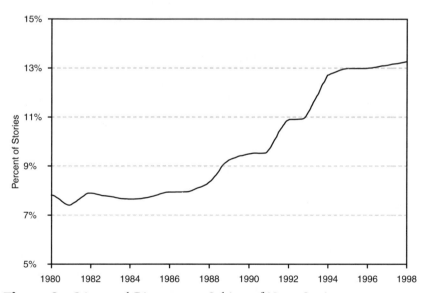

Figure 3   Crime and Disaster as a Subject of News Stories

From *Doing Well and Doing Good: How Soft News and Critical Journalism are Shrinking the News Audience and Weakening Democracy—And What News Outlets Can Do About It* by Thomas Patterson. Copyright © 2000 by Thomas Patterson. Reprinted by permission of the author.

being broadcast after this point in time reflects this change in attitude. Moreover, the news audience has been shrinking. News consumption has drastically fallen over the past 10 years. As news outlets "soften" their coverage and offer a more critical tone in their stories, there is a fear that they will hasten that decline and further weaken democracy (Patterson, 2000).

Are the Modern Media Helping or Hurting Democracy?

While the search for profit by private media corporations is not necessarily a technological issue, it does have its roots in technological development. The growth of technology in America has allowed for a modern media system to develop unlike any before. This has increased the volume of information but not necessarily the quality of it. Is the type of media proliferation seen in America a good or bad thing for democracy? Is it a good or bad thing for its citizens?

There have been a number of troublesome trends in American politics over the past 40 years. Since the 1960s Americans have reported higher levels of cynicism and mistrust toward government. Almost simultaneously, the number of Americans who turn out to vote has declined during this time. Can we blame some of these trends on the media? Some suggest that we can (Hart, 1994; Putnam, 1995). The rise of modern media seems to coincide with the decline in trust, increase in cynicism, and drop in voter turnout in America. In discovering the profitability of news reporting in America it may be possible that the media are having a negative influence on the citizenry. The deteriorating quality of news delivery may be impacting the quality of American democracy—what James Madison originally feared.

However, blame may be unfairly placed on the media. There may be institutional causes to the worrisome trends that have been seen (Bennett, 1998; Norris, 1996; Schudson, 1995). Some claim that we are blaming the messenger for the message, and that the trends just mentioned may actually be the result of government activity. In that sense, the news media are simply reporting activity that is already there. Government scandals such as Watergate, the Iran Contra Affair, and the Lewinsky scandal may have caused public trust in the government to erode. Additionally, unpopular military conflicts, such as the Vietnam War or possibly the second Iraq conflict, might be blamed as well. Political parties may also be to blame in failing to offer clear stances on political issues and failing to nominate quality candidates whose platforms resonate with voters.

As we saw with media effects earlier in this chapter, the answer is likely found somewhere in the middle. On this point, many agree that both the media and institutions are to be blamed for the problems that we face (Davis & Owen, 1998; Patterson, 1994; Sabato, 1991; Streich, 2000). Both groups have engaged in activity that has negatively affected the voter. Given that the media are at least partly to blame, what can be done to reverse this trend? How can the media reverse what has been called the spiral of disaffection, in which citizens abandon the news media in frustration only to have the resulting low levels of political information lead to further cynicism and alienation (Pinkleton & Austin, 1998)?

The cycle is likely to be broken only by the media successfully engaging the citizen through quality news reporting (Ibid.). There is a need for people to regain trust in the media's ability to fulfill its role as a socially responsible institution, rather than maintaining their view of the media as a partisan tool or profit machine.

Will the Internet Make Things Better or Worse?

The development of the Internet as a new mass medium causes us to reassess what is known about the media. The Internet employs the best of all other mediums that came before it and introduces a revolutionary new element—interactivity. Will this new medium cause us to change what we know about democracy or media effects? The theme of this section has been concerns about media's impact on democracy. There are those who suggest that the Internet and new digital communications will alleviate these concerns. Our attention will now turn to this topic.

How Will the Internet Affect the Media?

The Internet was originally seen as a tool which would break big media companies' stranglehold on news delivery. Much of this concern over media monopolies is based in the fear that a handful of major media corporations controlling the bulk of national media outlets could limit program diversity and diminish the quality of political discourse.

The Telecommunications Act of 1996 and the FCC Commission's loosening of ownership provisions in June of 2003 changed decades-old media regulations and had the cumulative effect of allowing fewer big media corporations to own more and more media outlets (see Table 1). The growth in the use of the Internet later that

⊜ Table 1

Media Ownership/Corporate Holdings as of October 2003

	AOL Time Warner	Viacom	Disney	General Electric Company	News Corporation	Vivendi Universal
Television	WB	CBS	ABC	NBC	FOX	USA
	HBO	MTV	Disney Channel	CNBC	FX	SciFi
	Cinemax	Nickelodeon	ESPN	MSNBC	Fox News	Universal TV
	CNN	TV Land	Soapnet	Telemundo	Fox Movies Channel	
	TNT	TNN		PAX	SKY	
	TBS	BET		MSG	National Geographic	
	TCM	UPN		Bravo		
	Cartoon Network	VH1				
Publishing	Time Magazine	Simon and Schuster	Hyperion		Harper Collins	Houghton Mifflin
	People				NY Post	Vivendi Universal
	Sports Illustrated				The Times of London	
	TimeLife					

Music	Warner Brothers Records Atlantic Elektra Rhino		Hollywood Records Mammoth Records Buena Vista Records		Festival	Universal Music Group Polygram Geffen Records A&M Island Decca Deutshe Grammaphore Verve Motown MCA
Movies	Warner Brothers HBO New Line Cinema	Paramount Pictures Showtime United International Pictures Famous Players	Walt Disney Pictures Touchtone Miramax		Twentieth Century Fox Fox Searchlight	Universal Studios
Other	AOL	Blockbuster Video CBS Radio Paramount Theme Park	Disney Theme Parks ABC Radio ESPN Radio Mighty Ducks Anaheim Angels	Madison Square Garden Knicks Liberty Rangers	Knicks Liberty Rangers LA Dodgers Staples Center	Universal Studios

Compiled from PBS.org. For a more thorough discussion of media mergers see:
http://www.mediachannel.org, http://www.commoncause.org, and http://www.pbs.org/now/politics/mediaconsol.html

decade and into the new millennium was heralded by many as an unstoppable threat to media monopolies. There were some who predicted that the Internet would become a true people's medium and would facilitate a revival in quality news dissemination and deliberation. This medium would be immune to monopolization by big media giants and would democratize the access to information in America.

While the potential for this occurrence is there, very little evidence supporting this position has been seen. In fact, there may be evidence to the contrary. The Internet may actually be facilitating the globalization of media industries.

The online media environment appears to be mimicking the more traditional media environment (Margolis & Resnick, 2000). Although there are a plethora of potential news sites online, most individuals use less than 10 specific ones (Ibid.). These 10 are coincidentally the same ones that dominate the traditional press. The reason for this is twofold. First, the existing media companies are referenced more frequently online because they already have the expertise to present political information in a way that is attractive and familiar. They have easily adapted the presentation style of their offline operations to operations online. Second, apart from the experience that they have at presenting news, they also have the added advantage of name recognition and credibility that smaller, upstart news sites lack (Ibid.).

It is clear that big media players are successfully adapting to being online. As the 1990s progressed, more and more traditional media companies established a presence online that Internet users willingly visited and supported. This begs the question: Is the Internet sapping the audience of traditional news outlets? There is disagreement on this issue. Some argue that it is inappropriate to think of the Internet as being in competition with more traditional forms of mass media, and some research finds no significant antagonism between online and offline media. One does not appear to threaten the other. In that case, we are not likely to see television or newspaper audiences significantly diminished by the presence of the Internet (Althaus & Tewksbury, 2000; Hughes, 2000). Also, there does not appear to be a strong relationship between the use of online and offline news sources. People do not substitute one medium for the other. In fact, there is evidence that the Internet may actually result in a small boost for newspaper sales (Hughes, 2000).

However, a larger body of evidence suggests the opposite is occurring. These studies show substantial evidence of Internet news sapping the audience of other national outlets (Pew Research Center for the People and the Press, 2000). Currently 33% of Americans go online for news at least once a week. In 1998 this number was 20%. During the same period, regular viewership of network news has fallen from 38% to 30% (Ibid.). Generally speaking, it appears that the more time people spend using the Internet, the less likely they are to use traditional media (Stanford Institute for the Quantitative Study of Society, 2000).

In sum, it is doubtful that the Internet will democratize news dissemination, nor will it break the media monopolies that currently exist (Davis, 1999; McChesney, 1999). With regard to monopolies in particular, we may see the Internet play a supportive role as news media agencies globalize and reach international markets. Media giants are adapting to the Internet and dominating cyberspace as well.

How Will the Internet Affect Journalism?

There are additional concerns that the field of journalism will also be affected by the Internet. Is it possible that the Internet will prompt a revitalization of a profession argued to be in a state of crisis?

The fact that the Internet is becoming a major source of information on government and world events has implications for journalists. News reporters hold a unique position in that they are not only charged with reporting information on events but are also charged with finding that information. News reporters require quality and reliable sources for information. Having a credible source is fundamental to the news reporter.

The Internet provides a challenge in this regard because the data available on the Internet is very difficult to verify. With government sources, such as the Federal Election Commission website, this issue of credibility is not such a problem. But for other types of news, it is. Some have suggested that as a general source of raw facts and figures, the Internet is less valuable than personal contacts and traditional connections (Selnow, 1998). The advantage that the Internet does lend to journalists is that it allows for very good information on follow-up leads and contacts (Ibid.). It also allows for easy retrieval of stored data and information for future reference, allowing reporters an ease in fact checking and referencing that is unprecedented (Ibid.).

A very interesting complication also arises out of the sheer volume of information that digital communications make accessible. Some suggest that the Internet will likely cause journalists to acquire a new role. Rather than simply reporting the who, what, when, and where of an event, reporters are expected to increasingly abandon their role as mere news reporter and evolve more aggressively into the role of news analyst (Wes Pippert in Selnow, 1998) As the volume of available information increases, the need to provide context and meaning also increases. Journalists are uniquely qualified for this task.

How Will the Internet Affect the Audience?

The need for news analysts in the days of information abundance suggests that the media consumers will also be affected by the creation of another mass information medium. There have been a number of studies that have suggested that the change in the media environment will substantially affect the way the consumers of information interact with it. The citizen, after all, is the true focus of this subject area. We study the media because we want to assess its impact on human beings.

The growth of the media seems to be having a substantial impact on citizens. We have already discussed some of the effects the media appear to have with regard to cynicism and mistrust. However, there are additional concerns involving the individual's ability to deal with the volume of information with which he/she is bombarded.

In America, there appears to be an information glut (Shenk, 1997). Twenty-four hour news media, endless political commentaries, and almost limitless numbers of news outlets deliver information on an almost continual basis. Information is no longer a rare commodity but something found in abundance and often taken for granted (Ibid.). Moreover, there is some concern that the volume of information that is now available will make the citizen's job more difficult; more information, after all, should not be confused with more understanding. It is possible that an abundance of information actually yields confusion and hinders understanding, in essence causing the individual to miss the forest for the trees.

The likely result of this trend will be a need for more news commentators, whose job it is to interpret the abundance of information for the average citizen. This potentially results in extended political debate among those who are news savvy for the benefit of those who are not. This may reduce the role of the average citizen to that of a spectator at a game, rather than a participant in it (Streich, 2000). This improperly redefines democratic debate as a spectator sport, which it is not.

Additional concerns involve fragmentation, not only of information but of audience. With so many news programs, the media is able to tailor their programming to fit well-defined subsets of viewers or readers, rather than the audience in general (Selnow, 1998). This will likely cause a severe dispersion of audiences who are exposed to very specific information rather than a wide range of issues and viewpoints.

For instance, it is now possible to watch only conservative news programs on television and arrange your online viewing to focus only on conservative issue stances and news alerts. Since democracies rely on consensus and tolerance, these information flows can potentially diminish the willingness of people to agree by allowing individuals to self-select not only the news, but the interpretation of the news that most fits their worldview.

The luxury to self-select news can result in citizens missing issues or views that fall outside their area of interest (Ibid.). A viewer who is exposed to a variety of news stories with varying topics and views will likely integrate those new issues and revise her opinions, or at least be forced to consider their applicability. Self-selection of the news will result in issues being defined too narrowly (Ibid.). Being exposed only to conservative news outlets, for instance, will result in all issues from that source being presented in a conservative frame that excludes or summarily dismisses other options or viewpoints. Democratic discourse strives for consensus and commonality, not particularism. The Internet may be an antagonist in this regard.

This trend has been described by one author as a "control revolution" (Shapiro, 1999). The Internet allows individualized access to political information to such an extreme, that there is a fear that polarization of public discourse will result. The Internet may facilitate division, not unity. Therefore, democracy, a system that relies on consensus and moderation, may suffer.

Summary

The impact technological developments have had on the media environment is substantial. There has been a quantitative and qualitative change in the media over the past decades. The number of communication mediums has increased which has multiplied the volume of information available for the voter. However, the quality of that information is generally lower than in the past. Media competition and the profitability of news have resulted in programming choices being influenced by sensationalism and negativism. News is delivered on the basis of ratings and sales, not solely on political importance.

The media's social role of informing citizens of public affairs has been deteriorating. While some hypothesize that digital communication technology can reverse this trend, evidence of this is lacking. Media mergers and the monopolistic tendencies of the media market have not been damaged or slowed by the Internet. In fact, media conglomerates appear to be thriving online there as well. The Internet is neither breaking up monopolies nor improving the quality of news delivery on a mass scale.

However, the Internet may affect other things more drastically. First, journalism as a profession will likely be impacted through the use of the Internet as a source of information. Verification of information remains an issue, but the ease of information retrieval, access to contact information, and the referencing capability it provides are extremely beneficial. Moreover, journalists are expected to find their roles expand into that of a political analyst. As the volume of information we have at our disposal increases, there is a growing need for people who can make sense of all this information for the individual.

Second, the media consumer will also be impacted greatly. As previously mentioned, more information does not necessarily yield more understanding. It is possible that the very opposite may occur. An increase in the volume of information available further challenges citizens' ability to make sense of the political world around them. Additionally, through the meticulous self-selection of news sources available through the Internet and the wide variety of programming options available with other mediums, citizens can deal with this abundance by selecting only the types of news programs that they wish to see. This can have the negative effect of narrowing issue exposure and issue analysis to a specific worldview or ideology. Liberals can avoid considering conservative views/interpretations and conservatives can avoid exposure to liberal views/interpretations. In a democratic society based on compromise and consensus, this could present a problem.

In sum, the modern media have poorly administered the application of technology. They have allowed the need for profit to guide their programming and cloud their social duty as an institution in America. The health of our democracy requires quality deliberation supported by a conscientious mass media, who have an interest in delivering worthwhile information from a variety of viewpoints. While technology can assist in this goal, it has yet to be fully utilized for this purpose.

Future of Technology and Government

10

Speculating about the future relationship of technology and government is not overly difficult, yet it is not without frustration. Summarizing the future of technology and government necessitates that we take a brief moment to look back at the theme we tried to develop in the preceding chapters: technology is prevalent in American politics and we need a better understanding of its influences. It also requires a discussion of the promises technology holds for government enterprise. These promises are both real and potential. We'll briefly look at both of them.

When Joe Trippi, manager of Howard Dean's campaign for President, intimated during an interview with C-Span that the Internet had the power to put back into American politics what television sucked out, we were intrigued (C-Span Interview, October 24, 2003). Our attention perked up even more as Mr. Trippi explained how he believed the Internet would empower citizens who had been left behind by the media age of politics. Could the manager of the most potentially transforming presidential campaign of the modern era be right about technology? Can technology put the political cat back in the bag so to speak? We are uncertain about such bold claims. What we are certain of is that technology and government will have interesting times in the near future.

Immediate Future

The most immediate political ramification of technology is opportunity costs associated with incorporating technology into American government and politics. In a larger context, the widespread use of information technology by governments is in its infancy. Like other technological advances that have improved the ability of government to deliver its core mission, there will be debates about how much technology is needed, when it is needed, and where. For example, governments have a fundamental duty to protect their citizens. If a multi-billion dollar weapons system will help with this function, shouldn't the money be invested to purchase it? The answer to this question depends on whom you ask.

The adaptation of technology to government operations is not much different from the weapons system example. As such, we believe that a budding debate about how much technology is appropriate will become a more permanent part of our political discourse. As long as there is scarcity of resources, debates will occur concerning the usefulness of spending on technology. Recent evidence suggests that technology spending at the federal level will be a political tug of war in the near future.

In addition to the prominent position technology will hold in budget debates, we anticipate a continued push by government leaders to explain the virtues of technology. Since one of the benefits of technology is management efficiency, we expect leaders to begin touting the ability of technology to streamline government operations and create management efficiencies that ease strained budgets. Simply put, technology will be touted as a "savior of government", among other things.

One of the other things in which technology will be seen as instrumental is economic development. The future growth industries are technological development and scientific discoveries. Governments at all levels are creating "corridors" that promote one aspects of the emerging "new" economy. These corridors are devoted to technology and life sciences. They promote the rapid economic advancement each of these industries holds. As we have mentioned, and so have others, the future of success (individual and collective) depends on our ability to capture technological innovations that will advance productivity and exchange of ideas. Therefore, technology has potential on several additional fronts.

Efficiency

Government has struggled with the notion of efficiency since the Progressive Era. Ideally, government should require no more resources than is reasonably necessary to discharge its duties. Critics of government claim that it costs too much, that government has over-stepped its boundaries, and that it is out of control and suppresses individual freedom. If these critics are correct, technology may not help government overcome its inefficient ways.

Efficiency is a somewhat subjective term. When an activity is efficient, such as government operations, it requires the least amount of resources. Therefore we can make comparisons of efficiency among almost all things. Some comparisons are easier, while others require an agreement. Comparing appliances, windows, and machines in terms of efficiencies are not difficult. Standardized levels of efficiency are determined by physical traits. With government operations, we don't have distinct physical characteristics to measure. For us, precise measurements of efficiency are elusive.

Despite the difficulties and arbitrary nature of gauging efficiency, we believe the technology programs being developed by governments at all levels are creating efficiencies. States such as Georgia and Virginia, for example, are experiencing population growth while still being able to serve more citizens without corresponding increases in staff. The Department of Motor Vehicles example we used demonstrated the efficiencies created by technology. Other state offices routinely address increased demand with technology. Not only does this create efficiencies (getting more out for essentially similar input), it also creates a more effective government.

Effectiveness

Government's ability to be effective is almost as elusive as the slippery notion of efficient government. Programs are said to be effective if they attain their goals. Likewise, a program is successful if it reaches its target audience. We therefore set out to gauge effectiveness in a number of ways. The reason for this infatuation with government performance stems from ideological concerns, as well as scarcity problems we mentioned throughout our discussion. Technology does not completely erase these issues or concerns, but it does provide tools for governments to become more effective with their efforts.

Technology allows government to become more effective through an increased ability to communicate with citizens. By being able to reach citizens at any time, governments can educate and inform the public, and make requests of them. Recently, the Commonwealth of Virginia began a campaign to collect back taxes owed to the Treasury. As part of the effort to collect delinquent taxes, the Commonwealth created a Tax Amnesty program which was advertised on television and other media. The publicity campaign was aimed at improving the effectiveness of collecting delinquent taxes, which was the overall goal of the program. Time will tell if the program was a success. At the federal level, a new program aimed at curbing the counterfeiting of money was launched by the Treasury Department. The bulk of the anti-counterfeiting program included an ad campaign describing the security features of the new $20 bill. Its purpose was to educate citizens about the security features with the hope that an informed citizenry could help the government become more effective at spotting and limiting counterfeiting. However, critics believe the campaign is a waste of money.

Governments can also use technology to become more effective in almost any area. Schools are rushing to harness the power of computing technology and its effects on learning. In our discussion of the digital divide, those who lack access to information technology are at a disadvantage in most respects to future economic success that is predicated on learning and gaining skills needed to compete globally. The military, police, and other organizations charged with our security routinely respond to technological advances that improve their effectiveness in protecting citizens. Technology has seemingly limitless bounds for helping us shape a more effective government. It also has tremendous potential for increasing the responsiveness of government.

Responsiveness

Over the course of our discussion, the idea of government being more responsive to its citizens through technology has been fairly consistent. Interestingly enough, events occur over the course of time that help to further illustrate how technology can improve government for everyone. As Mr. Trippi's comments indicate, technology has the potential to undergird the pillars of government that have been eroded over by the structural elements of American politics.

As we have pointed out, in an era of candidate-centered politics, campaigns are the essential source of information about candidates. Their campaigns have traditionally catered to television, but recent campaigns have tapped the Internet not only to spread their messages, but also to solicit campaign contributions. Howard Dean's campaign for president is making effective use of the Internet for fundraising. In the run-up to the 2004 presidential election, he has broken Democratic presidential fundraising records largely on the strength of a grassroots effort at connecting with potential voters through the Internet. Dean uses the Internet for fundraising, not only soliciting contributions through his website, but receiving them as well.

Fishing for campaign monies through the Internet is not what makes the Howard Dean story central to our discussion. The Dean campaign, as well as others, is effectively communicating with supporters through electronic means. Through the use of Blogs (short for Web Log), campaigns are receiving from and sharing ideas with supporters. When the Dean campaign realized they did not have a blog for specific voters, they created one. They did so in response to citizens living in Puerto Rico, the United Kingdom, and other parts of Europe. These tools of mass communication give campaigns the ability to communicate with citizens more effectively. Thus, as political scientists have cogently demonstrated, the quality of our politics increases. Moreover, candidate-centered politics places the onus of quality political discourse squarely on the shoulders of candidates. If our participation, interest, and views are not of quality, it is not the fault of voters or technology. The blame falls on those running for office.

Even though the success of the Dean campaign is evident, other candidates have had trouble replicating his model. The cause of their problem could be that there are very few active citizens interested in politics via the Internet. We don't fully subscribe to this argument. Retired General Wesley Clark's late insurgent campaign for the Democratic nomination was initially begun as a draft movement whereby tens of thousands of citizens wrote letters urging, even begging, the retired general to seek office. This movement went further by soliciting pledges to a potential Clark candidacy. Within two weeks of answering the call of the draft movement, the Clark campaign had raised 3.5 million dollars. Significant portions of the money came via the Internet. Clark's candidacy was a product of a grassroots movement conducted via the Internet.

The successes of Howard Dean and Wesley Clark in connecting with their supporters may explain their early luck in the presidential nominating process. The real measure of their success will be that of their continued dedication and their responsiveness to their Internet-connected supporters. Thus far they seem to be sticking to an unconventional strategy of firing up their supporters through the Internet while seeking the Presidency. Beyond Clark and Dean we do not see other candidates harnessing the power of the Internet with the same success. The other candidates' efforts have been perfunctory and rather bland.

Responsiveness to citizens goes beyond running for office. We expect candidates to pay attention to voters during campaigns. What about after the election? We are witnessing an increased usage of technology by government and elected officials to carry out their duties while in office. Our chapter on Congress and the Courts demonstrated that Members of Congress are using the Internet to brag about the work they do for their constituents while in Washington, D.C. They also ask that constituents relay any problems they have with government through the Internet.

Beyond Members of Congress (after all, they are elected and wish to remain in office), government in general has sought to become more agile and responsive to the needs of citizens. The responsive nature of government is rooted in a desire to be effective and efficient. We routinely see governments respond to public problems through "one-stop shops". The idea around one-stop shopping for government services is rooted in responsiveness. For example, recent wild fires in California caused the governor to call on the federal government to create rapid-response offices for citizens who were displaced because their houses were destroyed. These offices are set up in local places to provide counseling and application help, and to provide government relief as quickly as possible. These roving government offices can not ease the burden of loss, but by using technology, combined with a desire to be responsive to citizens needs, the pain endured by citizens can be lessened.

The mobile offices are an obvious example of government responsiveness. At a more basic operation level, governments are seeking to make interaction with government offices easier. We have discussed the problems a citizen may encounter when interacting with government. From intimidation to skepticism, citizens may recoil at the thought of such interactions. They may be put off by the bureaucratic maze that hinders their ability to directly connect a government service with the office that handles the program. Through search engines that match specific requests with offices that oversee a program and screening tools that help citizens determine their eligibility for a particular program, agencies are attempting to ease the stress of interacting with government. Technology is helping with this effort.

We believe our discussions of the various topics within American government pay particular attention to issues such as effectiveness, responsiveness, and efficiencies created by technology. At a rudimentary level, we are just beginning to understand how technology may or may not alter government. As such, and as we mentioned earlier, our treatment has been a snapshot of a fast moving target. For those of you with more of an interest beyond this snapshot, we suggest some avenues for future research as well as some questions to ponder as issues are raised concerning technology and government.

Where Do We Go from Here?

As we begin to adopt more technology for government operations, studies will need to address whether we are getting better government or just the same old services with a different delivery mechanism. Examinations that are designed properly, with appropriate methods used and generalizable results, will be desperately needed because of what we see as an exuberance factor whereby too much emphasis is placed on the benefits of technology for technology's sake. Abundant examples exist where government leaders view technology as a panacea for almost any government operation. Technology is not a panacea. Future studies will no doubt prove this claim.

Our suggestion for future analysis falls into a few broad categories: management analysis, cost benefit analysis, program analysis, and behavioral analysis. Technology can create efficient, effective, and responsive government. Our work here stakes out road signs that point to what is happening with government and technology. It is by no means a comprehensive examination. We hope our exploratory analysis prompts further interest in the subject matter. Technology, government, and politics are topics that have proven to be fertile ground for students of politics. Given the broad, yet justifiable, claims about the potentially transforming nature of technology, we think the attention is worthwhile.

Management analyses will reveal how technology is altering the administrative work of government. We have mentioned how hiring, advertising for jobs, and organizing communication are shaped by the ability to communicate. We need a firmer understanding of whether or not technology improves management abilities. This is important due to the heavy management requirements of government programs. Governments exist to manage problems. Does technology help in this endeavor?

Beyond the management question, we need a better model of the benefits of technology. Cost versus benefit analyses will move us closer to this understanding. Once we have this knowledge it will be up to students of government to synthesize the competing examinations regarding costs and benefits of technology in order to create a comprehensive framework that permits government leaders to make better decisions about whether to purchase technology.

As technology continues to grow, we should see valuable benefits with respect to better outcomes within policy evaluations. Cost effective evaluations reveal what we are getting back from our technology investments. Citizens and elected officials have a vested interest in government becoming better at improving the problems it sets out to address. Does technology improve our ability to apprehend criminals, treat drug abusers, prevent war, educate children, clean the environment, and improve the overall quality of life? These evaluations are ongoing and will occur naturally. We would advocate that technology be considered a variable that explains the improvement or degradation of our public policies.

Finally, we contend that concerns of political behavior are as equally important as the institutional concerns. Can technology make citizens feel more connected to the political process despite the distant nature of information technology? We are beginning to see people contribute to political campaigns who claim they have never donated to a campaign previously. Is the Internet responsible? Does technology ease the hassle of participating in politics? How might interest groups and mass movements harness the Internet to improve the feelings of efficacy on the part of citizens? As we saw with Senator Debbie Stabenow, her constituents flooded the Environmental Protection Agency with an online petition. When the Federal Communications Commission decided to relax media ownership rules, they did so after being electronically petitioned by hundreds of thousands of citizens. Are we seeing empowerment by technology, or are these folks participating in politics the usual suspects? Again, much potential is held within the power of technological advances. Is Joe Trippi correct? Can technology put the substance back into American politics? We need these answers.

Summary

Our intent here was to capture the nature of technology and government operations, and how political behavior is being altered by technological advancements. Hopefully, we have been successful in this endeavor. As we progressed with our discussion of fundamental topics, it became apparent that more work would need to be done beyond our undertaking. We believe that in the preceding pages the nature of politics and technology have been described, and an idea of where to go from here has been established. The changes on the information superhighway are rapid. Hang on as you travel down a very interesting road.

References

Abramson, J. B., Arterton, F. C., & Orren, G. R. (1988). *The electronic commonwealth: The impact of new media technologies on democratic politics.* New York: Basic Books.

Access America (2003). *Introduction* [On-line]. Available: http://govinfo.library.unt.edu/accessamerica/docs/introduction.html

Activists hold 'virtual march' on Washington. (2003, February 28). Retrieved August 30, 2003, from http://www.cnn.com/2003/TECH/ptech/02/26/virtual.protest/

Ahrens, F. (2003, May 28). FCC plan to alter media rules spurs growing debate. *Washington Post.* Retrieved August 30, 2003, from http://www.washingtonpost.com/wp-dyn/articles/A46442-2003May27.html

Althaus, S. L., & Tewksbury, D. (2000). Patterns of Internet and traditional news media use in a networked community. *Political Communication 17,* 21-45.

Alvarez, M. R., & Nagler, J. (2000). The likely consequences of Internet voting for political representation. *Center for the Study of Law & Politics.* Retrieved August 30, 2003, from http://lawweb.usc.edu/cslp/pages/papers.html

American Association of Retired Persons (AARP). (2003). *Fact sheet: What is AARP?* Retrieved August 30, 2003, from http://www.aarp.org/leadership/Articles/a2002-12-18-aarpfactsheet.html

Anonymous. (2001, July-August). Cyberactivism: 101. *The Futurist, 35*(4), 15.

Ansolabehere, S., Behr, R., & Iyengar, S. (1993). *The media game.* New York: Macmillan.

Anti-war protesters go digital. (2003, March 27) AP Wire. *CNN.com* Retrieved August 30, 2003, from http://www.cnn.com/2003/TECH/ptech/03/27/digital.protesters.ap/

Arterton, F. C. (1984). *Media politics: The news strategies of presidential campaigns.* Lexington, MA: Lexington Books.

Asher, H. B. (1984). *Presidential elections and American politics.* Homewood, IL: The Dorsey Press.

Astrom, J. (2001). Should democracy online be quick, strong, or thin? *Communications of the ACM, 44* (1), 49.

Attinger, T. (Senior Vice President of New Market Development, Visa USA). (2003, July 14). Phone interview.

Ayers, J. M. (1999, November). From the streets to the Internet: The cyber-diffusion of contention. *Annals, AAPSS, 566.*

Barber, B. R. (1998-99). Three scenarios for the future of technology and strong democracy. *Political Science Quarterly, 113* (4), 573-589.

Barelson, B. R., Lazarsfeld, P. F., & McPhee, W. N. (1954). *Voting.* Chicago: University of Chicago Press.

Beierle, T. & Cahill, S. (2000) *Electronic democracy and environmental governance: A survey of the states* (Discussion Paper 00-42) Washington, DC: Resources for the Future.

Bennett, L. (1996) the Governing Crisis: Media, Money, and Marketing in American Elections, St. Martins, New York.

Bennett, W. L. (1998, December). The uncivic culture: Communication, identity, and the rise of lifestyle politics. *PS: Political Science and Politics 31,* 741-61.

Berkowitz, L., Ed. (1978). *Cognitive theories in social psychology.* New York: Academic Press.

Bimber, B. (1998, Fall). The Internet and political transformation: Populism, community and accelerated pluralism. *Polity, 31*(1), 133-160. Retrieved August 30, 2003, from http://www.polsci.ucsb.edu/faculty/bimber/research/transformation.html

Bimber, B. & Davis, R. (2002, April 1). *Paper 5. The Internet in campaign 2000: How political web sites reinforce partisan engagement.* Retrieved August 30, 2003, from http://repositories.cdlib.org/isber/cits/5

Birdsell, D., Muzzio, D., Krane, D., & Cottreau, A. (1998, April-May). Web users are looking more like America. *The Public Perspective,* 33-35.

Brady, H. E., Verba, S., & Schlozman, K. L. (1995 June). Beyond SES: A resource model of political participation. *The American Political Science Review, 89*(2), 271-294.

Brody, R. A. (1978). The puzzle of participation in America. In A. King (Ed.), *The new American political system* (pp. 287-324). Washington, DC: American Enterprise Institute.

Brookings Task Force on the Internet. (2001). *The Economic Payoff from the Internet Revolution.* Washington, DC: Brookings Institution Press.

Brown, C. J., Brown, T. R, & Rivers, W. L. (1978). *The media and the people.* New York: Holt, Rinehart and Winston.

Browning, G. (1996). *Electronic Democracy: Using the Internet to influence American politics.* Wilton, CT: Pemberton Press.

Bush, G. (2002). *President signs E-government Act: Statement by the President* [On-line]. Available: http://www.whitehouse.gov/news/releases/2002/12/20021217-5.html

Campbell, J. (1997) *The Presidential Pulse of Congressional Elections,* University of Kentucky Press, Lexington.

Casey, C. (1996). *The hill on the net: Congress enters the information age.* Boston: AP Professional.

Capling, A., & Nossal, K. R. (2001). Death of distance or tyranny of distance? The Internet, deterritorialization, and the anti-globalization movement in Australia. *The Pacific Review, 14*(3), 443-465.

Case Management (2004) http://pacer.psc.uscourts.gov/cmecf/

Cavanaugh, J. W. (2000). E-Democracy: Thinking about the impact of technology on civic life. *National Civic Review, 89* (3), 229.

Census (2000) *www.census.gov*

Center for Digital Government (2003). *2002 Best of the web.* Available: http://www.centerdigitalgov.com/center/02top25states-pt3.phtml

Center for Digital Government (2003). *2002 Digital state survey, Part I.* Available: http://www.centerdigitalgov.com/center/bow02/

Center for Digital Government (2003). *2002 Digital state survey, Part II.* Available: http://www.centerdigitalgov.com/center/bow02/

Center for Digital Government (2003). *2002 Digital state survey, Part III.* Available: http://www.centerdigitalgov.com/center/bow02/

Center for Digital Government (2003). *2002 Digital cities survey.* Available: http://www.centerdigitalgov.com/center/02digitalcities.phtml

Center for the Study of Technology and Society. (2001, February 15). Special focus on Internet voting. Retrieved August 30, 2003, from http://tecsoc.org/govpol/focusnetvote.htm

Center for Voting and Democracy. (2000). *Presidential election voter turnout.* Retrieved August 30, 2003, from http://www.fairvote.org/turnout/preturn.htm

Chadwick, A. (2001). The electronic face of government in the Internet age. *Information, Communication & Society, 4* (3), 435-457.

Chopyak, J. (2001). Citizen participation and democracy: Examples in science and technology. *National Civic Review, 90* (4), 375-384.

Cohen, B. (1963). *The press and foreign policy.* Princeton, NJ: Princeton University Press.

Coleman, S. (2001). Online campaigning. *Parliamentary Affairs, 54,* 679-688.

Colletta, L. (Director of Field Operations, Common Cause). (2003, June 18). Phone interview.

Common Cause. (2003). REM and Pearl Jam join campaign to delay FCC vote. Retrieved August 30, 2003, from http://www.common-cause.org/news/default.cfm?ArtID=170

Conradi, M. (2003). Leadership, process and people. *Governing.com* [On-line]. Available: http://governing.com/conf/mtech3cr.htm

Congressional Management Foundation (2003) www.Congressonlineproject.org

Conway, M. M. (2000). *Political participation in the United States* (3rd ed.). Washington, DC: CQ Press.

Cook, T. E. (1998). *Governing with the news*. Chicago: University of Chicago Press.

The Council for Excellence in Government (2003). The new egovernment equation: Ease, engagement, privacy and protection. *Polls and Publications* [On-line]. Available: http://www.excelgov.org/displayContent.asp?Keyword=ppp041403

Davis, R. (1992). *The press and American politics: The new mediator.* New York: Longman.

Davis, R. (1999). *The web of politics: The Internet's impact on the American political system.* New York: Oxford UP.

Davis, R., & Owen, D. (1998). *New media and American politics.* New York: Oxford University Press.

Day, S. (2003). Electronic order in the court. The New York Times [On-line]. Available: http://www.nytimes.com

De Tocqueville, A. (1956). *Democracy in America, 1835-1839.* Ed. R. D. Heffner. New York: Mentor Books.

Deibert, R. J. (2000). International plug 'n play? Citizen activism, the Internet, and global public policy. *International Studies Perspectives, 1,* 255-272.

Delli Carpini, M. X., & Keeter, S. (1996). *What Americans know about politics and why it matters.* New Haven: Yale University Press.

Deloitte Consulting (2000). *e-Michigan Strategic Plan.* Michigan: Deloitte Consulting

Deloitte Research. (2003). *Cutting Fat, Adding Muscle: The Power of Information Technology in Addressing Budget Shortfalls* (ISBN 1-892384-60-8) Virginia: Deloitte Consulting.

Diani, M. (2001). Social movement networks: Virtual and real. In F. Webster (Ed.), *Culture and Politics in the Information Age: A New Politics?* New York: Routledge.

Dillehay, B. H. (2002). E-government as Virginia's vision. *Spectrum: the Journal of State Government, 75* (1), 24-26.

Dinin, M. (2002). Virginia and Tampa win best of web. Center for Digital Government [On-line]. Available: http://www.centerdigital-gov.com/center/highlightstroy.phtml?docid=3030000000021672.0

Dulio, D. A., Goff, D. L., & Thurber, J. A.. (1999, March). Untangled web: Internet use during the 1998 election. *PS: Political Science and Politics, 32*(1), 53-59.

Dunleavy, P. & Margetts, H. (2000) The advent of digital government: Public Bureaucracies and the state in the Internet age. *Annual Conference of the American Political Science Association.* London: University College London.

Dunham, R. S. (2002, October 29). A tougher cyber-campaign trail. Business Week Online. Retrieved August 30, 2003, from http://www.businessweek.com/technology/content/oct2002/tc20021029_7182.htm

Dye, T. (2000) Top Down Policy Making, Chatham House, New York.

E-gov (2003). *About E-gov.* Available: http://www.whitehouse.gov/omb/egov/about_backgrnd.htm

E-mail brings together flash mob at NY toy store. (2003, August 8). Reuters news service. Retrieved August 11, 2003, from http://story.news.yahoo.com/news?tmpl=story&cid=578&ncid=578&e=7&u=/nm/20030808/ts_nm/life_mob_dc

Elberse, A., Hale, M. L., & Dutton, W. H. (2000). Guiding voters through the net: The democracy network in a California primary election. In K. L. Hacker & J. van Dijk (Eds.), *Digital democracy: Issues of theory and practice* (pp. 130-148). London: Sage Publications.

Fairfield, R. P., ed. (1981). *The Federalist Papers: A collection of essays written in support of the Constitution of the United States: From the original text of Alexander Hamilton, James Madison, John Jay.* Baltimore: Johns Hopkins UP.

Federal Election Commission. (n.d.). *National voter turnout in federal elections 1960-1996.* Retrieved August 30, 2003, from http://www.fec.gov/elections.html

Federalist No. 10, The Federalist Papers, Madison, Hamilton, and Jay

Fenno, R. (1978) *Home Style: House Members and their Districts,* Little Brown.

Finkel, S. E. (1993, February). Reexamining the "minimal effects" model in recent presidential campaigns. *The Journal of Politics 55,* 1-21.

Fiorina, M. (1989) *Congress: Keystone of the Washington Establishment,* Yale Univesity Press: New Haven, CT.

Flanigan, W. & Zingale, N. (1998). *Political behavior of the American electorate* (8th ed.). Washington, DC: CQ Press.

Forman, M. (2003). Ask the White House. *The White House* [On-line]. Available: http://www.whitehouse.gov/ask/20030417.html

Foundation for Public Affairs. (2000, December 12). *Activist groups use the net to gain power and influence.* Retrieved August 30, 2003, from http://www.pac.org/pubs/cyberactivism.htm

Fountain, J. (2001) *Building a Virtual State: Information Technology and Institutional Change,* Brookings: Washington, D.C.

Fountain, Jane and Carlos A. Osorio-Urzua. (2001) "Public Sector: Early Stage of a Deep Transformation." *The Economic Payoff from the Internet Revolution.* Ed. Robert Litan and Alice Rivlin. Brookings Institution Press.

Friedman, M. (1962) *Capitalism and Freedom,* Univeristy of Chicago Press, Chicago, IL.

Georgia Department of State, Georgia Secretary of State. (2002). Exercise your right to choose our leaders—electronically. Retrieved August 30, 2003, from http://www.georgiacounts.com/zcolumn.htm

Georgia Department of State. (2002). Frequently asked questions. Retrieved August 30, 2003, from http://www.georgiacounts.com/faqs.htm

Governing.com (2003). *CIO's see opportunity in adversity* [On-line]. Available: *http://governing.com/4cios.htm*

Governing Magazine (2003) State and Local Sourcebook.

Graber, D. A. (1989). *Mass media and American politics.* Washington, DC: Congressional Quarterly Press.

Graber, D. A. (1997). *Mass media and American politics* (5th ed.). Washington, DC: Congressional Quarterly Press.

Greenberg, Anna. (1999). Reply to Pippa Norris's "Who surfs." In E. C. Kamarck & J. S. Nye, Jr. (Eds.), *Democracy.com: Governance in a Networked World* (pp. 95-98). Hollis, NH: Hollis Publishing Company.

Gronlund, A. (2001). Democracy in an IT-framed society. *Communications of the ACM, 44* (1), 22.

Grossman, L. K. (1995). *The electronic republic: Reshaping democracy in the information age.* New York: Viking/Penguin Books.

Grosswiler, P. (1998). Historical hopes, media fears, and the electronic town meeting concept: where technology meets democracy or demagogy? *Journal of Communication Inquiry, 22* (2), 133-152.

Gulick, Luther. 1937. "Notes on the Theory of Organization" in Luther Gulick and Lyndall Urwick Eds., *Papers on the Science of*

Administration, pp. 191-5. New York. Institute of Public Administration, Columbia University.

Hanson, W. (2002). Digital state 2002. *Government and Technology* [On-line]. Available: http://www.govtech.net/magazine/story. phtml?id=13182&issue=06:2002

Hanson, W. (2002). Digital state part III. *Government and Technology* [On-line]. Available: http://www.govtech.net/magazine/story. phtml?id+29358

Hanson, W. (2002). Digital state survey, pt. II. *Center for Digital Government* [On-line]. Available: http://www.centerdigitalgov.com

Hart, R. P. (1994). *Seducing America: How television charms the modern voter.* New York: Oxford University Press.

Hill, K. A., & Hughes, J. E. (1998). *Cyberpolitics: Citizen activism in the age of the Internet.* Lanham, MD: Rowman & Littlefield.

Ho, A. T. (2002). Reinventing local governments and the e-government initiative. *Public Administration review, 62* (4), 434-444.

Hovland, C., Lumsdaine, A., & Sheffield, F. (1949). *Experiments on mass communications.* Princeton, NJ: Princeton University Press.

Hughes, J. E. (2000). Going online: The future of the news media. In D. Schultz (Ed.), *It's show time! Media, politics, and popular culture* (pp. 245-263). New York: Peter Lang.

Institute for Politics, Democracy and the Internet. (2002a). *Online campaigning 2002: A primer.* Retrieved August 30, 2003, from http://www.ipdi.org/primer2002.html

Institute for Politics, Democracy & the Internet. (2002b). *Characteristics of 1998 campaign web sites.* Retrieved August 30, 2003, from http://www.ipdi.org/sites98.shtml

Institute for Politics, Democracy & the Internet. (2003, March 21). *Untuned keyboards: Online campaigners, citizens, and portals in the 2002 elections.* Retrieved August 30, 2003, from http://www. ipdi.org/untuned.pdf

International Institute for Democracy and Electoral Assistance. (n.d.). *Voter turnout: A global survey.* Retrieved August 30, 2003, from http://www.idea.int/vt/survey/voter_turnout1.cfm

Internet access gap closing, but other inequities remain. (2002, March 3). Associated Press Wire. *The Mercury News* web site. Retrieved August 30, 2003 from http://www.siliconvalley.com/ mld/siliconvalley/news/2785589.htm

Internet Voting Task Force Report. California Department of State. (2000). *The California online voting study.* Retrieved August 30, 2003, from http://www.ss.ca.gov/executive/ivote/final_report.htm#final-1

Iyengar, S. (1987, September). Television news and citizens' explanations of national affairs. *American Political Science Review 81*, 815-31.

Iyengar, S. (1990). Shortcuts to political knowledge: The role of selective attention and accessibility. In J. A. Ferejohn & J. H. Kuklinski (Eds.), *Information and democratic processes* (pp. 160-185). Urbana, IL: University of Illinois Press.

Iyengar, S., & Kinder, D. R. (1986). More than meets the eye: TV news, priming and public evaluations of the President. In G. Comstock (Ed.) *Public communication and behavior* (Vol. 1, pp. 135-171). New York: Academic Press.

Iyengar, S., Kinder, D. R., Peters, M. D., & Krosnick, J. (1984). The evening news and presidential evaluations. *Journal of Personality and Social Psychology 46*, 778-787.

Iyengar, S., & Simon, A. (1993, June). News coverage of the Gulf crisis and public opinion. *Communication Research 20*, 365-84.

Iyengar, S., Peters, M. D., & Kinder, D. R. (1982, December). Experimental demonstrations of the "not-so-minimal" consequences of television news programs. *American Political Science Review 76*, 848-58.

Jacobs, L. R., and Shapiro, R. Y. (1994, September). Issues, candidate image and priming: The use of private polls in Kennedy's 1960 presidential campaign. *The American Political Science Review 88*, 527-540.

Jacobson, (2002) The Politics of Congressional Elections, Longman, New York.

Jalonick, M. C. (2002, September). Consultant Q & A: Campaigning on the Internet. *Campaign and Elections, 23*(9), 51-61.

Johnson, D. R. & Post, D. G. (2003) The new 'civic virtue' of the internet. First Monday [On-line]. Available: http://www.firstmonday.dk/issue3_1/johnson/index.html

Joslyn, R. (1984). *Mass media and elections*. Reading, MA: Addison-Wesley.

Kamarck, E. C. (1999). Campaigning on the Internet in the elections of 1998. In E. C. Kamarck & J. S. Nye, Jr. (Eds.), *Democracy.com?: Governance in a networked world.* (pp. 99-123). Hollis, NH: Hollis Publishing Company. Retrieved August 30, 2003, from http://www.wired.com/news/politics/0,1283,13815,00.html

Kamarck, E. C. (2002). Political campaigning on the Internet: Business as usual? In E. C. Kamarck & J. S. Nye, Jr. (Eds.), *Governance.com: Democracy in the information age.* Washington, DC: Brookings Institution Press.

Kamarck, E. C., & Nye, J. S., Jr. (Eds.). (2002). *Governance.com: Democracy in the Information Age,* Washington, DC: Brookings Institution Press.

Katz, E., & Feldman, J. (1962). The debates in the light of research: A survey of surveys. In S. Krauss (Ed.), *The great debates, 1976: Ford vs. Carter* (pp. 173-223). Bloomington, IN: Indiana University Press.

Kettl, D. F. (2000). *The Global Public Management Revolution: A Report on the Transformation of Governance,* Washington, DC: Brookings Institution Press.

Klapper, J. (1960). *The effects of mass communication.* Glencoe, IL: The Free Press.

Knox, D. (2000, July 3). George Bush presents high-tech views: Presidential hopeful talks about Internet, taxation, privacy, campaigning. *eWeek, 17*(27), 31.

Kraus, S., & Davis, D. (1976). The effects of mass communications on political behavior. University Park, PA: Pennsylvania State University Press.

Krause, A. (1997, April 28). *The online activist: Tools for organizing in cyberspace.* Retrieved August 30, 2003, from http://www.motherjones.com/hellraiser_central/features/krause1.html

Krosnick, J. A., & Kinder, D. R. (1990, June). Altering the foundations of support for the President through priming. *American Political Science Review 84,* 479-512.

Krosnick. J. A., & Brannon, L. A. (1993). The impact of the Gulf War on the ingredients of presidential evaluations: Multidimensional effects of political involvement. *American Political Science Review 87,* 963-975.

Kuk, G. & Gow, I. (2002). Digital divide and quality of electronic service delivery in local government. *International Conference on the Digital Divide: Technology & Politics in the Information Age.* Nottingham, UK: Nottingham University Business School.

Lang, K., & Lang, G. E. (1981). The mass media and voting. In P. M. Hirsch & M. Janowitz (Eds.), *Reader in public opinion and communication* (pp. 327-340). New York: Free Press.

Larsen, E. & Rainie, L. (2002). *Digital town hall: How local officials use the Internet and the civic benefits they cite from dealing with constituents online.* Washington, DC: Pew Internet & American Life Project.

Larsen, E. & Rainie, L. (2002). *The rise of the e-citizen: How people use government agencies' Web sites.* Washington, DC: Pew Internet & American Life Project.

Lasswell, H. D. (1927). *Propaganda techniques in the World War.* New York: Alfred A. Knopf.

Lazarsfeld, P. E., Berelson, B., & Gaudet, H. (1948). *The People's Choice.* New York: Columbia University Press.

Legon, J. (2003, July 24). Electronic elections: What about security? Voters put touch screens to the test. *CNN.com* Retrieved August 30, 2003, from http://www.cnn.com/2002/TECH/ptech/11/05/touch.screen/

Lemert, J. B. (1981). *Does mass communication change public opinion after all?* Chicago: Nelson-Hall.

Lewicki, D., & Ziaukas, T. (2000, December 4). The digital tea leaves of election 2000: The Internet and the future of presidential politics. *First Monday, 5*(12). Retrieved August 30, 2003, from http://www.firstmonday.dk/issues/issue5_12/lewicki/

Lieberman, J. (2001). Electronic government act of 2001: Statement by Senator Joe Lieberman. *Joe Lieberman Press Office* [On-line]. Available: http://www.senate.gov/~lieberman/press/01/05/2001501810.html

Lippmann, W. (1965). *Public Opinion.* New York: Free Press.

Lipsky, M. (2003) Street-Level Bureaucracy: The Critical Role of Street-Level Bureaucrats, ed. Jay Shafritz Classics of Public Administration, Thomson Learning, New York.

Lubell, S. (2003, May 15). To register doubts, press here. *The New York Times* (Late Edition—Final), pp. G1.

Madison, J. (1910). 1900—1910: 4 August 1822. In G. Hunt (Ed.), *The Writings of James Madison* (Vol. 9, p. 103). New York: G. P. Putnam's Sons.

Marder, N. (2003). Cyberjuries: The next new thing? *InSITeS* [On-line]. Available: http://insites.heinz.cmu.edu/events/conferences/democracy/directory.html/abstract/marder.html/view

Maslow, A. (1943). A theory of human motivation. *Psychological Review, 50,* 370-396.

Margolis, M., & Resnick, D. (2000). *Politics as usual: The cyberspace "revolution."* Thousand Oaks, CA: Sage Publications.

Margolis, M., Resnick, D., & Tu, C. (1997, Winter). Campaigning on the Internet: Parties and candidates on the world wide web in the 1996 primary season. *The Harvard International Journal of Press/Politics* 2(1), 59-78.

McGregor, D. (1961), *The Human Side of Enterprise,* McGrawHill.

Mayhew, D. (1974) *Congress: The Electoral Connection,* Yale University Press, New Haven, CT.

McCarthy, E. (2003). Many Americans still aren't going online, survey finds. *The Washington Post.* [On-line]. Available: http://www.washingtonpost.com/ac2/wp-dyn/A41817-2003Apr16?language=printer

McChesney, R. W. (1999). *Rich media, poor democracy: Communication politics in dubious times.* Urbana, IL: University of Illinois Press.

McCombs, M. E., & Shaw, D. L. (1972, Summer). The agenda-setting function of mass media. *Public Opinion Quarterly 36,* 176-87.

Melitski, J. (2003). The world of e-government and e-governance. *Solutions for Public Managers* [On-line]. Available: http://www.aspanet.org/solutions/egovworld.html

Mendelsohn, M. (1993, May). Television's frames in the 1988 Canadian election. *Canadian Journal of Communication 18*(2), 149-171.

Mendelsohn, M. (1996, February). The media and interpersonal communications: The priming of issues, leaders, and party identification. *The Journal of Politics 58,* 112-25.

Moon, M. J. (2002). The evolution of e-government among municipalities: rhetoric or reality? *Public Administration Review, 62* (4), 424-433.

Morris, D. (1999). *Vote.com.* Los Angeles: Renaissance Books.

Murray, R., & Vedlitz, A. (1977, November). Race, SES and vote participation in large U.S. cities. *Journal of Politics 39*(4), 1064-1072.

National Center for State Courts (2003) http://www.ncsconline.org/

National Science Foundation. (2001, March 6). Internet voting is no 'magic ballot'. Retrieved August 30, 2003, from http://www.nsf.gov/od/lpa/news/press/01/pr0118.htm

National Telecommunications and Information Administration. Dept. of Commerce, (2002 February). A Nation Online: How Americans are expanding their use of the Internet. Retrieved August 30, 2003, from http://www.ntia.doc.gov/ntiahome/dn/nationonline_020502.htm

Nelson, T. E., Clawson, R. A., & Oxley, Z. M. (1997, September). Media framing of a civil liberties conflict and its effect on tolerance. *The American Political Science Review 91,* 567-583.

Neu, C. R., Anderson, R. H., & Bikson, T. K. (1999). *Sending your government a message: E-mail communication between citizens and government.* Santa Monica, CA: Rand.

Neuman, W. R., McKnight, L., & Solomon, R. J. (1997) *The Gordian Knot: Political Gridlock on the Information Highway,* Cambridge, MA: The MIT Press.

Newstrom, G. C. (2002). *The Global Digital Economy and the Bold Dominion: Commonwealth of Virginia Strategic Plan for Technology 2002-2006*, Virginia: Department of Technology.

Nixon, P., & Johansson, H. (1999). Transparency through technology: The Internet and political parties. In B. N. Hague & B. D. Loader (Eds.), *Digital democracy: Discourse and decision making in the information age* (pp. 135-153). New York: Routledge.

Norris, D.F., Fletcher, P.D., & Holden, S. H. (2001). *Is your local government plugged in? Highlights of the 2000 electronic government survey*, (Prepared for the International City/County Management Association and Public Technology, Inc.). Baltimore, MD: University of Maryland, Baltimore County.

Norris, P. (1996, September). Does television erode social capital?: A reply to Putnam. *PS: Political Science and Politics 29*, 474-480.

Norris, P. (1999). Who surfs? New technology old voters, and virtual democracy. In E. C. Kamarck & J. S. Nye, Jr. (Eds.), *Democracy.com: Governance in a networked world* (pp. 71-94). Hollis, NH: Hollis Publishing Company.

Norris, P. (2001). *Digital Divide: Civic Engagement, Information Poverty, and the Internet Worldwide* Cambridge, UK: Cambridge University Press.

Norris, P. (2001a). *Digital divide: Civic engagement, information poverty, and the Internet worldwide.* Cambridge: Cambridge UP.

Norris, P. (2001b). Preaching to the converted? Pluralism, participation, and party websites. Working paper located at the Harvard University website for the John F. Kennedy School of Government. Retrieved August 30, 2003, from http://ksgnotes1.harvard.edu/Research/wpaper.nsf/rwp/RWP01-040?OpenDocument

Noveck, B. S. (2000). Paradoxical partners: Electronic communication and electronic democracy. In P. Ferdinand (ed.), *The Internet, democracy and democratization* (pp.18-35). London: Frank Cass.

Oder, N. (2002, March 15). Benton: Feds retreat. Retrieved August 30, 2003, from http://libraryjournal.reviewsnews.com/index.asp?layout=article&articleId=CA199769&display=searchResults&stt=001&text=digital+divide

Office of Management and Budget (2003) *www.omb.gov*

Ogg, F. A., & Ray, P. O. (1951). *Introduction to American government* (10th ed.). New York: Appleton Century Crofts.

Orren, G., & Polsby, N. (1987). *Media and momentum.* Chatham, NJ: Chatham House.

Patterson, T. (2000). *Doing well and doing good: How soft news and critical journalism are shrinking the news audience and weakening democracy—and what news outlets can do about it.* Retrieved September 15, 2003 from the Joan Shorenstein Center on the Press, Politics, and Public Policy site: http://ksgnotes1.harvard.edu/research/wpaper.nsf/rwp/RWP01-001/$File/rwp01_001_patterson.pdf

Patterson, T. E. (1994). *Out of order.* New York: Vintage.

Patterson, T. E., & McClure, R. D. (1976). *The unseeing eye: The myth of television power in national elections.* New York: G. P. Putnam.

Perlman, E. (2003). Local governments: Time is ripe for IT investments. *Governing.com* [On-line]. Available: http://governing.com/4pti.htm

Pew Research Center for the People and the Press. (2000, June 11). *Internet sapping broadcast news audience.* Retrieved February 4, 2003, from http://people-press.org/reports/print.php3?ReportID=36

Pew Research Center for the People and the Press. (2003, January 5). *Modest increase in Internet use for campaign 2002.* Retrieved August 30, 2003, from http://www.pewInternet.org/reports/toc.asp?Report=82

Pinkleton, B. E., & Austin, E. W. Austin. (1998). Media and participation: Breaking the spiral of disaffection. In T. J. Johnson, C. E. Hays, & S. P. Hays (Eds.), *Engaging the public: How government and the media can reinvigorate American democracy* (pp. 75-86). Lanham, MD: Rowman Littlefield.

Porter, C. (2001, January 11). *Internet crosses a threshold in 2000 U.S. elections.* U.S. Department of State. Retrieved August 30, 2003, from http://usinfo.state.gov/topical/global/ecom/01011101.htm

Putnam, R. (1995, December). Tuning in, tuning out: The strange disappearance of social capital in America. *PS: Political Science and Politics, 28,* 664-83.

Putnam, R. (2000) *Bowling Alone,* Touchstone, New York, NY.

Ramasastry, A. (2002). Michigan's cybercourt: Worthy experiment or virtual daydream? FindLaw [On-line]. Available: http://writ.news.findlaw.com

Raney, R. F. (1998, November 6). Former wrestler's campaign got a boost from the Internet. *The New York Times Online.* Retrieved August 30, 2003, from http://www.politicsonline.com/coverage/nytimes2/06campaign.html

Reich, R. B. (1991). *The Work of Nations: Preparing Ourselves for 21st—Century Capitalism,* New York: Alfred A. Knopf.

Rhode, D. and Spaeth, H. (1976) Supreme Court decision making, W.H. Freeman, San Francisco.

Sabato, L. (1991). *Feeding frenzy: How attack journalism has transformed American politics.* New York: The Free Press.

Sadow, J. D., & James, K. (1999, September 2-5). *Virtual billboards? Candidate web sites and campaigning in 1998.* Paper prepared for the 1999 American Political Science Association meeting in Atlanta, GA. Retrieved August 30, 2003, from http://ball.tcnj.edu/pols291/readings/038001SadowJeffr.pdf

Sarasohn, J. (2003). Survey finds Americans split on 'E-government'. *The Washington Post* [On-line]. Available: http://washingtonpost.com/ac2/wp-dyn/A19407-2003Apr13?language=printer

Sardar, Z., & Ravetz, J. R. (Eds.). (1996). *Cyberfutures: Culture and Politics on the Information Superhighway,* New York: New York University Press.

Schudson, M. (1995). *The power of news.* Cambridge, MA: Harvard University Press.

Sears, D. O., & Chaffee, S. H. (1979). Uses and effects of the 1976 debates: An overview of empirical studies. In S. Krauss (Ed.), *The Great Debates, 1976: Ford vs. Carter* (pp. 223-261). Bloomington, IN: Indiana University Press.

Selnow, G. W. (1998). *Electronic whistle-stops: The impact of the Internet on American politics.* Westport, CT: Praeger.

Shapiro, A. L. (1999). *The control revolution: How the Internet is putting individuals in charge and changing the world we know.* New York: Public Affairs.

Shenk, D. (1997). *Data smog: Surviving the information glut.* New York: Harper Edge, an imprint of Harper Collins.

Simon, H.A. (1962) *The Architecture of Complexity, Proceedings of the American Philosophical Society,* v. 106, pp. 467-82.

Small, W. (1974). *To kill a messenger: Television news and the real world.* New York: Hastings House Publishers.

Southwell, P. L., & Burchett, J. (1998). Armchair voting: The vote-by-mail experiment in the state of Oregon. In T. J. Johnson, C. E. Hays, & S. P. Hays (Eds.), *Engaging the public* (pp.175-183). Lanham, MD: Rowan & Littlefield Publishers, Inc.

Stanford Institute for the Quantitative Study of Society. (2000, February 16). *Study of the social consequences of the Internet.* Retrieved August 30, 2003, from http://www.stanford.edu/group/siqss/Press_Release/InternetStudy.html

Stanford Institute for the Quantitative Study of Society. (2000, February 17). *Internet and society: A preliminary report.* Retrieved

October 1, 2003, from http://www.stanford.edu/group/siqss/ Press_Release/Preliminary_Report.pdf

Starling, G. (2002) *Managing the Public Sector,* 6th ed. Harcourt: Fort Worth, TX.

Stekettee, M.W. and Carlson, A. (2003) National Center for State Courts, http://www.ncsconline.org/, Center Report on IT and the Courts.

Stone, S. (2003, June 2). FCC set to vote on media ownership rules. National Public Radio's *All Things Considered* Retrieved August 30, 2003, from http://discover.npr.org/features/feature.jhtml? wfId=1283128

Strategic Plan (2003) Commonwealth of Virginia, www.myvirginia. org.

Streich, G. W. (2000). Mass media, citizenship, and democracy: Revitalizing deliberation? In D. Schultz (Ed.), *It's show time! Media, politics, and popular culture* (pp. 51-71). New York: Peter Lang.

Study: E-voting flaws risk ballot fraud (2003, July 25). Associated Press Wire. *CNN.com* Retrieved August 30, 2003, from http://www. cnn.com/2003/TECH/ptech/07/25/evoting.flaw.ap/index.html

Survey: Internet established as major news source in 2000 elections. (2000, December 4). *CNN.com* Retrieved August 30, 2003, from http://edition.cnn.com/2000/ALLPOLITICS/stories/12/04/pew. survey/

Taubman Center for Public Policy at Brown University (2000). *Analysis of 1,813 Web sites find 'e-government' far short of potential* [Online]. Available: http://www.insidepolitics.org/egovtrelease00.html

The White House. (2000). Press release. Retrieved April 2003 from http://www.digitaldivide.gov/2000-02-02.html

Thompson, D. F. (1970). *The Democratic Citizen: Social Science and Democratic Theory in the Twentieth Century,* New York: Cambridge University Press.

Thomas.gov (2003) *www.thomas.gov*

Towns, S. (2002). Digital dogfight. *Government Technology* [Online]. Available: http://www.govtech.net/magazine/story.phtml? id=29356

Tufte, Edward R., "Determinants of the Outcomes of Midterm Congressional Elections", *American Political Science Review,* Vol. 69 (1975), 812-826.

UCLA Internet Report. (2003). *Surveying the digital future (from Year Three).* Retrieved August 30, 2003, from http://www.ccp. ucla.edu

U.S. Bureau of the Census. (1998). *Voting and registration in the election of November 1996* (Current population reports P20-504). Casper, L. M., & Bass, L. E. Washington, DC:

Verba, S. & Nie, N. H. (1972). *Participation in America: Political democracy and social equality.* New York: Harper and Row.

Verba, S., Schlozman, K. L., & Brady, H. E. (1995). *Voice and equality: Civic voluntarism in American politics.* Cambridge, MA: Harvard UP.

Vote Here, Incorporated. (2001, October 30). Congressional panel addresses solution for disenfranchised military voters. Retrieved August 30, 2003, from http://www.votehere.net/news/archive01/103001.html

Warner, M. (2003) Commonwealth of Virginia's Information Technology Plan, Executive Summary.

Wattenberg, M. P. (1994). *The decline of American political parties.* Cambridge, MA: Harvard University Press.

Weare, C. (2002). The Internet and democracy: The causal links between technology and politics. *International Journal of Public Administration, 25* (5), 659-692.

Webb, C. (2003). Q & A with Matthew DeZee. *The Washington Post* [On-line]. Available: http://www.washingtonpost.com/ac2/wp-dyn/A29799-2003May8?language=printer

Webb, C. (2003). TechNews.com: Federal CIOs and the E-gov challenge. The Washington Post [On-line]. Available: http://washingtonpost.com

Webb, C. (2003). Government IT review. *The Washington Post* [On-line]. Available: http://www.washingtonpost.com/wp-dyn/articles/A26204-2003Sep4.html

Weber, M. (1978) *Economy and Society,* Guenther Roth and Claus Wittich, University of California Press, Berkeley, CA.

West, D. M. (2001). E-government and the transformation of public sector service delivery. *Annual Meeting of the American Political Science Association,* Providence, RI: Brown University.

West, D. M. (2001). *State and federal e-government in the United States, 2001* [On-line]. Available: http://www.brown.edu/Departments/Taubman_Center/polreports/egovt01us.html

West, D. M. (2000). *Assessing e-government: The internet, democracy, and service delivery by state and federal governments* [On-line]. Available: http://www1.worldbank.org/publicsector/egov/EgovreportUS00.htm

Westen, T. (1998). Can technology save democracy? *National Civic Review, 87* (1), 47-57.

Wilhelm, A. G. (2000). *Democracy in the digital age: Challenges to political life in cyberspace.* New York: Routledge.

Williamson, O.E. (1985) *The Economic Institutions of Capitalism,* Free Press, New York, NY.

Zaller, J. (1996). The myth of massive media impact revived: New support for a discredited idea. In D. Mutz, P. Sniderman, & R. Brody (Eds.), *Political persuasion and attitude change* (pp. 17-77). Ann Arbor: University of Michigan Press.

Zucker, H. G. (1978). The variable nature of new media influence. In B. D. Rubin (Ed.), *Communication Yearbook* (2nd ed., pp. 225-240). New Brunswick, NJ: Transaction Books.